D1595942

# Television Series of the 2000s

# Television Series of the 2000s

## Essential Facts and Quirky Details

VINCENT TERRACE

ROWMAN & LITTLEFIELD
*Lanham • Boulder • New York • London*

Published by Rowman & Littlefield
An imprint of The Rowman & Littlefield Publishing Group, Inc.
4501 Forbes Boulevard, Suite 200, Lanham, Maryland 20706
www.rowman.com

Unit A, Whitacre Mews, 26-34 Stannary Street, London SE11 4AB

British Library Cataloguing in Publication Information Available

**Library of Congress Cataloging-in-Publication Data Available**

ISBN 9781538103807 (electronic) | ISBN 9781538103791 (hardback : alk. paper)

♾™™ The paper used in this publication meets the minimum requirements of American National Standard for Information Sciences—Permanence of Paper for Printed Library Materials, ANSI/NISO Z39.48-1992.

Printed in the United States of America

# Contents

# Acknowledgments

The author would like to thank James Robert Parish, Steven Eberly, Bob Leszc-zak, Nicole Galiardo, and Madison Gorman for their help in making this book possible.

# Introduction

This is the sixth in a series of books that provide quirky (trivia) facts about select television programs. This book covers shows that were first broadcast between January 1, 2000, and December 31, 2009. Series prior to these eras can be found in *Television Series of the 1950s*, *Television Series of the 1960s*, *Television Series of the 1970s*, *Television Series of the 1980s*, and *Television Series of the 1990s*—each of which also contains the same details relating to the trivia facts associated with select, well-known series.

This is *not* a book of essays or opinions but rather a straight listing of facts for the represented programs. Did you know, for example, that on *According to Jim*, Jim's favorite writing instrument is "The Naked Lady Pen"; that, as a child, Adrian Monk's (*Monk*) favorite TV series was *The Patty Duke Show*; that on *Psych*, psychic Shawn Spencer carries a travel-size packet of Johnson's Baby Shampoo in his wallet; or that Lorelai Gilmore (*Gilmore Girls*) considers raising her daughter, Rory, "low maintenance like a Honda"?

How about Miley Stewart (*Hannah Montana*) using the catchphrases "Sweet niblets" and "Ya think!," serial killer Dexter Morgan (*Dexter*) considering himself "a very neat monster," Valerie and Lauren owning a shop called Sugar Babies Pastry on *What I Like About You*, Glen Matthews being Janitor's real name on *Scrubs*, or Sheldon Cooper (*The Big Bang Theory*) having set a specific time of the day (1:45 p.m. to 2:05 p.m.) as his "alone time"?

If these few facts intrigue you, you will be amazed at the many thousands of such facts that appear in the pages that follow.

Programs that were broadcast in the 1990s and extended their runs into the 2000s are not included here. Information on these programs can be found in *Television Series of the 1990s*:

*Ally McBeal*
*Angel*
*Buffy the Vampire Slayer*
*Charmed*

*The Drew Carey Show*
*ER*
*Everybody Loves Raymond*
*Frasier*
*Friends*
*Home Improvement*
*Just Shoot Me*
*The King of Queens*
*King of the Hill*
*Law and Order*
*Law and Order: Special Victims Unit*
*The Nanny*
*Nash Bridges*
*Sabrina, the Teenage Witch*
*7th Heaven*
*Sex and the City*
*Spin City*
*V.I.P.*
*Walker, Texas Ranger*
*Will and Grace*
*The X-Files*

# According to Jim
### (ABC, 2001–2009)

*Cast:* Jim Belushi (Jim), Courtney Thorne-Smith (Cheryl), Kimberly Williams (Dana), Larry Joe Campbell (Andy), Billi Bruno (Gracie), Taylor Atelian (Ruby), Connor Rayburn (Kyle).

*Basis:* The incidents that befall a married couple (Jim and Cheryl), their children (Gracie, Ruby, and Kyle), and Cheryl's siblings, Dana and Andy. It can be seen that characters have no last names; Cheryl later gives birth to twins Gordon and Jonathan.

## JIM

*Place of Birth:* Chicago on April 5.

*Middle Name:* Orenthal.

*Sister:* Roxanne (Jennifer Coolidge). Jim and Roxanne were raised by their mother (unnamed) after their father, Bill, deserted the family.

*Address:* 412 Maple Street.

*Occupation:* Architect and owner of the construction company Ground Up Designs.

*Character:* A fast-talker who bases much of what he says on the articles he reads in *Playboy* magazine. He has his own ideas about everything but never realizes they are preposterous and a constant cause of friction in his marriage.

*Philosophy:* "If a woman sees you are good at something, she will make it your job forever" (so he avoids doing anything really well).

*Escape Goat:* Gus Dimas. When Cheryl asks Jim to do something or plans a boring function, the nonexistent Gus suddenly comes to town, and Jim finds an excuse to be with him.

*Favorite Holiday:* Halloween.

*Prized Possession:* His eight-glass set of collectables from Chevron gas stations.

*Favorite Movies: Ice Station Zebra* and *A Fistful of Dollars.*

*Favorite Diner:* The Lunch Wagon (a sandwich, called "The Big Jim," has been named after him; it consists of fried bologna and sauerkraut on white bread).

*Favorite Pizza Parlor:* Speedy Tony's Pizza.

*Favorite Sport:* Bowling (on the team "Ball Masters"; he calls his bowling ball "Rolling Thunder"). He is also a fan of the Chicago Cubs, Bears, Bulls, and Blackhawks teams.

*Favorite Beverage:* Beer.

*Favorite Writing Instrument:* Bridget (a "Naked Lady Pen"; turn it upside down, and the pictured girl loses her clothing).

*Favorite Music:* Blues.

*Band:* The Sacred Hearts (Jim plays guitar and is lead singer).

*Trademark:* Flannel shirts.

*TV Appearance: Windy City Sunrise,* a Chicago morning program (on Channel 6) where Jim expressed his rather biased opinions about relationships between men and women ("I stand for being a man") and became known as "The Flannel-Sexual."

*Allergy:* MSG.

*Fear:* Spiders and dealing with Ruby's and Gracie's female issues as they grow up. It is first seen when Ruby asks Jim to buy her a training bra. Jim, freaking out, appoints Dana with "Mommy Powers" to "buy her the bra, but I don't want to hear about it, see it, or find it in the laundry" (Cheryl had been visiting her mother in Florida at the time). His second crisis: dealing with Ruby's first period (especially since her younger sister, Gracie, experienced hers first).

*Quirks:* Takes his shirt off to scare away Jehovah's Witnesses; has a "secret jelly donut" before dinner; hides "the good ice cream" in the back of the freezer behind the Brussels sprouts (so the kids will not find it). In college, Jim shaved his initials into a Shetland pony.

*Failed Moneymaking Ventures:* Self-folding pants; liquor-filled donuts; a doll called "Gassy Gus."

*Child Rearing:* Not the best of fathers. When it is his turn to mind the kids ("My Watch," as he calls it), he becomes "Frozen Man" (Ruby and Gracie play outside while Jim relaxes on the couch indoors) and "Hammock Guy" (Jim rests outside while Ruby and Gracie play inside).

*Catchphrase:* "Hold the phone" (said when something doesn't go his way).

*Flashbacks:* Young Jim (Elijah Runcorn, then Adam Cagley).

## CHERYL

*Place of Birth:* Chicago. Cheryl first mentions being born on June 6, then August 13.

*Mother:* Maggie (Kathleen Noone); her father is deceased.

*Middle Name:* Mabel.

*Siblings:* Dana and Andy.

*Occupation:* Housewife. Prior to her marriage, she was a claims adjuster for an unnamed insurance company.

*Education:* While schools are not named, she was a straight "A" student, a cheerleader, and in the National Honor Society in high school; she majored in business administration in college.

*Award:* Due to Cheryl's unrelenting desire to help people through her charity work, she was nominated as "One of the Women Who Cares" by *Playboy* magazine. She didn't enter but won the award when Jim wrote an essay and entered it as Cheryl's so that he could live his dream—"smoke a cigar with Hef" (Hugh Hefner, the publisher of *Playboy*).

*Bra Size:* Cheryl mentions 34C.

*Pet Cat:* Mr. Feeney.

*Quirks:* Worries that people will not like her (Jim claims that Cheryl needs to be liked by other people). She also has a compulsion to hold on to things, especially her outdated clothes ("Everything looks good on me"), and when she becomes depressed, she prepares spaghetti and meatballs for dinner.

*Constant Fear:* After her friends meet the uncouth Jim, will her friends still like her?

*Favorite Singing Group:* The Beatles.

*Belief:* "Jim pretends to be a moron to cover up being a jackass."

*Second Language:* French (speaks fluently).

*Medical Issue:* Totally tone deaf.

*Food Idiosyncrasies:* Must have her hamburger done medium well and her steak rare.

*Imperfection:* Cheryl has a scar on her forehead (when she was six years old, she was running around the house, fell, and hit her head on the refrigerator).

*DVD Appearance:* While in Fort Lauderdale, Florida, Cheryl and Dana drank a bit too much, wandered onto the set of a video called *Cuties Gone Crazy*, and flashed their breasts (Dana first), shocking Jim (as he and Cheryl were married at the time) and Andy (who believes he will have nightmares now that he saw his sisters topless).

*Classes:* Cheryl attends yoga classes.

## OTHER CHARACTERS

Dana, Cheryl's younger sister, works as the creative director for the Morris & Flatt Advertising Agency. She wears a 32B bra; stands 5 feet, 5 inches tall; and is a constant source of aggravation to Jim, as she is his total opposite. They argue over everything, and Dana has a bad habit of embarrassing herself in front of other people (like saying something and then realizing and regretting she actually agreed with Jim). She was accepted as a contestant on *The Bachelor* reality series and appeared topless (with Cheryl) in a DVD called *Cuties Gone Crazy* (mentioned earlier). Dana is very pretty but believes that only shallow men are attracted to her and she will never find a husband. Her life changes when she meets Dr. Ryan Gibson (Mitch Rouse), a gynecologist, and the two fall in love. They later marry, and Dana becomes the only regular character to acquire a last name (Dana Gibson). Dana and Ryan, however, leave the series in 2008 and move to Los Angeles.

Andy, Cheryl's older brother, is an architect and works with Jim at Ground Up Designs. Andy first dated Emily (Mo Collins), but without explanation she is replaced by Mandy (Jackie Debatin). Andy lives across the street from Jim and is his best friend and not only his stooge in the schemes he devises but also the one who often solves the problems that arise between Jim and Cheryl. Andy, the only unmarried member of his family, attended Stanford University (majoring in architecture). Final-season episodes are a bit strange, as the principal focus is on the antics of Jim and Andy. Cheryl is absent from most episodes, as are their children, who appear even less frequently. Jacob Nelson appeared as young Andy in flashbacks.

Ruby, the oldest of the children, was born in 1996. Like Gracie (born in 1997) and Kyle (born in 2000), virtually no information is given. Ruby (who takes piano lessons) and Gracie attend elementary school in the Unified School District (Ruby is on the school hockey team). She and Gracie appeared in a print ad for Delta Cruise Lines, and Gracie had a cockatoo (that responded only to her) named Daphne. Their main goal appears to not only try their father's patience but also drive Andy crazy with their antics. They made money with a sidewalk lemonade stand and have a *Hannah Montana* TV series calendar on their shared bedroom wall. It can be seen that Kyle is not the bright light in the family (he believes anything that anybody tells him but does love sports, especially baseball). Jim had no trouble having two daughters until Ruby began to develop and showed an interest in boys (something Jim has a hard time dealing with because "I was once a teenage boy"). Gracie looks up to Ruby and often follows her lead in doing something. Although a year younger than Ruby, Gracie still likes "girly things" (like dolls) and has "not discovered boys" in the same manner as Ruby. For the time being (even as the series ends), Jim fears little about Gracie as she grows. Kyle, on the other hand, has Jim wondering from which side of the family Kyle inherited his "dumbness." Hope Levy played Baby Kyle; Robert Belushi appeared as Adult Kyle.

# *Alias*
## (ABC, 2001–2006)

*Principal Cast:* Jennifer Garner (Sydney Bristow), Victor Garber (Jack Bristow), Michael Vaughn (Michael Vartan), Ron Rifkin (Arvin Sloane), Kevin Weisman (Marshall Flinkman), Carl Lumbly (Marcus Dixon).

Jennifer Garner as Sydney Bristow. *ABC/Photofest © ABC*

*Basis:* The assignments of Sydney Bristow, an agent for SD-6, a covert division of the CIA.

## SYDNEY ANNE BRISTOW

*Parents:* CIA spies Jack Bristow (see below) and Laura Bristow (alias Irina Derevko). Sydney believed that her father worked for Jennings Aerospace (selling airplane parts) and her mother died in an automobile accident. (In reality, Irina faked her death to distance herself from Jack and protect Sydney. She was a Russian KGB spy who married Jack [a CIA agent] to infiltrate the CIA and ferret out corruption. She was responsible for killing 25 agents before disappearing.)

*Adoptive Parents:* Arvin (see below) and Emily Sloane (taken in by them when Sydney's mother was "killed" in a car accident and Jack placed in protective custody when his cover was blown during a mission).

*Place of Birth:* Charleston, West Virginia, on April 17, 1975.

*Address:* 425 Cochran Place, Los Angeles.

*Measurements:* 34-25-35. She has brown hair, hazel eyes, and stands 5 feet, 8 inches tall.

*Education:* Attended an unnamed high school ("A" student except for one "D" in home economics); Berkeley College (acquired a master's degree in English literature).

*Life Changer:* One fall afternoon at Berkeley, Sydney was approached by a man. "He said he might be interested in talking to me about a job. When I asked why me, all he told me was that I fit a profile . . . I needed the money . . . and he offered me the job." The job was to become a spy. Sydney was trained and advanced quickly—"They said I was a natural," and her status as a student provided the perfect cover.

*The Christmas Project:* While living with Arvin and Emily, Sydney was subjected to an experimental CIA project designed to subconsciously train and program children for intelligence work in later life. As a result, Sydney cannot be brainwashed.

*Occupation:* Agent with SD-6 after graduating from college. Her cover is now that of a banker for Credit Dauphine (her father, Jack, poses as the bank's portfolio manager and Sydney's superior). SD-6 stands for "Section Disparue," "the section that has disappeared or doesn't exist." It is actually criminal and part of "The Alliance of Twelve," which is secretly headed by Arvin and seeks to access the secrets of the CIA. Sydney is unaware at first that she is actually a double agent—working for SD-6 to gather intelligence from the CIA for its nefarious operations. After seven years with SD-6, Sydney discovers that it is a terrorist organization and joins with the real CIA to bring it down. She then becomes an undercover agent with the real CIA, then with APO (Authorized Personnel Only), a black operations unit of the CIA.

*Character:* Sydney is extremely careful during assignments—"I have to be. If I get careless, it's over for me." She risks her life during every assignment and is not always prim and proper, as she uses her sexuality to accomplish a mission. She gets shot, tortured, and beaten up and is seen with bruises, cuts, and blood on her body and clothes. She is also careful about who she dates because one slip of the tongue, and it could cost someone close to her their life. Sydney is considered a rogue agent and rarely follows protocol. She does, however, want to serve her country as best she can.

*Undercover Aliases:* Kate Jones, Amy Tippin, Julia Thorne, and Joanna Kelly.

*Code Names:* "Bluebird" (SD-6); "Freelancer," then "Mountaineer" (CIA); and "Phoenix" (APO).

*Languages:* English, German, Dutch, Mandarin, Cantonese, Japanese, Korean, Italian, Spanish, Russian, Hindi, Swedish, and Greek.

*Expertise:* Weapons and self-defense. She has a photographic memory, carries lock picks in the heels of her shoes, and is proficient with explosives and a master of disguise.

*Discovery:* During her efforts to bring down SD-6, Sydney was kidnapped and brainwashed (although it was previously said that she was immune to this) to believe that she was Julia Thorne and programmed to do the unit's dirty work. Later, when Sydney discovers that her mother, Irina, is alive and in a prison at the CIA, she begins a relationship that also finds Irina helping Sydney with her missions.

*Flashbacks:* Sydney as a girl (Kristen Kaveney, then Rachel G. Fox).

## JONATHAN "JACK" DONAHUE BRISTOW

*Place of Birth:* Ontario, Canada (now lives in Los Angeles), on March 16, 1950.

*Wife:* Laura Bristow, alias Irina Derevko (Kate Anthony, April Webster, and Lena Olin).

*Daughter:* Sydney Bristow.

*Occupation:* Field agent for SD-6 and the CIA (he is Sydney's superior) and director of APO.

*Code Names:* "Black Bird" (for SD-6) and "Raptor" (with APO). At SD-6, Jack's cover was that of an airplane parts supplier. Jack was aware that SD-6 was part of "The Alliance of Twelve" and worked with Sydney and the real CIA to bring Arvin and SD-6 down.

*CIA Badge ID:* 2568463-87.

*Computer Log-In:* Mozart_182 (Irina's log-in is Handel_4ME).

*Skills:* Cryptology, engineering, aeronautics, physics, and linguistics.

*Languages:* English, French, Chinese, Spanish, and Russian.

*Flashbacks:* Young Irina (Angela DeAwn).

## MICHAEL VAUGHN

*Place of Birth:* Normandy, France (under the name Andre Micheaux, which he uses as an alias), on November 27, 1971.

*Parents:* William (a CIA agent) and Deloreme Vaughn. William moved his family to Los Angeles when his work in Paris threatened his family.

*Occupation:* Undercover agent for the CIA and APO; Sydney's handler during her time with SD-6. They later marry and become the parents of Isabelle and Jack (at which time Sydney retires from her affiliation with APO to raise a family). Vaughn was previously married to a now deceased double agent (working for the evil Covenant) named Lauren Reed (Melissa George).

*Code Names:* "Boy Scout" (with the CIA) and "Shotgun" (with APO).
*Languages:* English, French, Italian, Russian, and Spanish. He has a master's
degree in French literature from an unnamed university.
*Pet Dog:* Donovan.

## ARVIN SLOANE
*Wife:* Emily Sloane (Amy Irving).
*Daughter:* Jacqueline (but lived for only a few minutes after childbirth).
*Occupation:* Head of SD-6, a criminal division of the CIA that directs its operations against the U.S. government. It uses the cover of being a secret unit
of the CIA. He is later with "The Alliance of Twelve," the SD-6 unit that
controls each SD-6 cell.
*Languages:* English, French, Spanish, Italian, and Russian.
*Allergy:* Morphine.
*Background:* Arvin was first with the U.S. Army Corps of Engineers before
joining the CIA. It is revealed (but rather vaguely) that Arvin had a secret
affair with Jack's wife, Laura, from whom a daughter was born and became
known as Nadia Santos (Mia Maestro). Nadia was first a spy with Argentine
intelligence and then with APO; her computer log-in is 087_Santos, and
"Evergreen" is her code name.
*Vehicle ID:* 30947 28436.
*Obsession:* Milo Rambaldi, a fifteenth-century thinker whose papers, especially
page 47, contain a means by which to obtain immortality (through "The
Sphere of Life," which is supposedly contained within the unknown where-
abouts of the Tomb of Rambaldi).
*Flashbacks:* Young Nadia (Gisselle Castellanos).

## OTHER CHARACTERS
Marshall Flinkman, born on December 29, 1971, in Los Angeles, is a computer
whiz (first employed by the CIA and then APO) who is responsible for many
of the gadgets that Sydney (and other agents) use. He has the APO code name
"Merlin" and is skilled in physics, engineering, robotics, electronics, chemistry,
acoustics, explosives, computer networks, and inventing. He has a photographic
memory, and his special language skill is Ewok (from the *Star Wars* films). He
is married to Carrie (maiden name Bowman) and the father of four sons (only
one is mentioned by name—Mitchell). Marshall appears socially inept and often
uses visual aids for his technical briefings. He is basically a tech support operative
but does serve as a field agent on occasion.

Marcus R. Dixon is a field agent with SD-6 (unaware that it was part of
"The Alliance of Twelve"), the CIA, and APO (code name "Outrigger"). He was
born in Minneapolis, Minnesota, on August 14, 1955. He was married to Diane
(now deceased) and is the father of Robin and Steven. Marcus suffers from color

blindness in his left eye and is skilled in cryptology, kung fu, financial analysis, and linguistics. He is a graduate of Sarah Lawrence (business degree) and MIT (computer science degree). His language skills are English, Hebrew, Arabic, and Taiwanese, and 7836-B is his employee ID number. He worked with Sydney in destroying SD-6 and bringing Arvin down.

# *Arrested Development*
### (Fox, 2003–2006; Netflix, 2013, 2018)

*Cast:* Jason Bateman (Michael Bluth), Portia de Rossi (Lindsay Funke), Will Arnett (Gob Bluth), Michael Cera (George Michael Bluth), Tony Hale (Buster Bluth), David Cross (Tobias Funke), Jeffrey Tambor (George Bluth), Jessica Walter (Lucille Bluth), Alia Shawkat (Maeby Funke), Ron Howard (Narrator).

*Basis:* Michael Bluth, the only sane and responsible member of an eccentric family, tries to keep his sanity while attempting to look out for his family and keep the family-owned business running.

## MICHAEL BLUTH
Michael is the son of George and Lucille Bluth and now runs Bluth Enterprises in California. He was born on December 14, 1967, and his official name is "Nichael Bluth" (due to a misprint on his birth certificate). Bluth Enterprises

Jason Bateman leads the cast of *Arrested Development. Fox/Photofest © Fox; photographer: Gavin Bond*

was started by Michael's grandfather in 1953 when he opened Bluth's Original Frozen Banana Stand on Balboa Island in California (a frozen banana on a stick now costs $1). He turned the one stand into a franchise and built a family real estate empire. It is said that Michael's father opened the stand; this would be impossible, as George was born in 1944 and he would have been nine years old at the time.

As a youngster, Michael worked at the stand, learned the ins and outs of the business, and is now struggling to keep the company out of bankruptcy. He is a widower (late wife, Tracey) and lives with his son, George Michael Bluth (Michael Sera), in Newport Beach, California, in a model home of the proposed Bluth Development Company (the locale is also given as Sudden Valley in Orange County). The company is in such financial straits that the only vehicle they own is the Bluth Company Airplane Ladder Truck.

Michael cringes when he learns he is not right about something but remains cool despite the constant annoyances his family causes. He tackles each crisis with calm thinking and has concluded that the only way to save the company is to cut corners.

Ann, Michael's girlfriend, is first played by Alessandra Torresani, then by Mae Whitman (a totally different-looking actress). Michael could never remember what Ann looked like (hence the casting change), and because of this, his niece, Maeby, calls her "No Face."
*Flashbacks:* Young Michael (Michael Bartel).

## GEORGE OSCAR BLUTH

George, born in 1944, is married to Lucille and is the father of Michael and Gob; he is the adoptive father of Buster and Lindsay. He is a real estate mogul and built the family fortune from an idea that his father stole from a Korean immigrant—frozen bananas on a stick—and created Bluth's Original Frozen Banana Stand. George later took over the company and ran it quite illegally before he was arrested by the Securities and Exchange Commission for cheating investors (using his company funds as his personal piggy bank). George was tried, convicted, and sentenced to the Orange County Penitentiary. A year later, he escaped by faking a heart attack and found refuge in Mexico. Unhappy with his situation, he faked his death, returned to the United States, and hid in the attic of the model home in the Bluth Housing Development. Word got around that George was still alive and he again fled, this time taking refuge with the Blue Man Group (actors) and literally hiding in plain sight by painting himself blue. He was again captured and put under house arrest (watched over by Lucille) in her apartment at Balboa Towers.

George was called "The Muffin Man" when his kids attended school (for poisoning muffins to intimidate their teachers) and is manipulative, sarcastic, and demeaning to others. As he grew older, he felt he was meant to be a woman and started living life as one. He has cheated on Lucille numerous times and despises his twin brother Oscar (Jeffrey Tambor) because he has not gone bald as George has; Oscar, on the other hand, despises George for stealing Lucille from him. George also hates Buster, born out of an affair Lucille had, because he is not his biological son (Buster refers to George as "Uncle Father"). George is also responsible for creating a dangerous product called a Corn-Baller (a machine to make cornballs that was banned in the United States but is still sold in Mexico). *Flashbacks:* Young George (Seth Rogen).

## LINDSAY FUNKE
Lindsay is Michael's adoptive sister (they were originally led to believe they were fraternal twins until a scrapbook was uncovered and Lindsay learned that her real name is Nellie Stillwell). She was adopted for an idiotic reason by George and Lucille when she was three years old: to prevent a business competitor from acquiring her. Lindsay, a beautiful woman with no concept of money, is married to Tobias Funke and the mother of Maeby. They first live in Boston, then in Newport Beach, and rely on an allowance from Michael for their income after Tobias loses his job (see below). Having never worked a day in her life, Lindsay attempts several jobs, including a bead business, a pet grooming company (Dip-a-Pet), a beauty shop (What Will I Look Like?), secretary at Bluth Enterprises, salesgirl at a fashion boutique, and spokesgirl for Cloudmir Vodka (her mother's favorite drink). Lindsay, a Republican, later runs for a seat in Congress. She enjoys shopping, hosting charity events, and eating at fancy (and expensive) restaurants.

In 2004, when Lindsay and Tobias believe that having an open relationship will save their stagnant marriage, Lindsay releases her inner ambitions to have affairs with the family lawyer, a bounty hunter, an actor, and, most astoundingly, Marky Bark (Chris Diamantopoulos), an environmentalist and the owner of an ostrich farm (where she lived with him in a desert).

Lindsay was famous in high school for winning the annual Best Hairstyle Award. She is also proud of her lingerie pose as "Miss December" in the Ladies of Literacy Calendar. Lindsay is also an activist and not the best of mothers for Maeby, as she rarely keeps tabs on her and allows her to get away with everything.
*Flashbacks:* Young Lindsay (Somer Dice).

## TOBIAS BLUTH
Tobias, a hopeful actor, is married to Lindsay and the father of Maeby. Prior to this, he was a psychiatrist but developed a number of phobias and is now very insecure. (He lost his medical license while on a cruise, as he administered

cardiopulmonary resuscitation to a person he thought was having a heart attack. The Newport newspaper headline read, "Sleeping Tourist Has Sternum Broken.") He was chief resident in psychiatry at Massachusetts General Hospital for two years and did his fellowship in psychoanalysis at MIT. While he appears to like women, he may secretly be a homosexual, as he suffers from a rare psychological condition ("Never Nude") that makes him incapable of appearing without some type of clothing when being intimate with his wife (it is an actual condition called gynophobia, which is the fear of nude bodies).

His acting career has also suffered, as he rarely gets parts and steadily wore blue makeup for a hoped-for position (as an understudy comic) with the Blue Man Group. He appeared on the TV series *Scandal Makers*, staged his own show (*Fantastic 4: An Action Musical*), became a street performer known as "The Thing" (from the *Fantastic 4*), and directed Maeby's school production of *Much Ado about Nothing*.

Tobias lived at the Bluth model home development site until Lindsay evicted him. He found employment as a security guard at the Tantamount Film Studios and began living on the set of the mythical series *Wrench*. It is here, while exploring the wardrobe department, that he used the plot of the movie *Mrs. Doubtfire* to disguise himself as an English nanny (Mrs. Featherbottom) not only to prove that he is a capable actor but also to again become a part of his family, especially to Maeby (who calls him "Mr. Fingerbottom" when she realizes what her father is doing). He eventually gives up the disguise—but not before being praised as a great housekeeper.

Lindsay and Tobias lived previously in Boston (where they were famous for their cheese and wine fund-raisers) and had a band called Dr. Funke's 100% Natural Good Times Family Band Solution (wherein they sang about food and vitamins). It is hinted that Tobias may be African American "with a skin condition" due to Maeby's frizzy hair, Tobias having the middle name Onyango (common in Tanzania and Uganda), and Lindsay, attracted to black men, marrying Tobias to rebel against her father, who disapproved of interracial marriages.

## GOB BLUTH

George Oscar Bluth II, called Gob (pronounced "Jobe"), is Michael's older brother, a magician who prefers that his acts be called illusions, not tricks ("A trick is something a whore does for money"). He is a member of the Alliance of Magicians, rides a Segway (a two-wheeled electric vehicle), and has no friends. Gob has emotional issues (upsetting situations almost bring him to tears), and it seems that "hearing the song 'The Sound of Silence' in his head" soothes him. Gob does not make good choices and often says, "I've made a huge mistake!" or "Come on!" when he realizes he did something stupid.

Gob believes that he is a ladies' man but has great difficulty retaining a relationship. He claims that he became a magician to get out of gym class in high school and has ever since tried to make that scam a career. It worked until the Channel 6 news revealed the secret behind his Aztec Tomb Illusion and he became disgraced (dismissed from the Alliance of Magicians for revealing the secrets to an illusion). His confidence diminished to a point where even performing simple card tricks failed. He lives off money from the family company, although he tries to supplement his income with unusual jobs (like a stripper for "Hot Cops"). He created a character called "Mr. Banana-grabber" for his act and once used an African American puppet called "Franklin Delano Bluth" early in his career. To instill confidence in Gob, Michael made him the company president (which caused more harm than good). Gob next worked for Sitwell Enterprises (Bluth's main competition) but was fired in short order. He later forms (with Michael) a string of coffee shops called "Gobias Industries." For one of his failed illusions, the Magic Coffin Illusion, he was "honored" with the Poof Goof of the Year Award. He also appeared on a cable channel, the Miracle Network, where he performed his Jesus Crucifixion Illusion.

## BYRON "BUSTER" BLUTH

Buster is the middle brother. He is a bit strange, and doctors attribute his odd behavior to the 11 months he spent in the womb. He is a graduate of Milford Medical School ("where children should not be seen nor heard"). He studied everything from Native American tribal ceremonies to the mapping of uncharted territories. He is also cursed with crippling panic attacks. He lives with his mother, Lucille, who has cuddled him and made him neurotic, at Balboa Towers; he is also the result of an affair that Lucille had with George's twin brother, Oscar, while she was married to George. Buster has had some minor job experience but enjoys spending his time pursuing scholarly interests. He is so attached to his mother that they often wear matching color clothing, and each participates in "Mother-Boy" (an annual mother-and-son dance and dinner) and posing for covers of the *Balboa Bay Window* (the magazine of their apartment complex).

Buster is not very bright and has a difficult time with relationships (he is very close to his mother's friend, Lucille Austerio [Liza Minnelli], whom he calls "Lucille 2"). After discovering that his mother lied about Oscar being his father, Buster attempted to defy her by swimming in the ocean (something she never allowed him to do). A seal, which was part of Gob's magical act and which he set free, had acquired a taste for mammal blood and bit off Buster's left hand. It was replaced by a hook (which Buster chose to keep even though a prosthetic hand was available; he eventually replaced it with a bionic hand developed by the army).

*Flashbacks:* Young Buster (Jayden Maddux and Jason Aaron Tinero).

## MAEBY FUNKE

Maeby, born in Boston on September 22, 1990, is the daughter of Lindsay and Tobias Funke; they later move to Newport Beach. She has not been raised under the best of conditions, as her parents are irresponsible. Thus, Maeby has made a life for herself and excels in being a con artist. She has a fake sister named "Surely Funke," who is wheelchair bound, and has a disease called "BS" through which she gets charitable donations. She found that a cute, sexy smile and a big lie could get her what she wanted. She flunked out of high school (although her parents never noticed), worked at a Bluth Banana Stand (taking money from the register and throwing away bananas), and conned her way into an executive slot at Tantamount Pictures, where she oversaw production on the films *Almost Cousins, Love, Indubitably*, and *Young Man on the Beach*. When she was busted, she acquired a job with Imagine Entertainment (but was fired for not having a high school diploma). She then became a career high school student (attended various schools) and earned money by leasing out the Bluth Development model home to the crew of the TV series *To Entrap a Local Predator: Orange County Edition*.

Maeby won the Miss Inner Beauty Pageant and acted as her mother's pimp (supplying her with men) when Tobias and Lindsay tried to save their troubled marriage, and, while at Imagine Entertainment, she accompanied a film crew to India to shoot the movie *Gangie on the Ganges*. It was here that she saw her mother at a restaurant (the Four Seasons Mumbai), posed as a shaman, and convinced Lindsay to pay more attention to her daughter when she returned to America. She was also a member of the family band, Dr. Funke's 100% Natural Good Times Family Band Solution.

*Flashbacks:* Young Maeby (Danielle Cipolla).

## LUCILLE BLUTH

Lucille, maiden name Lucille Jenkins, is George's wife (she met George while working at Stucky's, a roadside convenience store). She is very critical and demanding (which frightens George) and an alcoholic (often seen with a drink in her hand). Although she dated George's twin brother, Oscar, she left him for George, as he was the more successful sibling. Michael is their only biological son. Lindsay is adopted, and Buster resulted from an affair Lucille had with Oscar. Lucille and George are also the parents of Annyong (Justin Lee), a boy they adopted to make George look sympathetic to the Securities and Exchange Commission while he was being investigated; Lucille soon got bored with him (using him as a fashion accessory) and sent him to the Milford Boarding School.

Lucille, a spoiled socialite, lives at the Balboa Towers (in an apartment the company can't afford). She has the distinction of being a reckless driver and was the role model for the reality TV series *The World's Worst Drivers*. Her car, with the license plate 4JBG, has a unique feature: a rock that Buster found on an expedition but can't get out of the car.

Lucille is very age conscious and seeks to always look younger than she really is. She has fake IDs (made by Gob) and regular chemical peels. She served as a USO (United Serviceman's Organization) hostess during the Vietnam War (where she met Oscar). George's yacht, *Lucille*, is named after her, and the Bluth Model Home Development road is named "Lucille Lane" (the model unit is located at 1 Lucille Lane in Newport Beach).

*Flashbacks:* Young Lucille (Ruby Jossen and Kristen Wiig).

# *The Bernie Mac Show*
### (Fox, 2001–2006)

*Cast:* Bernie Mac (Bernard McCullough), Kellita Smith (Wanda McCullough), Camille Winbush (Vanessa Thompkins), Jeremy Suarez (Jordan Thompkins), Dee Dee Davis (Bryana Thompkins).

*Basis:* A stand-up comedian (Bernie) and his wife (Wanda) struggle to raise his drug-addicted sister's (Stacy's) children (Vanessa, Jordan, and Bryana) after he sends her to rehab and their father is sentenced to a 10-year prison term for tax evasion.

## BERNARD "BERNIE MAC" McCULLOUGH

Bernie, born in Chicago in 1958, grew up in a tough neighborhood and was raised by a strict mother who would not tolerate disobedience (he feared "Big Mama's Black Belt because I was whooped when I was bad"). He liked to make people laugh but was a boxer in his youth. When he felt that the fight ring was not right for him, he turned his talents to becoming an actor and comedian. He starred in the feature film *The Kings of Comedy* but lost leading roles in *Training Day* to Denzell Washington and *Bagger Vance* to Will Smith. He gave up the lead in *Conrad's Prerogative* when he found he couldn't play an athlete who attempts to overcome a heart attack dramatically ("I want to only make people laugh").

Bernie and his family live at 811 Penrose Drive in Encino, California. He drives a car with the license plate 410R 1019, and golf is his favorite sport (it relaxes him). He watches movies based on settings; his favorites are *Car Wash* (set in Los Angeles), *Cooley High* (set in Chicago), and *Cotton Comes to Harlem* and *Claudine* (set in New York). He also uses "Claudine" as his home alarm system password.

Bernie enjoys his weekly game of poker with his friends and smoking a good cigar (illegal Cubans, which he gets "through the Cuban connection" for $20

The cast of *The Bernie Mac Show*. *Fox Broadcasting/Photofest © 2001 Fox Broadcasting*

each). He does charity work for the Children's Counsel and breaks the fourth wall by speaking directly to the home viewer (from his office to the side of the stage). He is the only one who is aware of an audience and calls them "America" (e.g., "Now I ask you, America"; "Listen, America").

## WANDA MCCULLOUGH

Wanda was born in Chicago in 1961 and was actually responsible for changing the course of Bernie's life. Bernie was working as a deliveryman for Atlas Parcel Service when he met Wanda Thomas, the daughter of a customer. Bernie was also performing as a comic on the "L" train and at Tickles, a comedy club. It was 1987 when Wanda encouraged Bernie to stop thinking small and go for the big time.

Wanda, a graduate of Littlefield High School and Chicago University, first worked as an executive at Chicago Telecom. It was at this time that she and Bernie married and moved to California, where Bernie became a hit on the stand-up comedy circuit. Wanda then became an executive at West Coast Wireless, then a vice president with AT&T. She drives a car with the license plate VP ATT (later 4JRY 932) and is very supportive in Bernie's efforts to help raise his sister's children. Wanda is quite glamorous (measures 38-28-39 and stands 5 feet, 10 inches tall) but rarely uses her attributes to get what she wants from others.

## VANESSA, JORDAN, AND BRYANA

Vanessa, born in 1988, attends Baha Vista Junior High School. Jordan, born in 1993, is enrolled at Damien Elementary School; and Bryana, born in 1998, attends the Wellington School. Vanessa, called "Nessa" by Bernie, is on the school's gymnastics team. All the children were born in Chicago, and because of their mother's drug addiction, Vanessa raised not only herself but Jordan and Bryana as well.

Jordan is a preasthmatic troublemaker and cries over everything. Bryana, called "Baby Girl" by Bernie, has a doll named "Precious" and won a good citizenship award (which Bernie proudly displays in "The Mac Hall of Fame," a trophy cabinet in his den; it also contains his football trophy from high school).

# The Big Bang Theory
## (CBS, 2007–)

*Cast:* Jim Parsons (Sheldon Cooper), Johnny Galecki (Leonard Hofstadter), Kaley Cuoco (Penny), Simon Helberg (Howard Wolowitz), Kunal Nayyar (Raj Koothrappali), Melissa Rauch (Bernadette Rostenkowski), Mayim Bialik (Amy Farrah Fowler).

*Basis:* Events that befall the lives of four science nerds who are also best friends: Sheldon, Leonard, Howard, and Raj.

## SHELDON COOPER

*Parents:* George Sr. (deceased) and Mary Cooper (Laurie Metcalf).

*Siblings:* Older brother (George Jr.) and twin sister, Missy (Courtney Henggeler).

*Place of Birth:* Galveston, Texas, on February 26, 1980, in a Walmart shopping center while Mary was shopping. Sheldon was brought to Lawrence

The cast of *The Big Bang Theory. CBS/Photofest © CBS*

Memorial Hospital, where Missy was born a short time later. The family later moved to Medford, Texas. Other episodes place his birth date between April 19 and 20, 1980, based on Sheldon's mention of being a Taurus.

*Education:* Johnson Grammar School and Medford High School (attending at age nine). A camera shot of a degree in Sheldon's office reveals he attended the California Institute of Technology (Cal Tech); he mentions teaching at the Heidelberg Institute in Germany (at age 15).

*Degrees:* PhD, MS, MA, and BS.

*IQ:* 187. Sheldon considers himself to be the smartest person in the world (except for his idol, Stephen Hawking).

*Pet Cat as a Child:* Lucky.

*Earliest Writing:* "A Proof That Algebraic Topology Can Never Have a Non-Self-Contradictory Set of Aeolian Groups" (at age five); his grade school science project was titled "A Rededication of Maxwell's Equations Regarding Electromagnetism"; and at the age of nine, he wrote "Rocket Reentry and Retro-Propulsion" in his school notebook.

*Occupation:* Theoretical physicist at Cal Tech (where he is trying to prove string theory and his own alter ego, M-theory). When the grant under which he was paid is depleted, he is promoted to junior professor to study dark matter and teach a class on analytical mechanics.

*Address:* 2311 Los Robles (Apartment 4A, which he shares with Leonard) in Pasadena, California.

*Religion:* Apparently an atheist (although he was raised as an Evangelical Christian by his mother and was a member of the East Texas Christian Youth Holy Roller Bowling Team).

*Nicknames:* "Shelly" (by friends) and "Shelly Bean" (by his mother); he has a tendency to refer to himself as "Einstein Von Brainstorm."

*Girlfriend:* Amy Farrah Fowler (see below). Amy is his intellectual equal, but "she is not my girlfriend. She is a girl who is a friend, not a girlfriend."

*Annoying Traits:* Displays his knowledge of historical and cultural antidotes; has no real concept of sarcasm or irony; when someone engages in sexual activity, Sheldon uses the word "coitus"; when he believes he is being smart and fools someone, he utters "bazinga." He lacks a sense of humor and empathy. He is a narcissist, selfish, self-righteous, and arrogant (apparently taking after his stubborn and egotistical grandfather, "Pop-Pop"). Sheldon will share an apartment only with someone who will adhere to his strict Roommate Agreement (Leonard being the only one who could abide by its rules—although he has manipulated it to his own benefit).

*Habit:* Knocking three times on a door and each time repeating the person's name he is attempting to see before entering (due to a childhood incident when he entered a room and saw his father in bed with another woman; he kept the incident to himself). He exhibits a strict adherence to routine procedures and relies on friends to drive him to wherever he needs to be.

*Alone Time:* 1:45 p.m. to 2:05 p.m. each afternoon (where he relaxes in the Cal Tech basement).

*Likes:* Trains (refuses to fly), model trains (Lionel "O" scale; he frequents the hobby shop, Jerry's Junction), comic books, video games, costumes, and science-fiction TV series. He deplores the series *Babylon 5* (he believes it lacks scientific integrity) but loves *Star Trek*, *Star Wars*, *Battlestar Galactica* (both versions), *Doctor Who*, *Stargate SG-1*, and *Firefly*. He claims to be an honorary graduate of *Star Trek*'s Starfleet Academy, and Mr. Spock (from *Star Trek*) also appears to be his hero.

*Sheldon's Log:* A journal (based on *Star Trek*'s "Captain's Log") of his interactions with certain people.

*Homemade Robot:* Shelbot.

*Dislike:* Sports (possibly due to his father making him watch football as a child).

*Most Prized Possession:* A napkin, used and signed by Leonard Nimoy at the Cheesecake Factory for Penny, that Penny gave him for Christmas (as Sheldon says, "I possess the DNA of Leonard Nimoy!"). Sheldon identifies himself as the real-life Mr. Spock (Nimoy's character on *Star Trek*), and if he could, he would create his own Mr. Spock from the napkin's DNA.

*Designated Nights:* Wednesday is Comic Book Night; Thursday is Pizza Night; Friday is Chinese food (which he orders from the Schrum Palace) and vintage video game night; Saturday is laundry night (which must begin at 8:15 p.m.). Any night that includes a movie must have popcorn be part of the event.

*Favorite Cookie:* Oreo (but only with a glass of milk).

*Favorite Dessert:* Chocolate cobbler.

*Favorite Pudding:* Chocolate tapioca.

*Favorite Cake:* Three-layer chocolate.

*Favorite Hamburger Joint:* Big Boy (he later switched to those served at the Cheesecake Factory).

*Favorite Cereal:* Honey Puffs of Wheat (which he must have with one-quarter cup of skim milk while watching the series *Doctor Who* on Saturday mornings).

*Mortal Enemy:* Actor Wil Wheaton (from the series *Star Trek: The Next Generation*). Sheldon traveled a great distance to get Wil's autograph at a *Star Trek* convention and was angered when Wil ignored the convention to appear on *Hollywood Squares.*

*Board Game:* Sheldon created "Research Lab" and a three-person version of chess. Glen is his video game battling ostrich.

*Self-Appointed Job:* Took it on himself to work as a waiter at the Cheesecake Factory (with Penny).

*Unusual Traits:* Everything in his life must be followed by the rules he has set. Although he won't admit it, it appears that Sheldon suffers from obsessive-compulsive disorder. He must do specific things at specific times each day. He is obsessed with flags (he has his own Web show called *Sheldon Cooper Presents Fun with Flags*) and has designed one for the apartment: a gold lion on a blue background. He invented the term "prevening" (the time between afternoon and evening) and only drinks hot chocolate on months with an "r" in them. Sheldon believes he is knowledgeable in all fields of science and hopes to win a Nobel Peace Prize. Not having the answer to a question is extremely upsetting to him, as he believes the universe owes him. He is often delusional (when he was a kid, he wanted a pet that he could train to kill through telepathic communication, and he yearns to conquer a planet so he can become its supreme ruler). If Sheldon is faced with a situation that baffles him, a facial tic emerges that grows worse until he can command control of the situation. He is an excessive neat freak, and everything must be in its proper place.

*Fears:* Germs (he constantly washes his hands), dogs, dinosaurs, and birds (due to such bird traumas as his neighbor's chicken chasing him up a tree, a parrot in a pet shop calling him "fat ass," and a magpie attacking him to take the retainer out of his mouth); a blue jay appears to be the only bird he will trust.

*Phobias:* Suffers from extreme stage fright if he must speak in a room with more than 35 adults (or 70 children)—no more of each though. Becoming sick terrifies him, and he must be mothered if he does become ill. The song "Soft Kitty" soothes him, but he must also have homemade chicken soup and Vicks VapoRub applied to his chest to relieve congestion from a cold.

*Safe Refuge:* He considers his bedroom his place of extreme solace and becomes furious if someone even enters it.

*Friendship Rules:* Sheldon keeps a record of people who violate any of his rules. If such a person should acquire three rule breaks, they could face banishment from his apartment for a year if they do not apologize. People virtually always see Sheldon as being crazy or insane, but he insists he is not: "My mother had me tested."

*That Spot on the Couch:* In his apartment Sheldon must sit on the right cushion (facing the screen) of the couch (which he says is the "single point of consistency in an ever-changing world"). Sheldon, however, will know if someone sat in his spot because, according to Leonard, "Sheldon has a very sensitive butt."

*Flashbacks:* Young Sheldon (Iain Armitage).

## LEONARD HOFSTADTER

*Parents:* Alfred (an anthropologist) and Beverly Hofstadter (a psychiatrist, played by Christine Baranski). Beverly wrote a book concerning Leonard called *The Disappointing Child.*

*Siblings:* A brother (Michael) and an unnamed sister.

*Place of Birth:* New Jersey on May 17, 1980.

*IQ:* 173.

*Favorite Dessert:* German chocolate cake.

*Childhood:* Had a dog named Mitzi, and his and Sheldon's favorite TV show was *Professor Proton* (Bob Newhart played the professor).

*Occupation:* Experimental physicist at Cal Tech.

*Girlfriend, Then Wife:* Penny (see below).

*Former Girlfriend:* Leslie Winkle (Sara Gilbert), Leonard's female counterpart (a physicist; works in the same lab as Leonard) but Sheldon's nemesis (her theories conflict with his).

*Nicknames:* "Sockmouth" (in high school; hoping to get the nickname "Duncan," Leonard carried a Duncan yo-yo with him that was stolen by school bullies who placed a sock in his mouth), "Lenny" (by an aunt), and "Ricardo Shilly-Shally" (by Sheldon). He was the president of his high school debate club, and his parents pushed him into becoming a scientist; in middle school, he wanted to become a rap star.

*Home:* Originally roomed with Sheldon in Apartment 4A (he later lives with Penny in Apartment 4B); Sheldon then shares Apartment 4A with Amy.

*Education:* Princeton University (previously attended advanced classes in high school; was considered a geek and bullied). He received a doctorate at the age of 24 with a Dissertation of the Year Award for his studies on experimental particle analysis.

*Favorite Hangout:* With Sheldon, Howard, and Raj: a comic book shop owned by Stuart Bloom (Kevin Sussman), a down-on-his-luck Rhode Island School of Design graduate who also lives in the back of the store.

*Character:* Wears glasses, not always sure of himself, often annoyed by Sheldon's antics, and acts as the mediator between Sheldon and whomever he annoys.

*Favorite TV Shows: Babylon 5, Buffy the Vampire Slayer, Star Trek*, and *Star Trek: The Next Generation* (he likes the original *Star Trek* better but prefers Captain Picard [from the next generation *Star Trek*] over Captain Kirk [from the original *Star Trek*]).

*Favorite Movies: Star Wars, Lord of the Rings*, and *Harry Potter.*

*First Award:* At age five, a blue ribbon for his project "Do Lima Beans React Better to Classical Music?"

*Favorite Video Game:* "Age of Conan." He is also team captain of the group's bowling team "Wifi."

*Paper with Sheldon:* "Paradoxical Moment of Inertia Changes Due to Putative Super Solid" (which they presented at the Institute for Experimental Physics, in short, showing that at temperatures of absolute zero, a solid becomes a super solid—something that was previously unknown).

*Study:* When Stephen Hawking became aware of Leonard's research, he invited him to join his team and become part of a group of scientists gathered to test hydrodynamic simulations of black holes (which led him to write a paper revealing that the space–time continuum is like a super liquid, always in a liquid state).

*Likes:* Comic books, superheroes, playing Klingon chess (from *Star Trek*) and Boggle, and *Star Wars* collectibles.

*Trait:* Proficient in history, English literature, music, and the sciences; he can play the cello and is intelligent and mature.

*Regret:* Being denied love from his parents (especially his mother, who had no admiration for him and ruined his moments of happiness as a child). His father would spend more time with a 2,000-year-old Egyptian mummy boy than with his own son.

*Conditions:* Leonard is sensitive, lactose intolerant, and prone to motion sickness and migraine headaches. Exercising (such as jogging) causes a bloody nose;

he has sleep apnea and numerous allergies and is prone to ear infections. He also appears to have asthma and a genetic inheritance of heart disease. As a child, Leonard was a bed wetter, and his parents gave him the middle name "Leaky" (after British anthropologist Louis Leakey, with whom Leonard's father worked); he hates his first name, as it contains the word "nerd." Leonard is sensitive to the fact that he is short (5 feet, 5 inches tall; stopped growing at age 14). He is insecure (tilts his head when he speaks and avoids eye contact, often squinting at the same time).

*Family:* Beverly is identical to Sheldon in personality, speech patterns, lack of social conventions, and attention to details. She never threw birthday parties for Leonard and, like Sheldon, thinks little of his work (as it has already been done by other people). Michael, his brother, is a Harvard law professor. His unnamed sister is a cutting-edge medical researcher hoping to find a cure for diabetes.

*Hope:* To win a Nobel Peace Prize.

*Doubt:* Skeptical of loop quantum gravity.

*Quirk:* Leonard uses *Star Wars* products, such as Luke Skywalker hair conditioner and Darth Vader No More Tears shampoo. He is a Superman fan, has a large Superman comic book collection, and even buys Superman underwear. His electronic password is Kal-El (Superman's Krypton name).

## PENNY

*Parents:* Wyatt (also said to be Bob; played by Keith Carradine) and Susan (Katey Sagal).

*Siblings:* Randall (brother, a drug dealer and ex-con); unnamed sister.

*Place of Birth:* A farm outside Omaha, Nebraska (on Perkins Street), on December 2, 1985. Penny, treated like a boy by her father (who wanted a son), learned how to fix a tractor by the time she was 12; was forced to play sports (until she began to develop breasts); and was finally allowed to become a girl when her brother was born. At this time, she had a pet pig named Moondance and a dog named Pepper. She was also a junior rodeo champion.

*Nicknames:* "P-Dawg" and "Bestie" (by Amy), "Patsy" (by Howard's mother), and "Slugger" (by her father).

*Occupation:* Waitress at the Cheesecake Factory (also works as a bartender); pharmaceutical sales rep at Zagan (where she often flirts with doctors to make sales); hopeful actress (when first introduced, it is revealed that Penny had written a screenplay about a girl from Lincoln, Nebraska, who, at the age of 18, leaves home to follow her dream of becoming an actress; Penny claims it is not autobiographical because "I come from Omaha, Nebraska").

*Husband:* Leonard Hofstadter (see above).

*Trait:* Somewhat naive at times with what appears to be a sparse education. She has common sense, is totally unaware what car maintenance means, spends beyond her means, and enjoys drinking (sometimes too much). She is kind and empathetic toward people (except, at times, to Sheldon, who often frustrates her). While Penny does earn money as a waitress, it can also be seen that Penny mooches off Leonard and Sheldon (borrowing their Wi-Fi, sharing their food, and having bills paid by Leonard). She is a Sagittarius and attempted to make extra money by starting a business called Penny Blossoms (flowerlike hair accessories for women).

*Acting Roles:* Prior to the series, she appeared topless in a horror film called *Serial Ape-ist.* She later stars as an ape in its sequel, *Serial Ape-ist: Monkey See, Monkey Kill.* During the series, she mentions performing in a TV commercial for a hemorrhoid product for women (rose-scented Preparation H) and acting roles in *The Diary of Anne Frank* (staged over a bowling alley), the musical *Rent,* and her acting class production of *A Streetcar Named Desire.* Her one chance at recognition came when she acquired a role on *NCIS,* but it ended when her scene was cut from the show. Her movies made her realize that she is a terrible actress.

*Clothes Shopping:* If Penny likes a blouse, she will buy it in two different colors.

*Beliefs:* Superstitious and believes in ghosts, voodoo, astrology, and psychics.

*Residence:* Apartment 4B (she replaced the former tenant, a 200-pound transvestite [Louie/Louise] who called Sheldon "Crazy").

*Food Preference:* Vegetarian—except for the occasional fish and steak—"I love steak." She upsets Sheldon when she eats Chinese food with a fork and double-dips her egg rolls (as he finds this unappealing; he also finds food unappealing if he does not have the right condiment for the right food).

*Ability:* Penny is an expert chess player and video game enthusiast (especially the games "Halo" and "Age of Conan"). She is constantly in a dither when Sheldon and Leonard speak (she simply doesn't understand them) and calls her new friends "beautiful mind genius guys." While Penny is trying to figure out Sheldon and Leonard, Sheldon and Leonard are trying to understand a girl who is well below their intellectual level.

*Car:* Penny owns a red 1980s Volkswagen convertible (she never pays attention to the red light engine warning, which constantly annoys Sheldon when riding with her).

*Education:* While schools are not named, Penny was somewhat of a bully in high school. She dropped out of community college but later returned to take courses in history and psychology.

*Catchphrase:* "Oh, my God!" or "OMG."

*Tattoo:* A Chinese character is on Penny's right butt cheek (she believes it stands for "Courage"; Sheldon believes it means "Soup").

*Favorite Music Groups:* The Spice Girls (especially "Baby Spice") and NSYNC (likes Justin).
*Favorite TV Series/Movie: Sex and the City.*
*Dislike:* Being awoken before 11:00 a.m.

## HOWARD JOEL WOLOWITZ

*Place of Birth:* Pasadena, California, on December 9, 1981.
*Religion:* Jewish (although he is not truly devoted to it, as he will eat pork and not attend Temple).
*Mother:* Debbie Wolowitz (voiced by Carol Ann Susi). She still treats him like a child and couldn't care less about his scientific accomplishments. She is grossly overweight, and, although she claims to live with her son, Howard contends that she lives with him. She is never seen (except for an overhead glimpse in one episode and her arm from a partially opened door in another). She is said to be somewhat masculine and communicates with Howard by yelling (and his yelling back). Howard must attend to his mother's physical needs (like helping her with her bath) and calls her "Crazy Old Lady." She passed away while visiting relatives in Florida. Sam, Howard's father, deserted the family when Howard was 11 years old (Howard believes it was because he didn't like him; his mother gave him an *ALF* TV series doll to comfort him).
*Occupation:* Aerospace engineer and ex-astronaut. He was also employed by the Jet Propulsion Laboratory's Deep Space Operations Center (where he created the Wolowitz Programmable Hand to make outside repairs to the International Space Station and the Wolowitz Zero Gravity Waste Disposal System [the Space Toilet]. As an astronaut (with the nickname "Froot Loops"), he designed a deep-field space telescope as a member of Expedition 31.
*Education:* MIT (master's degree in engineering).
*Wife:* Bernadette (see below).
*Childhood:* Debbie made Howard wear rubber gloves to kindergarten so he would not pick up diseases from other children. He was bullied in school and had a rather lonely childhood. His mother made him sleep in a bed with bars (protection from rolling off the mattress) until he was 17 years old.
*Character:* Before his marriage to Bernadette, Howard fancied himself a ladies' man and sought every opportunity to meet girls. He can speak a number of languages (Klingon, French, Russian, Mandarin Chinese, Japanese, and Arabic) and is obnoxious and arrogant. He likes video games, comic books, superheroes, and Klingon Boggle. His favorite video games appear to be "Age of Conan" (where he is the guardian "Sir Howard of Wolowitz") and "World of Warcraft" (where he is the elf hunter "Wolowizard" and has a

tiger named Buttons). He is fascinated by magic, rocket ships, and robots (made the "Mobile Omni-Directional Neutralization and Termination Eradicator" for the Southern California Robot Fighting League and Round Robin Invitational). He is perhaps most famous for sending a signal around the world via his computer to turn on a lamp on the roof of Sheldon's apartment building.

*Medical Issues:* Howard has asthma and is allergic to peanuts (causes severe face swelling), almonds, and walnuts. He suffers from motion sickness, has a tendency to get pinkeye, and inherited a risk of heart disease. Howard is one inch shorter (at 5 feet, 4 inches) than Leonard. He has brown hair and blue eyes and often wears loud clothes reminiscent of the 1960s. Howard gets aroused over pickled herring. He lost his virginity to his second cousin Jeannie in a car (a Toyota) after they locked eyes over a jar of pickled herring at his Aunt Barbara's house. He has also committed a number of illegal acts but has never been punished for them; these include numerous sexual harassment complaints, stealing government property, illegally spying on people with government surveillance cameras, and destroying multi-million-dollar government equipment (like the Mars Rover by steering it into a ditch on Mars).

*Likes:* Singer Neil Diamond and Beatles music (his hairstyle reflects that of Ringo Starr).

*Transportation:* A Vespa scooter.

*Online User Name:* Wolowizard.

*Residence:* A home with the street number 3150 (which he shares with his mother); with Bernadette in a home with the street number 845.

## RAJESH RAMAYAN KOOTHRAPPALI

*Parents:* V. M. Koothrappali (Brian George) and an unnamed mother (Alice Amter), with whom he communicates in India through Skype over the internet.

*Siblings:* Sister, Priya Koothrappali (Aarti Mann), a lawyer; another unnamed sister; three unnamed brothers. Priya appears in fourth-season episodes and began a relationship with Leonard after he and Penny broke up. Priya is a graduate of Cambridge University and can practice law in three countries.

*Place of Birth:* New Delhi, India, on October 6, 1981.

*Religion:* Hinduism.

*Nickname:* "Raj" (he calls himself "Brown Dynamite").

*Occupation:* Astrophysicist.

*Pet Dog:* Cinnamon.

*Character:* Although he comes from a prestigious background (his father is a wealthy gynecologist in India), he presents himself as growing up in poverty.

He speaks fluent English and Hindi but dislikes his country and its food (he even eats forbidden beef). He will degrade his own country but feels hurt when someone else does the same thing. Raj suffers from a form of social anxiety (pathological shyness) that makes him incapable of speaking directly to women outside of his own family (unless he is intoxicated). If he needs to say something and a woman is near, he whispers it into Howard's ear for him to relate. He likes America but is clueless when it comes to many of its customs and traditions. He refers to his skin tone as "Melt-in-Your-Mouth Caramel." He is addicted to internet pornography and enjoys a break from science fiction by reading *Archie* comics.

*Education:* Cambridge University (PhD in astrophysics).

*Accomplishments:* Member of Cal Tech's Physics Department and was part of a team that launched the New Horizons space probe to study Pluto and the systems beyond it. He appeared in *People* magazine's "30 Under 30 to Watch" issue (for his discovery of a planetary object in the Kuiper Belt region beyond Saturn that he called "Planet Bollywood") and won the Newcomb Medal for this research. He also performs research on dark matter, Trojan asteroids, and the Van Allen Belts. He believes the Hindu Code of Manu "is crazy."

*Likes:* Comic books, superheroes (except Aquaman because he is always chosen to appear as him at costume parties and in competitions), video games (he often questions the logic behind such forms of entertainment), and myths (such as how can vampires shave if they have no reflection?).

*Home:* An undisclosed apartment (3D) that he calls "Raj Mohall."

*Favorite Singer:* Taylor Swift.

*Favorite Number:* 5,318,008 (when turned upside down on a calculator, "it spells Boobies").

*Fears:* Spiders and bugs.

*Addiction:* Pedicures.

*Favorite Drink:* Grasshopper (gives him confidence to talk to girls).

*Family Shame:* Keeping a costume of Lieutenant Uhura (from *Star Trek*) in his closet.

*Favorite Real Bollywood Actresses:* Madhuri Dixit and Aishwarya Rai Bachchan.

*Favorite Girlie Magazine: Bombay Gadonka Donks.*

*Car:* A BMW with seat warmers.

## AMY FARRAH FOWLER

Amy, born on December 17 (year not given) in Glendale, California, and attended Harvard University (acquired her PhD). She currently lives in Glendale (Apartment 314) and works as a neurobiologist for the pharmaceutical company Zagan. Her childhood was lonely, as she had no friends her own age (in high school, she considered the janitor her only friend, as they had lunch together;

this ended when his wife found out and called her a whore). Her mother was the only person who signed her high school yearbook, and she paid their cousin to take Amy to the senior prom; he used the money to buy drugs.

Amy's lonely life changed when Raj and Howard, seeking to find a girl for Sheldon, secretly entered his profile into a computer dating site, and the two were matched (although it can be seen that they have very little in common, as Amy is not a fan of science fiction, comic books, trains, or wearing superhero costumes but does consider herself part of Sheldon's world when she uses phrases such as "My colleagues and I").

Amy is allergic to avocados and penicillin. She likes medieval poetry and movies with subtitles, and her love of the TV series *Little House on the Prairie* has led her to creating fan fiction. She is serious about everything she says and does but lacks emotion. She has hazel eyes and brunette hair and stands 5 feet, 4 inches tall. She also had an unnamed monkey that became addicted to cigarettes when she conducted an experiment on smoking.

Amy quickly became friends with Penny and believes "our menses are synchronized." It was with Penny that Amy became attracted to another girl (when Penny complimented her hair and aroused Amy's feelings of homosexuality). The two engaged in an innocent kiss that could be attributed to a number of scientific experiments in which Amy volunteered to have the pleasure center of her brain stimulated by artificial means.

While Amy seems well adjusted, she suffers from night terrors, fears constipation when traveling, and claims that the droll Sheldon is the most fun person she has ever known. As a child, Amy joined the Cub Scouts and went unnoticed for two years that she wasn't a boy. She has an electric toothbrush she calls Gerard and originally claimed that the only song she knew lyrics to was the theme from the TV series *Diff'rent Strokes*. She can play the harp and, with the exception of buying a sexy pair of leopard panties from Victoria's Secret, wears hand-me-downs from her grandmother. Amy also claims that she has created a number of what she calls "tension-relieving techniques for ladies."

Amy created a complicated rules game with Sheldon called "Counterfactuals" (questions that redefine historical facts). Neil Diamond is her favorite singer, and she was born with webbing between her toes (which she removed in a homemade operation with nitrous oxide). Amy has a pact with her mother that she will date at least once a year. As a teenager, Amy had a made-up boyfriend (Armand, the miniature horse breeder) to satisfy her family's curiosity about her having a boyfriend. Amy, like Sheldon, cannot tell a convincing lie.

## BERNADETTE MARYANN ROSTENKOWSKI

Bernadette has a PhD in microbiology and works for Zagan, a large pharmaceutical company (she also worked for a time as a waitress at the Cheesecake Factory to help pay her grad school tuition; it was here that she met Penny). She lives in Pasadena and later married Howard (at which time he moves in with her; later into his former home after his mother's passing). Howard and Bernadette later become the parents of a girl they name Halley.

Bernadette was born on June 23 (year not given) and is sensitive about her small stature (she believes it was caused by her mother smoking while she was pregnant with her). She has five siblings (only a brother, Joey, is named) and is the daughter of Mike (a retired cop who still carries a gun "as a fashion statement") and an unnamed mother (who ran an illegal day care center in the basement and left the responsibility of raising her siblings on Bernadette, thus Bernadette's dislike of children). While she is short (4 feet, 11 inches tall; also said to be 4 feet, 10 inches and 4 feet, 1 inch tall), she is very pretty and spent much of her teen years entering beauty pageants. She is a Catholic of Polish descent (Howard's mother calls her "The Little Polish Girl" and "That Little Catholic Girl"). She has blue eyes and blonde hair and is fond of the color red (expressed mostly in the clothes she wears). Bernadette drives a Nissan and is actually smarter than Howard but pretends to be less intelligent to protect Howard's standing with his friends. While the most exciting substance Bernadette gets to work with is yeast, she displays knowledge in experimental physics. She is a terrible liar and hates most of the things Howard and his friends hold dear, such as science fiction and magic.

## PREQUEL SERIES
*Young Sheldon* (CBS, 2017–). A look at Sheldon's life as a child in Texas (beginning in 1989).
*Cast:* Iain Armitage (Sheldon Cooper), Reagan Revord (Missy Cooper, Sheldon's twin sister), Zoe Perry (Mary Cooper, Sheldon's mother), Lane Barber (George Cooper Sr., Sheldon's father), Montana Jordan (George "Georgie" Cooper Jr., Sheldon's brother).

# Bones
## (Fox, 2005–2017)

*Principal Cast:* Emily Deschanel (Temperance Brennan), David Boreanaz (Seeley Booth), Michaela Conlin (Angela Montenegro), T. J. Thyne (Jack Hodgins), Tamara Taylor (Camille Saroyan), Eric Millegan (Zack Addy).
*Basis:* The work of Dr. Temperance Brennan, a forensic anthropologist with the Jeffersonian Institute in Washington, D.C. The fictional Jeffersonian is based on the real Smithsonian Institution.

Emily Deschanel and David Boreanaz. *Fox Broadcasting/Photofest © 2005 Fox Broadcasting; photographer: Carin Baer*

## TEMPERANCE BRENNAN

*Parents:* Max (Ryan O'Neal) and Ruth Keenan (Larisa Miller).

*Birthday:* January 10, 1976.

*Address:* 415 Ellsworth Street.

*Measurements:* 34-24-35; she stands 5 feet, 9 inches tall.

*Occupation:* Forensic anthropologist; author.

*Books: Bone Free, Cross Bones, Bred in the Bone,* and *Red Tape, White Bones.* Her books have made her wealthy, and although told by her publisher that she can retire, she continues to work, as solving puzzling crimes is what she needs to do.

*Fictional Book Character:* Brennan writes about an anthropologist she named Kathy Reichs. The character of Temperance Brennan is based on books by Kathy Reichs, whose fictional character in those books is Temperance Brennan.

*Obsession:* Solving crimes, especially extremely complex cases wherein the only evidence consists of skeletal remains.

*Background:* Brennan was born under the name Joy Ruth Keenan and is the daughter of Max and Ruth Keenan (later known as Max and Christina Brennan). She has a brother, Kyle Keenan (now Russ Brennan), and had a life like no other child: her parents were bank robbers, and her family lived as fugitives. Brennan's life changed when her parents abandoned their children and Brennan was raised in a foster home until her grandfather took her in. It is later learned that Brennan's mother was murdered; her father is now deceased.

*Husband:* Seeley Booth (see below for both Seeley and their children).

*Religion:* Atheist.

*Nickname:* Most commonly called "Bones" by Seeley. She is also called "Brenn," "Sweetie," and "Honey" by Angela and "Dr. B" by Hodge.

*Inspiration:* Brennan mentions the movie *The Mummy* as inspiring her to choose her profession (there are a number of "Mummy" movies, and, while not specified, it is most likely the 1932 version with Boris Karloff and Zita Johann).

*Education:* Northwestern University.

*Food Preference:* Vegetarian.

*License:* Possesses a hunter's license in four states; she claims to only hunt for food.

*Character:* Brennan has an extensive knowledge of anthropology. She adheres to the book when it comes to investigations, lacks tact (she has to tell it like it is no matter whose feelings she hurts), and, due to her sheltered upbringing and dedication to work, does not understand references to pop culture (she is forever saying "I don't understand that").

*Abilities:* Brennan is studying karate, has expertise in three types of martial arts, and at some point was trained as a high-wire circus performer.

*Music Preference:* New World jazz (she later develops an interest in hip-hop).

*Favorite Eatery:* The Royal Diner.

*Fear:* Snakes (although she says this, she is also seen holding one).

*Seat Belt Safety:* Whenever Brennan and Seeley are seen driving, only Brennan wears her seat belt.

*Note:* Emily's sister, Zooey Deschanel, played Temperance's second cousin Margaret Whitesell (who lived in Wisconsin).

## SEELEY JOSEPH BOOTH

*Place of Birth:* Philadelphia on August 23, 1971.

*Parents:* Edwin (mentioned he flew fighters during the Vietnam War; was later an alcoholic) and Marianne Booth (Joanna Cassidy); she composed commercial jingles for advertisers. Ralph Waite plays Seeley's grandfather Hank Booth.

*Brother:* Jared Booth (served in the navy; works for the Pentagon but has an addiction to alcohol).

*Ancestry:* Claims to be related to John Wilkes Booth, the man who shot Abraham Lincoln (highly unlikely, though, as Wilkes never married or had any children; could mean a reference to one of Wilkes's brothers and sisters, who did have children).

*Wife:* Temperance Brennan (see above). They met in 2004 on a case (finding the killer of a woman named Gemma Arrington; their first televised case was uncovering the killer of Cleo Eller).

*Children:* Christine Angela Booth (Sunnie Pelant) and Hank Booth (with Temperance); Parker (Ty Panitz) with ex-girlfriend Rebecca Stinson (Jessica Capshaw), who refused to marry him; it is later said that he and Rebecca were married.

*Address:* 101 Vermont Street, Apartment 2C in Washington, D.C. (over a liquor store called Sportsman's; he later lives with Temperance at her home).

*Occupation:* Special FBI agent and liaison between the FBI and the Jeffersonian Institute. He was formerly an Army Special Forces sniper (a sergeant major during the Gulf War; in some episodes, he is mentioned as being an Army Ranger [101st Airborne Division, 75th Ranger Regiment], skilled at knife throwing, and an FBI profiler). When he was with the Army Rangers, he was captured and tortured before being rescued.

*Religion:* Roman Catholic.

*Nickname for Temperance:* "Bones" (so called when Temperance's intellectual ramblings often tick him off and using "Bones" is the only way he can get her attention).

*Quirk:* He accepts Temperance and her team for what they can do, but deep down he mistrusts science and feels that instinct is also needed to solve crimes.

*Music Preference:* Rock.

*Favorite Music Group:* Foreigner.

*Fear:* Clowns.

*Office Wall:* Contains a framed "Wanted" poster of 1930s mobster John Dillinger and his fingerprint card.

*Education:* While schools are not named, Seeley enrolled in college on an athletic scholarship and was on the football team; he showed potential as a professional until he injured his shoulder and turned his attention to the military (wherein he enlisted after graduation; he earned money as a dance instructor while in college at $30 an hour).

*Character:* Seeley tries to be less robotic and more human in questioning suspects and capturing criminals. He does find the information Temperance gathers valuable to his investigation, but he dreads dealing with her restrictive methods based only on what science has to offer; he uses his own intuition and knowledge of people to guide him and thus constantly clashes with Temperance.

*Allergy:* Pollen.

*Personal Items:* When Seeley appears on camera, the following items can be seen with him at various times: a holstered gun, a girl-revealing pen (holding it upside down will cause a girl to disrobe, and she will appear nude), his FBI identification card, a $100 poker chip, a pair of dice, a St. Christopher medal that he always wears, his sunglasses, a cigarette lighter, and a 3-by-5 index card. He also has tattoos on both wrists.

*Van Bumper Sticker:* "Soccer Moms Kick Grass."

## CAMILLE SAROYAN

*Place of Birth:* Bronx, New York, in 1974.

*Occupation:* Forensic pathologist (and head of the Forensics Division of the Jeffersonian Institute; she was formally a police officer, then a coroner, for the New York Pathology Unit before transferring to Washington, D.C.; she claims the Jeffersonian facilities are much cleaner [up to date] and present a safer work environment).

*Nickname:* "Cam."

*Sister:* Felicia Saroyan (Rochelle Aytes); Camille's parents are not given first names.

*Husband:* Arastoo Vaziri (Pej Vahdat).

*Children:* Michelle (natural); Isaiah, Jordan, and Tyler (adopted).

*Character:* By the book and will not tolerate nonsense. She will also not deviate from the letter of the law even if she knows certain aspects of the law are wrong when applied to specific cases on which she is working.

*Measurements:* 34-23-34; she stands 5 feet, 7 inches tall.

*Fear:* Snakes and spiders.

*Hypnotic Trance:* As a younger woman, Cam volunteered to be the subject of a Las Vegas showman during his performance. When she heard the word "coffee," she would "cluck like a chicken." Although she claims to be over the suggestion, it still affects her on occasion.

*Actress:* To earn money while living in Manhattan, Cam appeared in a sleazy film called *Invasion of the Mother Suckers.*

*Past Habit:* Smoking.

## JONATHAN "JACK" STANLEY HODGINS IV

*Parents:* Anne and Jonathan Hodgins III. They are wealthy (owners of the Cantilever Group) and contribute to the Jeffersonian Institute (Jack is heir to the family corporation but keeps it a secret from his colleagues, as he wants to be respected for his work, not his wealth).

*Brother:* Jeffrey Hodgins (Jonno Roberts).

*Wife:* Angela Montenegro (see below). Jack wore his wedding ring on his left pinkie.

*Son:* Michael Staccato Vincent Hodgins.

*Occupation:* Entomologist at the Jeffersonian Institute.

*Expertise:* Insects, minerals, and spores.

*Nicknames:* Most often called "The Bug Guy" (but also "Hodgepodge" by Camille, "King of the Lab" by himself and Temperance, "Hodgey" by Angela, and "Slime Guy," "Bugs," and "Bugboy" by Seeley).

*Hobby:* Exploring conspiracy theories.

*Religion:* Episcopalian.

*Medical Issue:* In season 11, Jack is seriously wounded in an explosion that paralyzes him from the waist down.

*Political Affiliation:* The Green Party (although he votes Democrat "because they have a better chance of winning").

## ANGELA MONTENEGRO

*Date of Birth:* April 16, 1978.

*Birth Name:* Pookie Noodlin Pearly-Gates Gibbons (her name at the end of the series is Angela Pearly-Gates Hodgins-Montenegro). She changed her name to Angela Montenegro when she was 18 (when it came to her in a dream).

*Father:* Billy Gibbons, a guitarist with the group ZZ Top (she was named after Billy's guitar, "Miss Pearly Gates"); her mother is revealed to be Chinese. Real-life guitarist Billy Gibbons plays himself (although in a fictionalized version, as Angela is fictional).

*Husbands:* Grayson Barasa (divorced; they were married in Fiji); Jack Hodgins (current). It is revealed in season 8 that Angela is bisexual, having had a long-term romance with a woman named Roxie Lyon.

*Education:* University of Texas at Austin (bachelor's degree in fine arts; a minor in computer science); American University (studied biomedical illustration).

*Position:* Head of the Imaging Unit of the Medico-Legal Lab.

*Expertise:* A three-dimensional artist (she reconstructs victims' facial features from skull remains [from a program she created first called "The Angelator" and later "The Angelatron"]).

*Measurements:* 34-24-34; she stands 5 feet, 8 inches tall.

*Nicknames:* "Ange" by Temperance, "The Queen of Egypt" by herself, and "Angie" by Jack.

*Religion:* Agnostic.

*Character:* A free spirit who considers Temperance her best friend. She is caring and can sometimes be seen as the glue that holds her team together (although she is seen as not so normal at times due to the unsettling graphic nature of her job).

*Odd Ability:* Angela "can spit with deadly accuracy."

*Most Disturbing:* Having to reconstruct the facial features of a child.

## ZACHARY "ZACK" URIAH ADDY

*Place of Birth:* Michigan in 1981.

*Occupation:* Forensic anthropologist at the Jeffersonian Institute. He was originally Temperance's assistant (a graduate student) before earning his doctorate in forensic anthropology and mechanical engineering.

*Nicknames:* Most often called "Zacharoni" and "Z-Man."

*Specialty:* Determining the cause of death from skeletal remains.

*Religion:* Raised as a Lutheran; now an atheist.

*IQ:* 163 (he was a child prodigy and claims to possess a photographic memory).

*Past:* Wore an eye patch when he was six years old (presumably as part of a club) and was a singer in his youth.

*Medical Issue:* Lost mobility in his hands due to an accident (an explosion; he can be seen wearing gloves, presumably to hide the scars he sustained after his hands healed).

# *Burn Notice*

## (USA Network, 2007–2014)

*Principal Cast:* Jeffrey Donovan (Michael Westen), Gabrielle Anwar (Fiona Glenanne), Bruce Campbell (Sam Axe), Sharon Gless (Madeline Westen).

*Basis:* A former CIA operative (Michael Westen) uses his prior training to help people threatened by circumstances beyond their control.

## MICHAEL ALAN WESTEN

*Place of Birth:* Miami, Florida.

*Parents:* Madeline Westen and Frank Westen (deceased).

*Brother:* Nate Westen (Seth Peterson).

*Background:* Michael and his father simply did not get along. Frustrated with living at home, Michael joined the army at the age of 17 (he left with a change of clothes and $50; his mother signed the consent form, as Michael was underage, so he could get a fresh start in life). His skills from boot camp earned him a position as an Army Ranger, service with the Special Forces and the Army Combat Applications Group and then a position as a covert

Jeffrey Donovan, Gabrielle Anwar, and Bruce Campbell. *USA Network/Pho-tofest © USA Network*

intelligence operative for the CIA (operating mostly in the Middle East and eastern Europe).

*The Change:* While in Nigeria, Michael discovers that he is no longer recognized by his agency. He receives a burn notice (services no longer required) while on a dangerous undercover assignment. The mission goes sour, but Michael manages to escape and returns to his hometown of Miami Beach, Florida. He seeks out a friend (Fiona) and learns that the CIA has frozen his bank accounts, canceled his credit cards, and refuses to acknowledge he even exists. But why? (Miami Beach was chosen as the background "because it is his hometown and the feds can easily keep tabs on his every move—and it's a great location for showing bikini-clad babes with bouncing boobs running along the beach every two seconds.") Other than watching girls, Michael decides to do something constructive. Through an agency contact (not part of the conspiracy), Michael meets Sam Axe, an alcoholic ex–military intelligence agent (and "ex–everything else" as he says). Sam has contacts (although he is unable to help Michael with his CIA problems) and sets Michael up as a private detective to solve the problems of other people and, it is hoped, find out why he was given the burn notice and who is responsible for it. Sam and Fiona then become his team.

*The Business:* Michael establishes his office (and home) in a run-down loft over a nightclub that is anything but comfortable or appealing. There is no air-conditioning, little furniture, and a refrigerator that seems to contain only beer and yogurt (blueberry being his favorite). He uses an out-of-date 1990s computer and rarely complains about his living conditions.

*Character:* Because of his abusive childhood, Michael is reluctant to commit to any long-term relationships with a woman. Although taught to kill by the CIA, Michael has a sense of justice that will not allow him to do that in civilian life. He uses everything at his disposal to avoid killing during a case but will kill if there is no other choice or his client's life is in imminent danger. Michael also has a strange habit of helping himself to the food in the refrigerators of homes he breaks into during a case.

*Abilities:* Skilled in explosives, firearms, military weapons, chemical warfare, espionage, torture, and devising weapons from ordinary devices (like cell phones and toasters) to the unthinkable (like cake frosting and potatoes). He can speak Russian, Arabic, and some Spanish and is skilled with accents that allow him to impersonate any character and blend into any setting a situation calls for. He is a highly trained strategist and carefully plans each maneuver before acting on it. He finds employing psychological warfare the best means of defeating the enemy (as he feels that getting to know his target and learning their weaknesses will cause the least collateral damage). His training has also afforded him knowledge of the human body, enabling him to act quickly to address any injuries that may occur during a mission.

*Legend:* Michael's name is feared in Russia (Russian intelligence believes that "Michael Westen is the code name for U.S. Special Ops because no one man could do such damage").

*Wardrobe Feature:* His Victory-style sunglasses were custom made by Oliver Peoples for the series (Michael claims he did not buy them but "borrowed" them from an Algerian special operations soldier he battled "who did not need them anymore").

*Quirk:* Whistles when impressed by something.

*Car:* A 1973 Dodge Charger (once owned by his father).

## FIONA GLENANNE

Fiona, born in Dublin, Ireland, is a former member of the Irish Republican Army who now assists Michael in his effort to uncover the people behind his burn notice. She was also a gun runner and is an expert on all types of explosives. Fiona, called "Fi" by Michael, has a brother, Sean, and a sister, Claire. Although Michael and Fiona have a past relationship (that Michael broke off when his cover was blown during a mission), Fiona appears determined to renew that relationship when he returns to Miami after being burned.

Fiona has little patience when it comes to dealing with her enemies (the people who are harassing Michael's clients). She is a shoot-first-ask-questions-later type of gal (in her case, however, it is blow something up, then ask questions). Michael often opposes Fiona's reckless endangerment of people's lives but has little influence in stopping her. She is proficient in hand-to-hand combat, an excellent mimic (can adapt to any dialect or personality), and an excellent (but somewhat reckless) driver. Seeing abused children or children placed in dangerous situations is Fiona's Achilles' heel. She won't wait for the police to resolve such situations and takes it on herself (with Michael and Sam's help) to do so.

Fiona is a very beautiful woman and uses that advantage to infiltrate "the enemy" and acquire information for Michael. Michael and Fiona are two of a kind—they are attracted to each other and meant to be with each other but afraid to make a commitment, as Fiona, more than Michael, thrives on disorder (but she also believes that she and Michael belong together for better or worse; it happens in the final episode, when they are together in Ireland).

## SAMUEL "SAM" AXE

Sam has many military connections (having served as a navy SEAL and with military intelligence) but is unable to uncover the people responsible for Michael's burn notice. Sam was considered one of the world's best intelligence operatives but since leaving the military has become a slacker and a ladies' man. He is addicted to alcohol but still maintains the sharp talents he learned and used serving with the SEALs. While he does help Michael and Fiona, he is not one for rushing into a situation and is more cautious than both Michael and Fiona. While it would appear that with his background Sam would be living comfortably on a pension, the FBI has frozen that pension in an effort to get Sam to inform on Michael (something he won't do); he gives them just enough information to please them without exposing Michael.

Sam has also become Michael's mother's (Madeline's) protector, as Michael assigns him to safeguard her when he feels that a mission will hit too close to home and put his mother in harm's way. Madeline is a heavy smoker (of Morley cigarettes) and embraces Sam and Fiona and often goes undercover for Michael on assignments.

Sam's style of dress is also very casual, most often Hawaiian shirts, linen pants, a Rolex watch (accompanied by seemingly expensive jewelry), and sunglasses. While it is not apparent, Sam does possess some unique skills: wiretapping, burglary, hand-to-hand combat, forgery, interrogation, surveillance, and an endless source of contacts. Sam also possesses the ability to assume personalities with the name "Charles Finley" (his favorite undercover alias). Sam mentions that he played football while attending high school in California.

*Note:* In the episode "A Dark Road" (January 21, 2010), Sharon Gless (Madeline) was reunited with her former *Cagney and Lacey* costar, Tyne Daly, in a story that found Madeline teaming with her friend Tina (Daly) to acquire information for Michael at a senior citizen center.

# Castle

(ABC, 2009–2016)

*Principal Cast:* Nathan Fillion (Richard Castle), Stana Katic (Kate Beckett), Molly Quinn (Alexis Castle), Susan Sullivan (Martha Rodgers).

*Basis:* Mystery novelist Richard Castle accompanies New York police detective Kate Beckett to not only acquire story material but also help her solve crimes.

## RICHARD CASTLE

*Place of Birth:* New York City in April 1969.

*Occupation:* Former private detective turned crime novelist.

*Book Characters:* "Derrick Storm," then "Nikki Heat." When Richard feels that writing the Derrick Storm character has become more like work than fun, he kills him off. When a series of murders occur that duplicate those found in Richard's books, New York police detective Kate Beckett (see below), an avid reader of Richard's books, approaches him and asks for his help in solving the crimes. Finding renewed interest in writing, Richard creates a new detective for his books—"Nikki Heat" (whom he patterns after Kate).

*Publisher:* Black Pawn Publishers.

*"Derrick Storm" Books: In a Hail of Bullets* (his first novel), *Death of a Prom Queen, Hell Hath No Fury, Storm Fall,* and *Flowers for Your Grave.*

*"Nikki Heat" Books: Heat Wave* (the first novel), *Naked Heat, Heat Rises,* and *Frozen Heat.*

*Birth Name:* Richard Alexander Rodgers.

*Pen Name:* Richard Edgar Castle (because he felt it sounded better for a writer; he took the middle name of Edgar after his favorite writer, Edgar Allan Poe).

*Mother:* Martha Rodgers (see below); Jackson Hunt (an alias) is his father (a CIA spy who distances himself from his family to protect them).

Stana Katic and Nathan Fillion. *ABC/Photofest © ABC*

*Address:* 595 Broome Street in the Soho district of Manhattan.

*Wives:* Meredith (Darby Stanchfield), his first ex-wife and an actress; Gina Cow-
ell (Monet Mazur), his agent, then publisher (second ex-wife); Kate Beckett
(current wife).

*Children:* Alexis (with Meredith; see below); Lily and twin sons Jake and Reese
(with Gina).

*Reason for Writing:* To understand how criminals operate.

*Writing Inspiration:* As a child, when he was cared for by various nannies
(who would watch daytime soap operas), the ABC serial *One Life to
Live* inspired him. He later claims that in 1983, when he was 11 years
old and on a trip to New Hampshire, he became lost in the woods and
stumbled on the body of a murdered woman. On his return to New York,
he anonymously called the police. When he learned that an investigation
turned up no evidence of the woman's body, Richard became interested
in the case and studied missing-persons cases, determined to solve the
crime. While he never did, he did write a short story about his experiences
called *A Death in the Woods.* It could also be seen that as a high school
student, Richard spent much time in the New York Public Library reading stories by Carolyn Keene (Nancy Drew mysteries), Edgar Allan Poe,
and Sir Arthur Conan Doyle (Sherlock Holmes mysteries). This too could
have been his inspiration. Still another scenario finds Richard, now age

14, attending Edgewick Academy, where, to pass the time (homesick and without friends), he developed an interest in writing. He also attended Faircroft Academy (but here it is mentioned he was quite mischievous and spent more time in detention than in classes). In his unnamed college, he apparently returned to his love of writing, finding the local bar, The Old Haunt, his favorite place to write. He also says that his first rejection letter is his motivation for writing. Yet again, Richard says that the novel *Casino Royale*, given to him by his father during one of the few times he met with him (at the library), was his inspiration.

*Unusual Interests:* The macabre, murder, and death.

*Honor:* Voted New York's ninth top eligible bachelor by *Ledger* magazine.

*Flashbacks:* Richard, age 11 (Webb Baker Hayes).

## KATHERINE HOUGHTON BECKETT

*Parents:* Jim (Scott Paulin) and Johanna Beckett.

*Place of Birth:* Manhattan on November 17, 1979.

*Husbands:* Rogan O'Leary (divorced) and Richard Castle.

*Occupation:* Homicide detective with the 12th Precinct of the New York Police Department (NYPD). Before being promoted to captain, she was one of the youngest women to become a detective and has a reputation for tackling crimes that seem to fall outside the box. She was a former model turned federal government agent.

*Badge Number:* 0334 (later 41319).

*Character:* Smart, tough, and determined; she joined the police force after her mother's unsolved murder. Her firsthand experience with tragedy has fueled her desire to bring closure to the victims of tragedy and their families. She and Richard constantly bicker, as she is a by-the-book officer and must work with his nonprocedural, theorized approaches to solving crimes. Kate is honored to be the inspiration for a book character but dislikes the name "Nikki Heat," as she feels it is a stripper's name. Although Kate asks Richard to change it, he never does.

*The Partnership:* Although Richard was teamed with Kate only to solve the case of a killer using his books as a guide, he became intrigued and used his influence with the city's mayor to continue as Kate's "unofficial consultant." Kate is not as enthused as Richard, as she feels that "he's like a nine-year-old with a sugar rush, incapable of taking anything seriously." But Kate, a control freak, has no choice and must work with "the annoying, self-centered, egotistical" Richard Castle.

*Fascination:* Magic (as a child, her grandfather would take her to the Drake Magic Shop) and comic books (she envisioned herself as the superhero Electra).

*Education:* Stuyvesant High School; Stanford Law School (she dreamed of becoming the first female Supreme Court justice). She transferred to New York University to study law enforcement after her mother's murder (stabbed to death by an unknown assailant for an unknown reason in 1999 when she was on her way to meet Kate and Jim for dinner). She now wears her mother's wedding ring as a remembrance of a life she lost (she also helped her father, who turned to alcohol after the murder, become sober; she now wears his wristwatch as a reminder of saving a life). Kate also mentions that Richard's books as well as two fictional TV series, *Temptation Lane* and *Nebula 9*, helped her overcome what happened and became part of her inspiration to join the police force (and to also have the opportunity to solve her mother's murder).

*Favorite Sport:* Baseball.

*Favorite Real TV Show: Saved by the Bell* (as a teenager).

*Favorite Music Group:* KISS (she even wore a Gene Simmons costume for one Halloween).

*Transportation:* A 1994 Harley motorcycle (which she purchased with the money she earned while modeling).

*Coffee:* A skim latte with sugar-free vanilla creamer.

*The Unknown:* Kate has a tattoo (apparently small and not visible; she never reveals what it is).

## OTHER CHARACTERS

Martha Rodgers is Richard's mother, a New York City socialite who gained fame as a Broadway actress (famous for her stage work, which won her a Tony Award). She had to move in with Richard when her ex-husband swindled her out of her life savings. She is a bit controlling and feels the need to point Richard (and Alexis) in the direction she thinks is right. She operates the Martha Rodgers School of Acting and is noted for her performance as Titania in a Shakespeare in the Park production of *A Midsummer Night's Dream*.

Alexis Castle is Richard's 18-year-old daughter (by his first wife Meredith), a college student who claims that "it's a curse being so irresistible." Alexis displays wisdom and insight beyond her years, and while she inherited her father's charm, she is not overly pleased by his devil-may-care attitude. She also appears to be inheriting her father's adeptness at solving crimes.

Javier Esposito (Jon Huertas) is a homicide detective with the 12th Precinct (works with Detective Kevin Ryan). He previously served with Special Forces and as an officer with the Organized Crime Task Force of the NYPD's 54th Precinct. He considers himself a ladies' man, is a loyal and dedicated cop, and is full of wisecracks. He is the prototype for the "Nikki Heat" book series character "Detective Ochoa." He is a victim of a broken home (his parents divorced when he was five years old) and became a juvenile delinquent (a record for numerous petty misdemeanors). He can speak English, French, and Spanish; was raised by his mother; and is a Catholic. He likes watching the Spanish telenovelas and is a big fan the Animal Planet channel's *Shark Week* specials.

Kevin Ryan (Seamus Dever) is a homicide detective with the 12th Precinct of the NYPD. He works with Javier as part of Kate's unit. He worked with the Narcotics Division of the police department before the Homicide Unit. He possesses a unique knowledge of obscure facts, which, at times, help Kate and Richard solve a crime. Kevin wears badge number 42344 and dislikes watching horror films (frightened as a child by one such movie and now fears characters like Freddy Kruger [*Nightmare on Elm Street*]; he also mentions being weary of nuns, who taught him in Catholic school). He was born in the Bronx and served as an altar boy at church. His favorite color is blue, and he took piano lessons as a child. He is from an Irish family and has two sisters (Karen and Stacy), and Richard based his "Nikki Heat" book series character "Detective Raley" on him. He is allergic to feathers, liked the TV series *Curious George* as a kid, and even wanted his own pet monkey. Kevin is married to Jenny Ryan and is the father of Sarah Grace and Nicholas.

Victoria Gates (Penny Johnson Jerald) is the 12th Precinct captain. She replaced Captain Roy Montgomery (Ruben Santiago-Hudson), who was killed while investigating a case. She is "as by the books as they come." She is determined to do what it takes to reach a high-ranking position at police headquarters at One Police Plaza. She was previously with the Internal Affairs Division, where she earned the nickname "Iron Gates." She prefers to be addressed as "Captain" or "Sir." She is somewhat bitter, as Kate beat her out for the honor of becoming the youngest female detective by six weeks. Gates is a stickler for following the rules and is not too thrilled with Richard, whom she feels is a professional embarrassment but puts up with him due to his friendship with the mayor. She is a fan of the mythical TV series *The Wives of Wall Street* and collects Gemini dolls.

# *The Closer*
## (TNT, 2005–2012)

*Principal Cast:* Kyra Sedgwick (Brenda Leigh Johnson), G. W. Bailey (Louie Provenza), Jon Tenney (Fritz Howard), Michael Paul Chan (Mike Tao), Mary McDonnell (Sharon Raydor), Gina Rivera (Irene Daniels), J. K. Simmons (Will Pope).

*Basis:* A team of detectives, headed by Brenda Leigh Johnson, investigate crimes as part of a special unit created to better serve the public and bring homicide cases to a successful conclusion.

## BRENDA LEIGH JOHNSON

*Parents:* Clay (Barry Corbin) and Willie May Johnson (Frances Sternhagen). Clay was in the air force (for 25 years), and Brenda was born on a military base in August 1966.

*Hometown:* Atlanta, Georgia.

*Brothers:* Bobby, Clay Jr., and Jimmy Johnson.

*Niece:* Charlene "Charlie" Johnson (Sosie Bacon). Sosie is actually Kyra Sedgwick and her husband's (Kevin Bacon's) daughter. Charlene lives with Brenda after a falling-out with her parents (Bobby, Brenda's brother, and his wife Joyce).

*Husband:* FBI agent Fritz Howard (see below).

*Occupation:* Deputy chief of the Los Angeles Police Department's (LAPD's) Major Crimes Division (originally called the Priority Homicide Division). She first worked for the Atlanta Police Department, then the U.S. State Department, and finally the CIA. She turned down a job with the Department of Homeland Security for the Major Crimes position. When Brenda retires (final episode), she becomes chief of the Bureau of Investigation for the Los Angeles district attorney's office.

*Nickname:* "The Closer," a person who has the ability to interrogate suspects and solve cases.

*Character:* Very pretty, tough, and dedicated to her job of arresting criminals. She is a rather sloppy housekeeper but fastidious when it comes to her job. Brenda never bluffs—"I just express my optimism forcefully." She says what is on her mind and rarely shows any compassion for suspects. While she goes by the book during investigations, she appears to have her own set of rules when cases become puzzling. Brenda must take charge of every assigned case and, because of the work she puts into a case, claims she would like to quit at times because it overwhelms her—"It's so frustrating to work so hard for so long with so little appreciation."

*Office Number:* 935.

*Wardrobe:* Very stylish dresses and skirts; she rarely wears jeans or slacks (she first wore them in the season 4 episode "Dial M for Provenza").

*The Johnson Rule:* Established after Brenda released a suspect and he was killed: "The LAPD cannot knowingly release a suspect or witness into a hostile environment."

*Addiction:* Sweets (especially donuts and chocolate bars; she carries some in her purse wherever she goes and has a stash in her desk drawer). In times of stress, her willpower to resist sweets tends to desert her.

*Major Fault:* Bad at keeping in touch with people—"I can't even keep an address book together."

*Pet Cat:* Kitty (she can also be heard calling it "Joe").

*Ringtone:* Brenda has a T-Mobile phone, and the ringtone is the same as the one heard in their commercials (an example of product placement).

*Measurements:* 35-25-35; she stands 5 feet, 5 inches tall.

*Medical Issue:* In season 3, Brenda begins acting erratically and, after seeing a doctor, is diagnosed with polycystic ovarian syndrome (a hormonal disorder that causes the ovaries to enlarge with small cysts on the outer edges). It is treatable, and Brenda suffers no aftereffects (she can still have children).

*Security Blanket:* Her oatmeal-colored sweater (she wears it when she is under stress and overwhelmed by a case).

## OTHER CHARACTERS

Louis Provenza, called "Louie," is a lieutenant and second in command of the Major Crimes Division. He has been married five times (Liz, Heather, Sharon, and Heather [whom he remarried]; he is eventually married to Patrice Perry). He is a 40-year veteran of the LAPD and joined Brenda's unit when it was first formed (under the name Priority Homicide Division). He was previously with the Robbery-Homicide Division.

He is the oldest member of the unit and won't retire; he claims the only way he'll leave is when he is killed on the job. Louie appears cynical as well as lazy but has an eye for noticing small and seemingly insignificant clues (that often lead to breaking a case). Prior to his first name being mentioned, Louie was called either "Provenza" or "Lieutenant." He has been on the force (and still on active duty) longer than anyone from his original academy graduating class. He has a strange habit of naming the crime scene reconstruction mannequins after his former wives and, due to his attitude, has been sent to sensitivity training classes. Although Louie mentions that "snitching on people" is how he started his career, he has been awarded several medals: the Medal of Valor, the Police Distinguished Service Medal, the Meritorious Service Medal, and the Police Star. His badge number is 35082.

Andrew "Andy" Flynn is a lieutenant and was formerly with the Robbery-Homicide Division of the LAPD before becoming a member of the Major Crimes Division. He is divorced from Sandra and will ultimately marry his second wife, Sharon Raydor (see below), at St. Joseph of Nazareth's Church. He and Sandra have a daughter named Nicole. Andy was an alcoholic (now sober for 15 years) and sometimes gets too emotionally involved in his cases. He wears badge number 2805.

Fritz Howard is the FBI special agent (Organized and Special Crimes Unit) who married Brenda (he was a former deputy chief with the Special Operations Bureau of the LAPD). He has a sister named Claire (Amy Sedaris), who believes she is a psychic (she assisted Brenda on a case). Fritz had been working for the LAPD before receiving his FBI training (he now assists Brenda with acquiring information from the FBI through his contacts). Love develops between Brenda and Fritz, and during season 2 they move in together (residing in Brenda's home) and marry shortly thereafter. Fritz, a recovering alcoholic, has two DWIs and is called "Fritzy" by Brenda. Although they work together, Fritz sometimes becomes upset with Brenda when their cases cross and Brenda doesn't always live up to her bargain to share information (Brenda will often ignore professional boundaries and even risk her job to see that a case is closed).

William "Will" Henry Pope was originally Brenda's love interest before Fritz (they had an affair when they worked together in Washington, D.C., while Pope was still married). He has been divorced twice (only his second ex-wife, Estelle, is mentioned). He held the rank of assistant chief of the LAPD, director of operations, interim police chief, and chief of police. He is responsible for recruiting Brenda to head the Major Crimes Division (originally the Priority Homicide Division when Brenda first joined). His reasoning: Brenda could provide prosecutors the evidence they needed to win cases.

Julio Sanchez is a detective with the Major Crimes Division (a member of Brenda's team); he previously worked with the Gang Intelligence Unit (he is an expert marksman and the source for information on local gangs). Ramona, his mother, as well as his older brother, Oscar, are deceased. His younger brother, Alonso, is currently in prison. Julio has been a widower for two years but hasn't taken off his wedding band. His work with the LAPD earned him the Medal for Valor. Julio is especially fond of children, and cases involving children always upset him. He is a third-generation American (as he states) and became the foster father of a boy named Mark Jarvis. He wears badge number 34150.

Michael "Mike" Tao is a lieutenant with the Major Crimes Division. Tao is Chinese and married to Kate, a Japanese woman; they are the parents of Kevin (and two additional unnamed sons). He completed one year of medical school and is a forensic specialist (processes crime scenes). He originally worked with the Scientific Investigation Division and then with homicide and vice. Mike also works as the technical adviser on a TV series called *Badge of Justice*. He wears badge number 2641.

Irene Daniels is a detective with the Major Crimes Criminal Division. Her specialty is forensic accounting (finding evidence in other forms of documents); she often works with the Department of Homeland Security. She has an unknown past, and nothing else is revealed about her.

Sharon O'Dwyer Raydor was introduced on *The Closer* during season 5 and spun off into the series *Major Crimes* (taking over Brenda's team when she resigned). Jackson Raydor is her ex-husband (they are the parents of Ricky and Emily); she is also the legal guardian of a boy named Rusty Beck, a witness to a homicide. Sharon and Andy Flynn later marry, but complications arise when she is diagnosed with a heart condition. She is given a pacemaker and placed on a list for a heart transplant. She is the commanding officer of the Major Crimes Division but worked previously as the commanding officer of the Force Investigation Division of the LAPD (attached to the Professional Standards Bureau and scrutinizing shootings or other violent acts involving officers). Sharon mentions that she wanted to become a lawyer but took a job as a police officer to pay her husband's law school tuition. He graduated but never returned the favor to help her through law school. He left her after their children were born. However, she found that she liked law enforcement better and chose a different profession. Sharon wears badge 951753. She is very strict and feared by her team (as she appears to have no sense of humor and things must be done as she says). She lives at 4411 Los Feliz Boulevard in Los Angeles; 555-0112 is her phone number; O'Dwyer is revealed to be Sharon's maiden name.

# Cold Case
## (CBS, 2003–2010)

*Cast:* Kathryn Morris (Lily Rush), Tracie Thoms (Kat Miller), Danny Pino (Scotty Valens), Nick Vera (Jeremy Ratchford), John Finn (John Stillman).

*Basis:* Lily Rush, a policewoman fascinated by unusual unsolved crimes that have been labeled "cold cases," uses her abilities to bring closure to the victims of such cases by exerting all her energies to solve them.

## LILLIAN "LILY" RUSH

*Place of Birth:* Philadelphia in January 1969. She grew up on Kensington Avenue, an area "where a child could grow up in tranquil surroundings." "Today," she says, "it is an area infested with hookers and drug dealers."

*Sister:* Christina Rush (Nicki Aycox).

*Childhood:* Lily was raised by an alcoholic mother (Ellen Rush [Meredith Baxter]; passed away in 2007) but apparently without a father. Lily and Christina were virtually ignored by their mother, and Lily's first traumatic experience occurred when she was 10 years old: Her mother sent her out late one night to buy her alcohol (apparently from an illegal source); she was beaten and robbed and suffered bruises and a broken jaw.

*Occupation:* Detective with the Homicide Bureau of the Philadelphia Police Department.

*Inspiration:* The "cop shows" she watched on TV as a child.

*Education:* Kensington High School; the University of Pennsylvania.

*Belief:* "Cold cases are more important because they have been waiting longer." She prefers these unsolved crimes to current crimes "because I don't like

Kathryn Morris, Thom Barry, Jeremy Ratchford, Danny Pino, and John Finn.
CBS/Photofest © CBS

bastards getting away with murder." Then-and-now footage is used to highlight Lily's case investigations with a ghostlike image of the victim being seen when Lily solves the case.

*Character:* Lily is optimistic when it comes to solving cold cases. She feels that new evidence, coupled with the cold case file, holds the answers to a crime. It is that enthusiasm that drives her and eventually allows her to close the file on a previously unsolved crime. When Lily feels there is a new direction, it means there is hope of solving a cold case—"People shouldn't be forgotten; they matter. They should see justice too." Lily is beautiful and never uses that asset to influence a case investigation. Her private life is just that: private. She enjoys evenings at home and an occasional date but reveals little else about herself.

*Measurements:* 36-26-35; she stands 5 feet, 7 inches tall.

*Food Preference:* Vegetarian.

*Favorite Drink:* Scotch and soda.

*Despises:* People who believe that because she is a woman, she became a cop "because of a bad education and limited talent." Lily is highly educated and very talented and never gets praise, as a cold case does not appear to be a newsworthy event.

*Flashbacks:* Young Lily (Madison Meyer, Christina Cellner, Makenna Barrett, Megan Helin, and Harley Graham).

## KATHERINE "KAT" MILLER

Kat, as she is called, is a detective with the Philadelphia Police Department and a member of Lily's Homicide Unit. She first worked as an undercover cop and, while attempting to bust a gang, had an affair with a gang member (Jarrod Jones) that resulted in a pregnancy and the birth of her daughter, Veronica Miller. It was in 2005, when Kat was assigned to the Narcotics Unit, that her case crossed paths with one of Lily's cold cases (that of the 1973 murder of Carl Burton), and together they solved both cases.

John Stillman, a lieutenant and Lily's superior, was impressed and offered Kat a position with Lily's unit. Kat mentioned she grew up in Kensington (as did Lily), but apparently, after the area went bad, she had a difficult childhood in the crime-ridden area and was deprived of a good education.

## SCOTT "SCOTTY" VALENS

Scotty became Lily's partner in 2003 after he was transferred from Philadelphia's West Detective Precinct to the Homicide Unit. He is the son of Ramiro (Ismael "East" Carlo) and Rosa Valens (Terri Hoyos) and has an older brother named Mike Valens (Nestor Carbonell), a professional boxer. While exact years are not mentioned, Scotty was born in the late 1970s and joined the department in the early 1990s (he was promoted to detective in 1998; his first case was to infiltrate a drug cartel). Scotty's induction into Lily's unit was traumatic. He had remained friends with his childhood sweetheart, Elisa (Marisol Nichols), and they began dating in the early 2000s. Elisa was afflicted with schizophrenia, and her constant hospitalization simply began to wear Scotty down. In 2004, after being admitted to the hospital, Scotty was relieved to hear that Elisa was getting better and able to handle her condition. Several months later, however, Elisa's body was found floating in the Schuylkill River, with her death being declared a suicide. Scotty, informed by Lieutenant Sullivan as to what happened, is unable able to accept this and believes she was murdered. He apparently joins Lily's unit to solve not only Elisa's murder but other cold cases as well (Scotty has created a box on Elisa and stores it with the unit's other cold case box files).

## NICHOLAS "NICK" VERA

Nick was born in Philadelphia in the late 1960s. His grandparents emigrated from Russia, and through his grandfather, he can understand and speak Russian—even "the curse words," as his grandfather often used foul language. While his high school is not named, he was on the hockey team. He joined the Philadelphia Police Department in 1989 and was first assigned to its Ninth Precinct. Ten years later, he would become a detective and assigned to the department's homicide squad. One of his first cases involved finding a serial rapist whose crimes became deadly when he killed one of his victims (Gail Chimayo). Nick's driving ambition to find the killer never came to fruition, and Gail became a cold case that he is determined to solve. At that time he was transferred to the department's cold case unit.

## JOHN STILLMAN

John, a Vietnam War veteran, is a lieutenant with the Homicide Division of the Philadelphia Police Department and in charge of the cold case squad. His commitment to the job caused a strain on his marriage, and he is now divorced. He has a daughter and a grandson (not named) and an equally unnamed brother who is a Catholic priest.

# *Criminal Minds*
## (CBS, 2005–)

*Principal Cast:* Thomas Gibson (Aaron Hotchner), Mandy Patinkin (Jason Gideon), Joe Mantegna (David Ross), Paget Brewster (Emily Prentiss), Matthew Gray Gubler (Dr. Spencer Reid), A. J. Cook (Jennifer "J. J." Jareau), Lola Glaudini (Elle Greenway), Kirsten Vangsness (Penelope Garcia).
*Basis:* The cases of the BAU (Behavioral Analysis Unit; based in Quantico, Virginia, of the FBI) as they investigate horrific crimes.

## AARON HOTCHNER

*Wife:* Haley (Meredith Monroe); killed by fugitive serial killer George Foyet (C. Thomas Howell). Hotchner later begins a relationship with Beth Clemmons (Bellamy Young).
*Son:* Jack (Cade Owens).
*Sister-in-Law:* Jessica Brooks (Molly Baker).
*Brother:* Sean Hotchner (Eric Johnson).
*Occupation:* Profiler and unit chief of the BAU (and the media liaison officer). He was a former prosecutor (following in the steps of his father) and was originally assigned to the FBI field office in Seattle, Washington. As a prosecutor, Aaron felt that his services were stymied by red tape and joined the BAU to enable him to do what he wanted to do: capture killers.
*Change:* During season 12, Aaron and his son Jack are placed in the FBI's witness protection program when Jack becomes the victim of an unknown stalker (Emily Prentiss then takes over Aaron's position). When the stalker is killed, Aaron and Jack are taken out of protective custody, but Aaron elects not to return to the BAU and instead to raise Jack as a full-time father.
*Education:* Degree of jurist doctor from George Washington University in Washington, D.C.
*Work Philosophy:* "To catch a killer, you have to think like a killer."

*Character:* Totally dedicated to work at the cost of having a normal family life. He is serious, determined, and focused on leading his team. He rarely smiles (although a camera shot of his ID card does picture him with a smile). He carries a backup gun in a hidden ankle holster (although he is left-handed, both his service gun and his concealed gun are on his right side). Aaron is an expert with a sniper rifle and appears to have some knowledge of the Bible (as he often quotes from it).

*Hobby:* Collected coins in his youth.

*Favorite Music Group:* The Beatles.

*Blood Type:* O-negative.

*Sideline:* Teaches crisis negotiation from the book he cowrote, *Children of the Dark.*

## DR. SPENCER REID

*Parents:* Diana and William Reid. Jane Lynch plays Diana, who is suffering from schizophrenia and confined to a mental institution in Las Vegas; his father deserted the family when he could no longer deal with Diana's condition. Diana was a college professor (of fifteenth-century literature).

*Place of Birth:* Las Vegas, Nevada, on October 29, 1981.

*Occupation:* Supervisory special agent with the BAU.

*IQ:* 187.

*Address:* Apartment 23 at the Capital Plaza Apartments.

*Education:* Las Vegas High School (graduated at the age of 12); MIT, and Cal Tech (where he acquired degrees in engineering, mathematics, psychology, and sociology). An outcast growing up, Reid claims he learned everything he knows from reading books.

*Ability:* Can read 2,000 words a minute and has a photographic memory. He is also an expert at sleight-of-hand magic and sometimes uses that to trick suspects into revealing more than they would normally. He appears to have knowledge of forensic anthropology (as he is able to determine sex and race from skeletal remains). He demonstrates knowledge on historical serial killers (able to give statistics off the top of his head), geographic profiling, and body language. He has an ability to card count and has thus been banned from Las Vegas casinos.

*Character:* Clearly seen as socially awkward with an uncanny tendency to fixate on things. It is hinted that he shows signs of schizophrenia and autism (Asperger's syndrome). He dislikes the beach (too sunny and bright) and hospitals (due to bright lighting). He wears mismatched socks (believing it means good luck) and was nicknamed "Crash" by his grandmother (for his habit of bumping into things as a child).

*Favorite Movie: Star Wars.*

*Favorite TV Shows:* Doctor Who, Star Trek, and soap operas.
*Car License Plate:* WG S654.
*Favorite Drink:* Coffee (later seen drinking tea).
*Fear:* The dark ("Because of the inherent absence of light").
*Medical Issue:* Chronic headaches (he takes riboflavin and magnesium plus sporadic shots of E2 to hopefully prevent them).

## EMILY PRENTISS
*Mother:* Ambassador Elizabeth Prentiss (Kate Jackson); her father is not named.
*Date of Birth:* October 12, 1970.
*Occupation:* BAU unit chief and communications director. She was formerly with the FBI (Midwest field agent) and a BAU supervisory special agent. She resigned from the BAU after being shot to take a position with Interpol in London; she later returned to the BAU to become the unit chief.
*Religion:* Catholic.
*Languages:* English, French, Italian, Spanish, and Arabic.
*Expertise:* Terrorism and linguistics; she is also an expert at chess.
*Education:* Garfield High School; Yale University.
*Character:* Highly professional but tends to let her emotions interfere with her case investigations (she shows empathy for the victims of crime). She has a sarcastic sense of humor and takes unnecessary chances, often placing her life at risk. When she becomes frustrated over a case, she relieves anxiety by going to the unit's firing range and shooting.
*Measurements:* 37-26-37; she stands 5 feet, 8 inches tall.
*Pet Cat:* Sergio.
*Flashbacks:* Young Emily (Danielle Lester).

## PENELOPE GRACE GARCIA
*Place of Birth:* San Francisco in 1977.
*Occupation:* Technical analyst for the BAU and the media liaison officer (works in an office in Quantico and is not usually a part of field operations).
*Education:* California Institute of Technology.
*Background:* An orphan. Penelope, age 18, was out past her curfew when her parents came looking for her. They were killed when a drunk driver ran into their car. Penelope couldn't continue the life she had previously led and dropped out of college. She began to teach herself computer coding and became so skilled that the FBI placed her on a list of talented but dangerous hackers. Penelope dressed in black and called herself "The Black Queen." She was a member of Star Chamber and used hacking to expose companies she felt were engaged in criminal activities. Her attempt to access one such

organization, the BAU, failed when she was caught, but in lieu of prison, she was offered a job with Aaron's unit.

*Fear:* Clowns (when she was 12 and attending a birthday party, a clown grabbed her breast and made a honking sound; she has been fearful ever since).

*Hobby:* Knitting and "making soup."

*Service:* Heads a support group to help people who have lost loved ones.

*Car:* Calls it "Esther."

*FBI Badge Number:* 001-9-0.

*Food Preference:* Vegetarian.

*Vision Issue:* Nearsighted.

*Favorite TV Show: Small Wonder* (a real series about a 10-year-old robot named Vicki).

*Favorite Film Director:* Federico Fellini.

*Favorite Writer:* Joseph Campbell (a mythologist).

*Pet Cat:* Simba.

*Flashbacks:* Penelope, age five (Maddison Davis); Penelope, age nine (Christina Gabrielle); Penelope, age 20 (Rebecca Egender).

## DAVID STEPHEN ROSSI

*Place of Birth:* Commack, Long Island, on May 9, 1956.

*Occupation:* Senior supervisory agent and profiler with the BAU (he replaced Jason Gideon). He worked for the BAU in its early stages of development (20 years prior) but left to write books and lecture about criminal analysis.

*Military Service:* Marine private during the Korean War. He is later promoted to sergeant major.

*Marriage:* Has three ex-wives. His first wife, Carolyn Baker (Isabella Hofmann), suffers from Lou Gehrig's disease and later dies from a drug overdose. Hayden, an African American, is his second wife (a U.S. diplomat at the embassy in France). Krystal is his third wife (whom he met in Las Vegas and married after they both got drunk; the following day, they realized it was a mistake and divorced).

*Children:* James David (with Carolyn; he died shortly after birth on April 16, 1979); Joy (with Hayden).

*Specialty:* Hostage negotiation.

*Sport:* Bird hunting.

*Books:* Mentioned as writing *Evil Never Rests, Eyes of a Predator, Deviance: The Secret Desires of Sadistic Serial Killers, Understanding Evil,* and *Frenzy: America's Worst Spree Killers.*

*Belief:* True evil really exists (through his interviews with Charles Manson and Ted Bundy).

*Hobby:* Appears to be video games (as he expresses knowledge on the subject). As a child, he would take apart TV sets and radios to see what made them work.

*Favorite Sport:* Soccer.

*Favorite Meal to Cook:* The Italian dish Carbonara.

*Favorite Actors:* Dean Martin, Peter Lawford, Frank Sinatra, and Sammy Davis Jr. (members of the Rat Pack). He also mentions that he dislikes gangster movies (as he experienced gangsters in real life) and that as a child the silent movie *The Phantom of the Opera* (with Lon Chaney) frightened him (especially the scene "where the girl takes off the Phantom's mask").

*Dislikes:* Snakes (as did his grandmother); he also says he dislikes Los Angeles.

*Heritage:* Italian.

*Religion:* Catholic.

*Flashbacks:* Young David (Robert Dunne).

## DEREK MORGAN

*Parents:* Hank (African American) and Fran Morgan (Caucasian).

*Place of Birth:* Chicago on June 6, 1973.

*Sisters:* Desiree and Sarah Morgan.

*Wife:* Savannah Hayes.

*Son:* Hank Spencer Morgan.

*Occupation:* Supervisory special agent with the BAU. He was formerly a Chicago police officer (assigned to the Bomb Unit) and temporarily served as the acting chief of the BAU. He resigns (in season 12) to be with his family.

*Expertise:* Explosives, obsessive behavior, and fixations. He holds a black belt in judo and teaches FBI self-defense classes.

*Character:* Totally dedicated to his job, but his personality changes over the course of the series. He is first seen dressing in three-piece suits and always seeking to gain attention. This changes to a ladies' man type of character and concludes with his becoming serious and grim faced and rarely cracking a smile. It can also be seen that Morgan is particularly fond of Penelope.

*Education:* Northwestern University (attended on a football scholarship; graduated with a law degree; a knee injury ended his potential football career).

*Favorite Novel: Mother Night* (by his favorite author, Kurt Vonnegut).

*Favorite Music:* Rap.

*Favorite Sport:* Hockey (he dislikes baseball).

*Pet Dog:* Clooney.

*Trait:* Impatient and kicks down doors to enter a premises.

*Flashbacks:* Young Derek (Sterling Ardrey, Jordan Carroll, Tyree Brown, and Amaar Wooten).

## ELLE GREENWAY

Elle, born in New York on June 24, 1977, was called "Peanut" by her father (Robert) as a child. She is half Cuban, and her father, a police officer, was killed in the line of duty. She first worked for the FBI field office in Seattle before becoming a supervisory special agent for the BAU. She is an expert profiler, and her expertise is sexually based crimes. Elle becomes the victim of an unsub and suffers emotional trauma after being shot. Later, after confronting a serial rapist and shooting him at point-blank range, she resigns, saying, "This is not an admission of guilt" (the shooting is declared self-defense). Grace Kathryn Murdock plays Elle as a child.

## JASON GIDEON

Jason is the senior supervisory special agent with the BAU; he is also the team's most proficient profiler (which he has been doing since 1975). He was the first agent to leave after a series of troubling cases got the best of him and he felt no longer capable of handling the pressure, especially after the death of his friend Sarah at the hands of serial killer Frank Breitkopf. Jason is last seen in a Nevada diner where he is heard telling a waitress that he has no specific plans. He leaves the diner and drives off, but he is later killed (off-screen) by Donnie Mallick, who feared Jason would expose him for killing a woman. Mint chocolate was Jason's favorite flavor of ice cream, and he had an obsession with birds (and bird watching), disliked hunting, and regularly visited the Smithsonian Institution. He was known for taking toiletries from the hotels where he stayed and kept a journal of the people he encountered during his case investigations. Ben Savage played Jason as a teenager in flashbacks.

## JENNIFER "J. J." JAREAU

J. J. was born in East Allegheny, Pennsylvania (her mother is Sandy, but her father is unnamed). Her sister, Rosaline, committed suicide when she was 17 (J. J. was 11 at the time). She is a graduate of East Allegheny High School (where she was on the soccer team), the University of Pittsburgh (on an athletic scholarship), and Georgetown University in Washington, D.C. (where a speech by Rossi inspired her to join the FBI). She is married to William LaMontagne Jr. and is the mother of Henry and Michael. She first works as the communications liaison for the BAU, then as a liaison for the Pentagon, and finally as a profiler for the BAU. As a child, she collected butterflies, was (and still is) a fan of the Washington Redskins football team, and uses the screen name CheetoBreath (after her love of Cheetos snacks) to play online video games.

# Crossing Jordan
## (NBC, 2001–2007)

*Principal Cast:* Jill Hennessy (Jordan Cavanaugh), Ken Howard (Max Cavanaugh), Miguel Ferrer (Garrett Macy).

*Basis:* The cases of Jordan Cavanaugh, an unorthodox Boston medical examiner.

## DR. JORDAN CAVANAUGH

*Parents:* Max (a retired cop after 38 years on the force) and Emily Cavanaugh (deceased).

*Place of Birth:* South Boston (she is 32 years old when the series begins).

*Occupation:* Chief medical examiner for the Commonwealth of Massachusetts ("I cut up dead people for a living").

*Address:* 43 Victor Drive, Apartment 311. A poster of the singing folk duo Indigo Girls can be seen on her kitchen wall.

*Education:* St. Inez High School; University of Massachusetts, Amherst; Tufts University School of Medicine; her schooling is also said to be Boston University (top five in her medical class).

*Religion:* Irish Catholic.

*Favorite Color:* Purple.

*Imperfection:* A chipped tooth from an accident in the second grade.

*Skills:* Expert diagnostician.

*Problem:* Insubordination. She constantly clashes with her superiors, as she has an obsessive desire to solve crimes and do things her way.

*Award:* A commendation from the Chicago Police Department for solving five murders. She is opposed to injustice ("That pisses me off").

*Background:* When Jordan was born, her father followed an old Irish-Catholic tradition and gave her a rosary for her confirmation. As a child, Jordan would sneak out of her room at night to spy on her father as he sat at the kitchen table with a glass of scotch and all the evidence in the case he was investigating placed before him. Max would stare at the evidence and envision himself as both the killer and the victim in an attempt to solve the crime. Max always knew that Jordan was watching him and one night asked her, "Would you like to be the victim or the killer?" "And that's how it started," says Jordan. "It was like our very own game of Clue, only it wasn't Colonel Mustard in the drawing room with a knife." Max was forced into early retirement when he became obsessed with finding the man who killed his wife and Jordan's mother (mysteriously killed with no motive or culprit ever found). Max now helps Jordan through their game of role playing and with the contacts he has in the police department.

When Jordan and Max play their game, the audience sees a reenactment of the crime with Jordan as the killer and Max as the victim. Max now lives with a woman named Evelyn (Lois Nettleton), an old friend from high school who is a widow, and runs a bar called Cavanaugh's. His favorite dinner is vegetable lasagna, and he believes that Jordan is "pig-headed and stubborn."

*Contradiction:* Jordan later says that the book *Catcher in the Rye* changed her life when she read it at age 15 and that it—not the game she played with her father—prompted her to become a medical examiner.

*Character:* Jordan spent a year in Italy and speaks perfect Italian. She doesn't like to be challenged in her work and gets very emotional when a murder baffles her. She assures the victim, "I'm gonna find out who did this to you." She can take the simplest assignment and turn it into a murder investigation. She often works closely with Woody Hoyt (Jerry O'Connell), a detective with the Boston Police Department.

*Ability:* Plays the guitar and sings folk songs.

## DR. GARRETT MACY

*Position:* Chief medical examiner (Jordan's superior). He believes, "This place [coroner's office] is going to hell, and it's about to get crazier" (due to budget cuts). He says, "I'm more than a medical examiner; I'm an interesting guy."

*Substitute:* When Max is unable to join Jordan for their crime game, Garrett fills in but is not too happy to do so ("The last time I did this, I had nightmares for a week").

*Daughter:* Abby (Alex McKenna). Garrett is divorced from Maggie (Lindsay Frost) and struggling to raise Abby, a rebellious girl. Abby attends Loyola High School, and she and Garrett have a yearly tradition of eating at Yang Chao's Restaurant.

*Hobby:* Collects old vinyl records—mostly jazz and blues from the 1920s and 1930s. As a kid, he had a comic book collection (the series sound track features many classic songs, including those sung by Rosemary Clooney, Miguel Ferrer's mother).

*Car License Plate:* 50F VB1.

*Medical Issue:* High blood pressure from his job. He keeps a bottle of Pepto-Bismol in his desk drawer, has insomnia, and has a hand puppet dog "that my shrink gave to me to say things that I can't say to other people."

*Allergy:* Strawberries.

*Assistant:* Lily Lebowski (Kathryn Hahn), the intake girl who coordinates matters; she is later the office grievance counselor.

# CSI: Crime Scene Investigation
## (CBS, 2000–2015)

*Principal Cast:* William Peterson (Gil Grissom), Marg Helgenberger (Catherine Willows), Jorja Fox (Sara Sidle), George Eads (Nick Stokes), Gary Dourdan (Warrick Brown), Paul Guilfoyle (Jim Brass).

*Basis:* Stark portrayal of the work of the Crime Scene Investigation (CSI) Unit of the Las Vegas Police Department.

## OVERALL SERIES INFORMATION

The unit, also known as the Criminalities Division of the Metropolitan Las Vegas Police Department, is located on North Trop Boulevard. It is considered the number two crime lab in the country and solves crimes that most labs believe are unsolvable. Gil Grissom is its chief investigator and oversees the "Body Farm" in conjunction with the Department of Anthropology of the University of Western Nevada. It is a morbid, desolate area where bodies donated to science are studied and tracked by a team of scientists. "It's not creepy," Gil says. "It's a controlled study of situational decomposition in a very helpful place." The sign posted on the farm reads, "Private Property—Keep Out. All Persons in Violation Will Be Prosecuted Under Section 42.4.323.8470 of the Nevada Penal Code."

## GILBERT ARTHUR "GIL" GRISSOM

*Place of Birth:* Santa Monica, California, on August 17, 1956.

*Education:* University of California, Los Angeles (bachelor of science degree in biology).

*Position:* Originally supervisor of the graveyard shift of the CSI Unit; promoted to the unit's head (level 3) when Captain Jim Brass (see below), the former head, was transferred to the police department's Homicide Division.

*Special Skills:* Entomology (the study of insects).

*Background:* At the age of eight, Gil would frequent the beach at Marina Del Rey to collect dead birds to perform autopsies. As he grew older, he would find dead cats and dogs and do the same thing, teaching himself the ins and outs of death. Gil worked his way through college and at the age of 22 became the youngest coroner in the history of Los Angeles County. Eight years later, he was recruited by the Las Vegas Police Department to run their CSI field office. Gil mentions that his father (unnamed) was in the import/export business and that his mother (Betty) ran an art gallery in Venice.

*Character:* Gil does not like people in his house, gets frustrated if a case baffles him, and likes to be in command of his team. He gets a migraine headache about once a year and enjoys chocolate-covered grasshoppers for a needed

The first-season cast of *CSI: Crime Scene Investigation*. *CBS/Photofest © CBS*

burst of energy. He can also speak sign language (taught to him by his mother, who was partially deaf; as the series progressed, Gil began to develop the same condition as his mother). He is an expert at poker and often wins—"It's how I funded my first body farm at college."

*Quirks:* Experiments with the "why" and the "how" of a killing but focuses more on the "how," as the "why" doesn't make sense to him. He leaves his experiments in the unit's community refrigerator when the lab's refrigerator is full. He also likes to believe he is smarter than a criminal and can find the evidence he or she may have left behind. "I hate it when the criminal is smarter."

*Greatest Challenge:* Finding Paul Millander (Matt O'Toole), a brilliant serial killer he is unable to apprehend. As a child, Paul saw his father killed over a money dispute. He now kills on a specific day each year—the day of his father's murder—which is also Gil's birthday.

*Religion:* Catholic.

*Hobbies:* Reading, solving crossword puzzles, riding roller coasters, and insect (roach) racing.

*Hates:* Abusive husbands, child predators, and drug dealers who target children.

*Belief:* "Evidence is like a fine wine: you can't just drink it, you've got to let it breathe." He and his team call themselves forensic criminologists and handle each case they receive "with no regard to race, creed, or bubble gum-flavor." But, as Gil says, "we also handle cases involving alive people—from drunk drivers to a child who is a victim of molestation to robberies. When the pieces of a puzzle don't fit, they call us in." He also believes the weather plays an important role in what they do: if it should rain, as an example, the team has three minutes to bag the body and gather evidence. In a missing-persons case, Gil says, "the first 24 hours are gold; after that, it's quicksand, and the worst it can get is a dead end." While Gil is reluctant to admit defeat, he does say of rain-soaked cases, "The killer got lucky tonight."

*Marriage:* Gil and coworker Sara Sidle (see below) marry and eventually leave the CSI Unit when Sara joins with Gil to help save sharks in international waters.

## CATHERINE WILLOWS

*Place of Birth:* Bozeman, Montana, on March 26, 1963.
*Parents:* Lily Flynn and Sam Braun.
*Maiden Name:* Catherine Flynn.
*Ex-Husband:* Eddie Willows (Timothy Carhart).
*Daughter:* Lindsay Willows (Madison Reynolds); she attends Butterfield, a private school.
*Education:* West Las Vegas University (bachelor of science degree in medical technology).
*Background:* Catherine was born on a farm and craved excitement; a rural life was not for her. She left home at an early age and headed for Seattle, Washington, where she found work as a waitress. When this failed, she returned to Montana to find that her parents had divorced and sold the farm. With no place to call home, she settled in Las Vegas, where she first worked as a waitress, then as an exotic dancer. With the money earned there, she entered college. It was at this time that she met a sleazy music producer (Eddie) and had a daughter (Lindsay). Constant bickering between Catherine and Eddie led to their marriage breaking up. When Eddie split, Catherine was left with $10, a cocaine habit, and a daughter to raise. She then woke up, realized what had happened, and turned her life around. Catherine's birth history is later changed to reflect her being born in Las Vegas when her mother, Lily, a casino showgirl, had an affair with Lloyd Braun, the casino owner. Lloyd took no responsibility for Catherine, and Lily raised her on her own.
*Position:* Senior investigator. She was first an officer with the Las Vegas Police Department, where she was spotted by Gil Grissom, a field service

officer, who recruited her for his CSI Unit. Over a 10-year period, she worked her way up from assistant technician to her current status: CSI, level 3. She became an FBI agent in Quantico when she resigned from CSI.

*Interest in Police Work:* It is seen that when Catherine worked as a stripper, she befriended a regular customer named Jimmy Tadero (Felonious Monk), a police detective who piqued her interest in crime solving when he would tell her about the cases he was working; it changed the course of her life.

*Expertise:* Blood-spatter analysis. Catherine scrutinizes every crime scene and says of herself and her team, "We're like a bunch of kids getting paid to work on puzzles. You feel like King Kong on cocaine when you solve a puzzle." Catherine often photographs the evidence she finds and re-creates what happened by piecing together that evidence.

*Belief:* Human behavior plays a part in solving a crime (Gil believes that only the forensic evidence is necessary to solve crimes).

*Religion:* Catholic.


## SARA SIDLE

*Place of Birth:* Tamales Bay, California, on September 16, 1971.

*Education:* Harvard University (bachelor of science degree in physics). She also attended graduate school and has a degree in theoretical physics.

*Position:* Investigator. She first worked at the San Francisco Coroner's Office for five years before being transferred to the crime lab.

*Specialty:* Material and element analysis.

*ID Number:* 037-784

*Expertise:* Arson. Gil believes that Sara becomes too involved in a case, especially when a victim survives and she vows to find the culprit who is responsible. If an unknown substance is found at a crime scene, she delights in trying to figure out what it is.

*Background:* Sara's hippie parents ran a bed-and-breakfast, and she became interested in police work as a child. She listened to police scanners at home and studied forensic magazines in her spare time. She likes houseplants but now, obsessed with solving crimes, maxes out each month on overtime. In the episode "Goodbye and Good Luck" (aired on November 15, 2007), Sara chooses to leave her job with the CSI Unit. It is apparent by her somber attitude that Sara has become disenchanted with her job and realizes that no matter how many murderers she captures, she will never be able to stop the killing. Sara was attracted to Gil, and it is later revealed, when Sara returns to the unit, that she and Gil are married.

*Car License Plate:* 019 ATO.

## NICHOLAS "NICK" STOKES

Nick, a field operative, was born in Dallas, Texas, on August 18, 1971. His father was a district attorney before becoming a judge, and his mother worked as a public defender. He mentions having five brothers and one sister. He has a bachelor of science degree in criminal justice from Rice University, and his specialty is hair and fiber analysis. Another episode mentions he is a graduate of Texas A&M University. Nick previously worked with the Dallas Police Department before being transferred to its crime lab (CSI, level 1). He was then assigned to the Las Vegas Crime Lab. Nick likes being around people but is easily frustrated over a case. "Sometimes I hate this job," he says. He dislikes peanut butter and finds watching the Discovery Channel beneficial to his work.

## WARRICK BROWN

Warrick was born in Las Vegas on October 10, 1970, but his father abandoned the family when Warrick was still an infant. His mother died when he was seven, and he was raised by his grandmother. He had a normal high school education but had to work to put himself through college (jobs included taxicab driver, grave digger, bell captain at the Sarah Hotel and Casino, and selling helicopter rides over the Grand Canyon). He possesses a bachelor of science degree in chemistry from the University of Nevada, Las Vegas, and immediately went to work for the Las Vegas Police Department (where he was recruited by Gil for his CSI Unit). His specialty is audio-video analysis. He is also the team's crime scene photographer and is an expert at figuring out what item was used to do what. He is a stickler for gathering evidence and brilliant at piecing together fragments of objects to make them whole or identifiable. Warrick can visually detect evidence others may have overlooked but suffers from a gambling problem that is not fully under control.

## JAMES "JIM" BRASS

Jim was born in Newark, New Jersey, on January 3, 1953. He has a bachelor of arts in history from Seton Hall University and has logged 22 years on the police force—first in New Jersey and then with the Las Vegas Police Department. He was mainly an administrator at CSI before being transferred to homicide. He is most often assigned to the same cases as Gil's unit. Jim lives at 554 Applegate Way and believes that every police recruit should experience an autopsy on their first night to see if they have what it takes to be a CSI investigator. Although he is a captain, Jim introduces himself to suspects as Detective Brass.

## OTHER CHARACTERS

In the episodes aired from January 18, 2007 to February 8, 2007, Michael Keppler (Liev Schreiber) was brought on to temporarily replace Gil Grissom, who took a leave of absence to teach at Williams College in Williamstown, Massachusetts (a seminar called "The Seasonal Behavior of the Walden Pond Swamp Mosquito"). Michael was a forensics investigator who joined the Las Vegas Police Department after having served in Baltimore, Philadelphia, and his hometown of Trenton, New Jersey. He was killed off when a rapist he had been tracking shot him.

In the episode "19 Down" (aired on December 11, 2008), Gil Grissom announces to his team that he is leaving the unit (no specific reason given) and that his replacement will be Raymond Langston (Laurence Fishburne), a criminal pathologist Gil met while attending one of Raymond's teaching classes. Langston is a former medical doctor who, after assisting in a murder investigation, becomes a level 1 CSI operative (later level 2). Ray, the son of a Korean War veteran, was raised in Korea. Ray left the series to help his ex-wife, the victim of a brutal kidnapping, overcome the trauma.

D. B. Russell (Ted Danson) replaces Catherine as the night shift supervisor when Catherine chooses to leave the unit. Like Catherine (and Gil), D. B. is totally dedicated to the job despite the fact that his work sometimes means being away from his wife and four children. D. B. previously worked in the CSI Unit in Washington State and finds that no matter how much knowledge one may possess regarding crime detection, there are cases so unconventional that you sometimes have to make it up as you go along to solve them.

# CSI: Miami

## (CBS, 2002–2012)

*Principal Cast:* David Caruso (Horatio Caine), Emily Procter (Calleigh Duquesne), Adam Rodriquez (Eric Delko), Rory Cochrane (Tim Speedle), Khandi Alexander (Alexx Woods).

*Basis:* The investigations of the members of the Crime Scene Investigation (CSI) Unit of the Miami-Dade Police Department.

### HORATIO CAINE

*Place of Birth:* Miami, Florida, on April 7, 1957; another episode mentions his birthday as April 17, 1960.

*Occupation:* Lieutenant with the CSI Unit of the Miami-Dade Police Department.

*Education:* Florida State University (bachelor of science degree).

*Expertise:* Arson and explosives.

*Background:* As a child, Horatio grew up in an era of drugs, race riots, and Cuban freedom fights. When Horatio was 17, his mother (unnamed) stood up to a drug dealer and was killed. Horatio knew from that moment on that he had to do something and helped the police find her killer. He also realized that he found his true calling: protecting the city he loves. He enrolled in the Miami Police Academy after graduating from high school. However, when he was assigned to walk a beat, he had found it boring and unrelated in what he wanted to do. Soon after, when he discovered it was the CSI Unit that actually solved major crimes, he enrolled in a four-year criminology program at the University of Miami. He graduated as a level 1 criminologist and eventually became the head of the CSI Unit. Another story line reveals that Horatio was raised by an abusive mother and father and, after high school (1995), traveled to New York City, where he joined the New York City Police Department (and became a detective). After being injured (stabbed by a culprit), Horatio moved to Miami and joined the police department's bomb squad, then the CSI Unit.

*Character:* Horatio is a three-dimensional thinker and has the ability to place pieces of a puzzle together. He knows that science provides the solutions to a crime, and he incorporates all the field has to offer. When he catches a killer, he is satisfied; the motive doesn't appear to matter to him.

*Favorite Leisure Activity:* Fishing.

*Nickname:* Called "H" by his colleagues.

*Wife:* Marisol Delko (Alana de la Garza), the sister of Horatio's colleague, Eric Delko; she died after being shot by a sniper.

*Obsession:* Capture Esteban Carlos Navarro (Kuno Becker), a serial killer nicknamed "The Miami Taunter."

## CALLEIGH DUQUESNE

*Place of Birth:* Darnell, Louisiana, on February 28, 1974.

*Occupation:* Detective with the Criminal Investigation Unit of the Miami-Dade Police Department (she is also the assistant day shift supervisor).

*Expertise:* Ballistics (firearms and tool marks).

*Education:* Tulane University (physics degree).

*Second Language:* Spanish.

*Background:* Calleigh grew up in a small, rural town and was the daughter of rich parents (her father, Kenwall "Duke" Duquesne, was a public defender with a drinking problem). Her parents constantly bickered, but Calleigh's father taught her the ins and outs of guns. She learned that she was capable of doing everything a man could and that upholding justice was the highest call of all. After graduating from college, Calleigh attended police rookie school and began her career as a street cop with the New Orleans Police Department. Her knowledge of firearms earned her the nickname "Bullet Girl," and she was reassigned to the crime lab. She became a member of the Miami CSI Unit when its head, Horatio Caine, recruited her.

## ERIC DELKO

*Place of Birth:* Miami, Florida, on December 19, 1976.
*Occupation:* Detective with the CSI Unit.
*Education:* University of Miami (degree in chemistry).
*Expertise:* Fingerprint analysis and drug identification.
*Background:* Eric was conceived in Cuba but born in the United States. His
   father, Pavel Deletrosky, was a Russian engineer working in Cuba (early
   1970s). There, he met Clorinda, a young Cuban woman he later married.
   They had three daughters. When Pavel learned that their fourth child was
   to be a boy (Eric), he smuggled his family out of Cuba across the Straits
   of Florida. It was the only way Pavel knew how to give his unborn son a
   future. Pavel found work as an engineer, while Clorinda worked with the
   various Cuban charities in Florida. Eric learned to help others from this.
   Although Eric excelled in science in grammar and high school, he discovered his true love, swimming, in high school. He graduated with a swimming degree and enrolled in college. After graduating, he used his skills
   as a swimmer for the Miami Police Department's Underwater Recovery
   Unit. During a bomb scare investigation, Eric met Horatio Caine, who
   became impressed with Eric's work and recruited him as the first member
   of his CSI team. He calls Horatio "Boss" and often doubles as the unit's
   crime scene photographer.

## TIMOTHY "TIM" SPEEDLE

*Place of Birth:* Syracuse, New York, on June 24, 1973.
*Occupation:* Chief investigator for the CSI Unit.
*Education:* Columbia University (in New York; a degree in biology).
*Expertise:* Trace and impressions evidence.
*Background:* Tim's father was an entrepreneur and ran a chain of family restaurants; his mother was a volunteer in social services. He grew up around
   abandoned and neglected children and gained a sense of compassion to
   help people solve problems beyond their control. The library became his
   hangout during high school. He read everything science had to offer and
   won the state science championship four years in a row. In college, Tim
   devoted himself to the science of paralysis (as the result of a friend's being
   stricken). A year later, while vacationing in Florida, Tim accompanied his
   police officer uncle to the Miami Crime Lab and became fascinated by
   what he saw. He studied and observed and knew what he had to do. He
   interned at the Miami Crime Lab for six months before being recruited by
   Horatio Caine.
*Departure:* Rory Cochrane left the series in 2004 for other ventures; Tim was
   written out when he was shot and killed during an investigation.

**ALEXX WOODS**

*Place of Birth:* Queens, New York, on August 13, 1960. She is the oldest of five
brothers and sisters.

*Occupation:* Medical examiner with the CSI Unit.

*Education:* New York University (bachelor of science degree in chemistry); Rut-
gers University (an MD).

*Background:* When her parents worked long hours to keep the family out of
poverty, Alexx became a substitute mother and cared for her siblings. As a
result, she became compulsively neat. By the age of 12, she wanted to become a doctor, and her parents encouraged this; her determination earned
her a college scholarship. She began work with the New York City Coroner's Office but left that position for a job with the state-of-the-art crime
lab in Miami-Dade County.

*Quirk:* An unusual affinity with the victims of violent crimes, to whom she
promises closure.

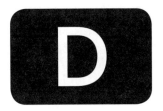

# Dark Angel
(Fox, 2000–2004)

*Principal Cast:* Jessica Alba (Max Guevara), Michael Weatherly (Logan Cale), John Savage (Colonel Donald Lydecker), Jensen Ackles (Alec McDowell), Nana Visitor (Dr. Elizabeth Renfro).

*Basis:* A girl (Max), genetically created to be the perfect soldier, escapes her bonds to live free and destroy the organization that created her.

## MAX GUEVARA

*Background:* Technically, Max is a chimera (a mythological creature) and has 11 brothers and sisters (children who were created at a secret genetics lab called Manticore located in the mountains of Gillette, Wyoming). Its scientists sought to produce superior humans for the military. Women were used to produce the children whose DNA was altered. The mother and child were never permitted to meet, and thus Max has no knowledge as to who her biological mother is. Max was placed in Block 12 with a group of children designated as "X-5."

*The Escape:* On a snowy night in February 2009, Max, now nine years old (Geneva Locke), and 11 other children manage to escape from Manticore and separate. Max is found by Hannah Sukovic (Eileen Pedde), a nurse at Manticore who rescues and shields her (as she felt Manticore was wrong in what it was doing). A short time later, after leaving Hannah, Max continues her escape, stowing away on a supply truck headed for Casper, Wyoming. It was here that she befriended a girl her own age, Lucy Barrett (Kristen Marsden), and was taken in by Lucy's mother, Joann, when Max told her she was "running away from a bad place." The years pass, and Max eventually finds her way to Los Angeles and then Washington State in search of those who had also escaped. It is the year 2019 when the series begins, and Max finds herself in a world that is in a depression. Computers and other electronic devices have been wiped out by an electromagnetic pulse (designated as "The Pulse") by terrorists, and the United States is now a Third World country.

*Home:* Max now resides in Seattle, Washington, and is "living a life on the run and always looking over my shoulder."

*Job:* Although Max is a bike messenger for Jam Pony-X-Press Messenger Service, she is actually a thief. ("I steal things in order to sell them for money. It's called commerce.")

*Greatest Fear:* Donald Lydecker, an army colonel assigned by Manticore to apprehend Max and the other escapees. Lydecker has a plan for Max and others like her: "Instead of sending 1,000 soldiers into battle and losing 100, send in 10 perfect soldiers and lose none."

*Manticore ID:* A bar code on the back of her neck: X5-452-332960073452. Max is considered to be a rogue X-5 by Manticore. She is top of the line (other X-5s have been affected by an aging process, an acceleration of the genes that ages them dramatically, and Max's DNA is needed to create flawless soldiers).

*Abilities:* The pupils in Max's eyes work like a telescope lens and can pinpoint distant objects. She is able to dodge a bullet and has a photographic memory. Although Max was genetically engineered to kill, she is opposed to guns and will kill only if there is no alternative. She can see in the dark and prowl like a cat and doesn't need to sleep. She also has an immune system that makes her incapable of catching disease.

*Blood Type:* All X-5s contain O-negative blood.

*Measurements:* 34-24-34. She stands 5 feet, 6 inches tall and has black hair.

*Genetic Flaw:* Seizures (she must take the medication tryptophan to control them).

*Mode of Transportation:* A Kawasaki motorcycle (plate JG 154).

*Catchphrase:* "Gotta Bounce" (which she says when she rides her motorcycle).

*Human Trait:* Will steal, cheat, and lie to get what she wants.

*Lip Balm Preference:* Cherry flavor.

*Alone Time:* When Max feels she needs serenity, she seeks it at the top of the Seattle Space Needle ("I look down at the people and think how everybody has problems, and if I sit up here long enough, I start to feel like I'm one of those people, a normal girl").

*Childhood Memory:* When imprisoned at Manticore, Max found faith in "The Lady of the Sacred Heart" (whom she called "The Blue Lady" [for the blue garments she wore]; she is a variation on the Virgin Mary).

*Childhood Fear:* The Nomilees (supposed creatures who drank blood; they are actually Manticore genetic mistakes concealed in the basement).

*Assistant:* Logan Cale (see below), a cyber-journalist seeking to bring criminals to justice.

*Series Change:* In the first-season finale (May 22, 2001), it is revealed that the mysterious Madame X (Dr. Elizabeth Renfro) heads Manticore. She frames Lydecker for a killing in an attempt to capture Max. Her plan backfires when Lydecker teams with Max and Logan to bring Manticore down by destroying the DNA lab. The episode ends with Max being captured by Renfro as she attempts to destroy the lab. The second-season opener (September 28, 2001) reveals that Madame X requires Max's unique DNA to create flawless soldiers and that Manticore is thought of by the outside world as a VA hospital (Max was found to have no junk DNA; each one of her cells is coded for a specific use). Before Madame X can control Max, she escapes through a secret tunnel and not only destroys Manticore but also unleashes the Nomilees that were concealed in the lower level of the building and feared by Max. There is now a threat to the city—unearthly creatures who prey on innocent people. Max and Logan are now followed as they attempt to expose Manticore as a government cover-up and protect people from the Nomilees.

## LOGAN CALE

Logan is a cyber-journalist who secretly operates a nontraceable cable broadcast called *Streaming Freedom Video*, wherein he reveals information to authorities to help them catch criminals (he hacks under the name "Eyes Only" in a post–"The Pulse" world when technology has been mostly restored). His telecasts, which last exactly 60 seconds, "cannot be traced and cannot be stopped."

One night, while attempting to rob Logan, Max is caught in the act. Logan, however, does not call the police. He notices the bar code on the back of Max's neck, realizes who she is, and offers to help her find her roots if she will help him. Max refuses until Logan is shot and crippled by one of the criminals he is seeking to catch. He is able to walk after a blood transfusion from Max (her cell-enriched blood enables new tissue growth, but the effect is not permanent, as it will not fuse his severed spinal cord). Logan was born in 1988 and is the son of a wealthy family. He is afraid of heights and is divorced from Valerie.

## ALEC MCDOWELL

Alec (Manticore ID number X5-494-331845739494) was created to become a soldier of the future (through genetic manipulation). He is one of 10 such Beta Soldiers programmed to use flirtation as a weapon. He escaped in 2020 (when Max destroyed Manticore) and joined with her in an effort to find other Manticore escapees and give them refuge in Terminal City (also known as Transgenetic City and T.C.).

Although Alec appears as an ordinary human, he possesses a number of unique abilities: an enhanced immune system, telescopic eyesight, an accelerated healing system, and enhanced hearing, agility, speed, stamina, strength, and coordination. He also has a very high IQ and a photographic memory. Like Max, he has the universal blood type O-negative, but if he should become injured beyond his enhanced healing abilities, he can receive a blood transfusion only from another X-5. Alec was trained for military combat, strategy, and espionage (with knowledge of weapons, martial arts, and the ability to withstand brainwashing).

# *Desperate Housewives*
## (ABC, 2004–2012)

*Principal Cast:* Teri Hatcher (Susan Mayer), Felicity Huffman (Lynette Scavo), Eva Longoria (Gabrielle Solis), Marcia Cross (Bree Van de Kamp), Nicollette Sheridan (Edie Britt), Andrea Bowen (Julie Mayer), Steven Culp (Rex Van De Kamp), Brenda Strong (Mary Alice Young and narrator), Ricardo Antonio Chavira (Carlos Solis), Doug Savant (Tom Scavo).

*Basis:* A look at the lives of five vastly different women (Bree, Edie, Gabrielle, Lynette, and Susan) living on Wisteria Lane, a seemingly meticulous neighborhood in the city of Fairview. The Wisteria Lane ZIP code is 00057, and car license plates show Fairview to be in "Eagle State, U.S.A."

## SUSAN MAYER

*Unmarried Parents:* Addison Prudy (a feed store owner) and Sophie Bremmer (who raised Susan on her own).

*Address:* 4353 Wisteria Lane.

*Education:* Mentioned only as Community College (in high school, she was a cheerleader and class valedictorian).

*Occupation:* Children's book author and illustrator; owner of the Double D Strip Club (which she inherited). She also worked as a school art teacher and for a risqué website (an "internet model") that led to her losing her teaching job (as school officials thought she was setting a bad example).

*Book: Ants in My Picnic Basket.*

*Ex-Husband:* Karl Mayer (a divorce attorney who left her for his younger secretary). Susan eventually remarried (plumber Mike Delfino), and together they had a son they named M. J.

*Daughter:* Julie. Susan is raising Julie alone and appears to live on "store-bought meals," as Susan can cook only macaroni (and not very well).

Marcia Cross, Eva Longoria, Teri Hatcher, and Felicity Huffman. *ABC/Photofest* © *ABC*

*Character:* Known for her streak of bad luck, especially when a romance happens and a dark cloud casts its shadow and Susan is alone again. Twelve-year-old Julie is very knowledgeable and looks out for her mother, even offering her dating advice.

*Measurements:* 34-24-34; she stands 5 feet, 6 inches tall.

*Exercise:* Jogging.

*Car:* Volvo XC 70.

*Flashbacks:* Young Julie (Coral Conroy).

**LYNETTE SCAVO**

*Parents:* Stella Lindquist and an unnamed father.

*Sisters:* Lucy and Lydia Lindquist.

*Address:* 4355 Wisteria Lane.

*Husband:* Thomas "Tom" Scavo.

*Children:* Porter (Shane Kinsman, then Charlie Carver), Parker (Zane Huett), Preston (Brent Kinsman, then Max Carter), and Penny (Kerstin and Darien Pinkerton, Jordan Cline, Angelina Ganiere, Darcy Rose Byrnes, and Kendall Applegate). Lynette calls them "Little Monsters."

*Education:* Northwestern University.

*Occupation:* Executive at the Parcher and Murphy advertising agency. She worked previously at an unnamed ad agency (where she met Tom; she gave up her career to raise her children), then Scavo's Pizzeria (started by her husband). She and Tom later move to New York when Lynette's friend Katherine Mayfair (Dana Delany) offers her a job as the CEO of her interior design company (a sideline she started during the series). They now live in a penthouse overlooking Central Park.

*Affiliation:* Wisteria Lane Book Club.

*Character:* Neurotic and stressed out. Lynette is always on the go, finds little time for relaxation, and had a miscarriage and a bout with cancer. She is a Boy Scout troop leader and finds herself involved with her children's school only when they get in trouble and she needs to see the principal. For relaxation, Lynette takes her children's ADHD medication. Despite it all, she says, "It's the best job I ever held."

*Measurements:* 34-26-33. She stands 5 feet, 5 inches tall and has blonde hair and blue eyes.

## GABRIELLE SOLIS

*Place of Birth:* Los Colinas, Texas, on December 8, 1976.

*Parents:* Lucia Marquez and an unnamed father.

*Husband:* Carlos Solis (they later divorce); Gabrielle then hooks up with Victor Lang (John Slattery), a politician running for governor.

*Children:* Celia Solis, Lily Helm (adopted), Juanita Solis, and Grace Sanchez (Grace, Gabrielle's biological daughter, was switched at birth with Juanita and raised by Hector and Carmen Sanchez). Gabrielle's first pregnancy ended in a miscarriage; she and Carlos had planned to name the baby Aurora (if a girl) and Charlie (if a boy).

*Address:* 4349 Wisteria Lane.

*Occupation:* A high-fashion model who gave up her career for a rich husband (Carlos) and life as a housewife.

*Character:* Beautiful, manipulative, deceitful, cunning, and unfaithful to Carlos. As a model, Gabrielle had a taste for rich food and rich men and admits she was a slut and had hoped her old ways would vanish when she married Carlos.

*Background:* Gabrielle, also called "Gaby" and "Gabriella," grew up in a very poor home (with several unnamed siblings) where her parents struggled just to make ends meet. Her father was diagnosed with cancer when she was six years old, and she developed a smug attitude. Following her father's passing, her mother married a man named Alejandro Perez, but the situation became intolerable for Gabrielle when Alejandro sexually assaulted her. Her mother believed it was Gabrielle who seduced him. No longer able to be in the same house as her mother, Gabrielle, now 15 years old, left home and, believing that her beauty was the ticket to her success, traveled to New York City. There, she met a photographer who saw model potential in Gabrielle and took her on as a client. Her pictures appeared in various fashion magazines, leading her to become a model and befriend people in the entertainment and fashion industry. It was at a runway show that Carlos Solis became attracted to Gabrielle, and the two married after their third date (although Carlos's mother, Juanita "Mama" Solis [Lupe Ontiveros], hated Gabrielle and became a constant source of aggravation in their married lives). Gabrielle, however, pretends to love Carlos to cover up her affairs with other men.

*Blood Type:* O-positive.

*Allergy:* Lilies.

*Favorite Drink:* Merlot wine.

*Favorite Dance:* Salsa.

*Measurements:* 34-23-33; she stands 5 feet, 7 inches tall.

## BREE VAN DE KAMP

*Place of Birth:* Rhode Island.

*Parents:* Henry Mason and an unnamed mother (killed by a drunk driver when Bree was 10). Henry later married his mistress (Eleanor).

*Address:* 4354 Wisteria Lane; she later moves to Louisville, Kentucky.

*Husband:* Rex (a doctor).

*Children:* Andrew, born in 1988 (Shawn Pyfrom), and Danielle (Joy Lauren), born in 1989.

*Occupation:* Cookbook author and caterer.

*Education:* Chicago area Lake Forest College (where she met Rex during a Young Republican's speech).

*Measurements:* 34-24-34. She stands 5 feet, 10 inches tall and has red hair and green eyes.

*Pet Dogs as a Child:* Taffy, Munchie, and Coco.

*Hobby:* Gardening.

*Character:* Always impeccably dressed and tries to be the perfect wife and mother. She makes her own clothes and prepares exotic meals for her family. She is a sentimentalist and enjoys celebrating holidays. She also has an alcohol problem.

*Habit:* Presenting a basket of freshly baked muffins to new neighbors.

*Childhood Demons:* Felt guilty for not getting straight "A's" in school; as a teenager, she felt guilty for letting her boyfriend take advantage of her sexually; as an adult, she first felt guilty about taking three weeks to send out thank-you notes for her wedding gifts.

*Secrets:* Concealing the facts that her son (Andrew) killed Juanita—Gabrielle's mother-in-law—in a hit-and-run and that her daughter (Danielle) had a baby out of wedlock.

*Life Change:* As the series progressed, Bree turned to alcohol after Rex's death (killed by a jealous pharmacist), turned her catering business into an empire, married for a second time (Orson Hodge, a dentist played by Kyle MacLachlan), and became a cougar after her divorce from Orson (resulting from Bree's extramarital affair and Orson becoming paralyzed after a plane crash). She later marries Trip Weston (Scott Bakula), a lawyer (they moved to Kentucky, where Bree entered politics and was elected to the Kentucky State Legislature).

*Affiliation:* A member of the National Rifle Association and the monthly Wisteria Lane Book Club.

*Cars:* A Saturn, Chrysler, Lexus RX, and finally a Lexus LS.

*Medical Issue:* Allergies (needs to take antihistamines).

*Flashbacks:* Bree, age 10 (Mackenzie Brooke Smith).

## EDITH "EDIE" BRITT

*Parents:* Ilene Britt and an unnamed father.

*Ex-Husbands:* Charles McLain and Umberto Rothwell.

*Son:* Travers McLain (cared for by Charles, as Edie has given up parental custody, feeling it would be better if Charles raised him).

*Occupation:* Realtor for the Fairview Realty Company.

*Company Address:* 125 North Main Street.

*Cell Phone Number:* 555-0199.

*Home Address:* 4362 Wisteria Lane (later 4350 Wisteria Lane).

*Background:* Edie had a difficult childhood, as her parents seemed not to care for her and she would spend her adolescent years hanging out with the wrong crowd at the docks (where Edie would smoke and drink). It is also said that Edie's family has a musical background, but she grew up without a father (deserted the family) and became promiscuous, something that has followed her in her adult life. At one point, after her mother was arrested, a court-appointed social worker cared for Edie.

*Character:* Considered the black sheep of the neighborhood. She is single (divorced) and very flirtatious (a "slut," according to some residents, as she is always boasting of her romantic conquests). Edie doesn't like to worry because she feels it will give her wrinkles. She feels the need to show others her fabulous body by wearing seductive clothes and explains her numerous sexual escapades as "a healthy sex life."

*Measurements:* 36-26-37; she stands 5 feet, 7 inches tall.

*Church:* First Methodist Church.

*Death:* When Edie swerves to miss hitting another car, she crashes her car into a utility pole. Unknown to her, standing water is under her car. Electrical lines are dangling around her, and when she steps out of the car, she is electrocuted when the car door touches the power line.

*Flashbacks:* Young Edie (Kara Stribling).

## MARY ALICE YOUNG

Mary (real name Angela Forrest) is the series narrator who weaves her own story into the lives of Bree, Gabrielle, Lynette, Susan, and Edie. She knows their hopes, dreams, fears, and desires but also, most importantly, their secrets. Mary Alice worked as a nurse and lived at 4352 Wisteria Lane. She was married to Paul (Mark Moses) and was the mother of Zach (Cody Kasch). Her dark past and desperation to find a normal life led her to commit suicide (self-inflicted gunshot wound to the head; mentioned as being on a Thursday, but a camera shot of her gravestone reads September 26, 2004, as the date of her passing, which was a Sunday). Her spirit has not left Wisteria Lane. She has returned from beyond to watch over and reveal the intimate details of her former friends and their families.

# *Dexter*

### (Showtime, 2006–2013)

*Principal Cast:* Michael C. Hall (Dexter Morgan), Jennifer Carpenter (Debra Morgan), Lauren Velez (Maria LaGuerta), James Reemar (Harry Morgan), Julie Benz (Rita Bennett), Erik King (James Doakes).

*Basis:* A blood-spatter specialist (Dexter Morgan) takes the law into his own hands by systematically killing the murderers who beat the system (and leaves no trace behind as to who did it).

## DEXTER MORGAN

*Place of Birth:* Miami Beach, Florida, on February 1, 1971.

*Biological Parents:* Laura Moser and Joe Driscoll.

*Adoptive Parents:* Harry and Doris Morgan.

*Biological Brother:* Brian Moser.

*Adoptive Sister:* Debra Morgan (see below).

*Wife:* Rita Bennett (see below).

*Stepchildren:* Astor (Christine Robinson) and Cody (Preston Bailey, then Daniel Goldman), Rita's children from a first marriage.

*Son:* Harrison Morgan (Luke Andrew Kruntchev) with Rita.

*Present Address:* 8420 Palm Terrace, Number 108 (in Miami).

Michael C. Hall (center) and the first-season cast of *Dexter*. *Showtime/Pho-tofest © Showtime; photographer: Christian Weber*

*Phone Number:* 744-3078.

*Childhood Address:* 1235 Mangrove Drive in Miami.

*Occupation:* Blood-spatter analyst for the Homicide Division of the Miami Metro Police Department (he collects, processes, and interprets evidence).

*Background:* When he was three years old, Dexter witnessed the murder of his mother, Laura, a police informant for Detective Harry Morgan (who was investigating the Estrada cartel). Laura, Dexter, and Brian were captured and placed in a shipping container with three other drug dealers. Dexter and Brian were spared, but Laura and the other three were slain with a chainsaw. Dexter and Brian sat in a pool of blood for two days before being found by Harry. Dexter and Brian appeared unaffected by the incident—at first. Because of Dexter's father's inability to care for him (being a recovering drug addict), Dexter was taken in by Harry and his family and officially adopted by them when Dexter was seven years old; it appears that Brian was sent to a foster home. When Harry noticed that Dexter had an unnatural urge to kill animals (and would most likely become a serial killer), he encouraged

Dexter and taught him how to focus on criminals, especially serial killers, and how not to leave any evidence behind.

*The Code of Harry:* Dexter, now with the police department, lives by the rules Harry taught him: never kill an innocent person (make sure the target is a killer who evaded justice), avoid getting caught, blend in, never appear suspicious, never leave behind any clues, and never make it personal (as it can lead to a capture). Dexter always follows the code; as he says after a killing, "I'm a very neat monster."

*Fascination:* Watching blood flow from a killer.

*Keepsake:* Taking a blood-slide sample of each victim (which Dexter calls "a blood trophy").

*First Kill:* After suffering a heart attack and being confined to a hospital, Harry noticed that a nurse (Mary) was purposely overdosing patients (including him). While visiting his father, Dexter (now 20) was told what was happening, and Harry gave him permission to kill Mary. Dexter then began his signature ritual (although he did not take a blood-slide sample from her).

*Victims and Disposal:* Once a killer escapes justice, Dexter targets that person. He stalks them to learn their routines, gathers evidence, and prepares his "kill room." After capturing his victim, he collects his "blood trophy," then thoroughly enjoys the next two steps: conduct the "kill ritual" and "dismember the body" (linking this part to his mother's murder). After making sure there is no evidence whatsoever, he places the body pieces in a black plastic bag and dumps the remains in the ocean from his fishing boat. When the police discovered 18 such bags, they labeled them the work of "The Bay Harbor Butcher" (which Dexter disliked). His blood collection is kept in his "Blood Slide Box" (each sample was obtained by drawing blood from a surgical cut on a victim's cheek). Dexter's victims were labeled as missing persons by the police before they were found.

*Kill Attire:* Dexter often uses the same disposable apparel that he incorporates in his police lab work: latex gloves, shoe coverings, hooded coveralls, and a face shield (mask and goggles) to protect him when using a power tool. He subdues each victim with a tranquilizer he calls "M-99."

*Character:* Dexter needs to be in control. If he cannot control himself or others, he can become careless and expose his true self. His lab notes are meticulous, his home is very neat and clean, and his kills are expertly planned and executed; as he says, "I'm a control freak." He is also a skilled manipulator and well versed in the martial arts, a computer hacker, and an accomplished hunter and tracker (taught by Harry how to use a gun, although he prefers a knife—"It's more intimate").

*Blood Type:* AB-negative.

*Fishing Boat:* Originally called *Slice of Heaven* and then *Slice of Life* when he began disposing of victims. It is docked at Coral Cove.

*Religion:* Atheist (he believes he would go straight to hell for what he is doing if he chose a religion). He has enrolled his son, Harrison, in a Catholic school (hoping it would present him with a structured lifestyle).

*The Dark Passenger:* Dexter calls his inner feelings about what he does "The Dark Passenger," something he believes is real and uses as his scapegoat for what he does.

*The Narration:* Dexter's narration relates each stage of what is happening in a personalized manner to what he is doing and plans to do.

*Secret Exposed:* Over the course of the series, a number of people stumbled on Dexter's secret. The most notable are Brian Moser, Dexter's older brother (who became the Ice Truck Killer; he avoided capture by hiding his normal self behind a mask of deception); Debra Morgan, who stumbled on Dexter's capture of the Doomsday Killer on a church altar; James Doakes, the police detective who deduced that Dexter was the Bay Harbor Butcher; Lumen Ann Pierce (Julia Stiles), a woman who saw Dexter kill the evil Boyd Fowler but whom he did not harm (Dexter held her hostage, but after learning that she was raped and tortured by members of the Barrel Girl Gang, he helped her dispose of the gang members); and Hannah McKay (Yvonne Strahovski), captured by Dexter for poisoning several people but spared when he discovered that she was actually disposing of bad people.

*Education:* While schools are not mentioned, he has a degree in forensic science. He has also taken courses in anatomy, chemistry, and biology.

*The Change:* Following Rita's death by the Trinity Killer, Dexter gives custody of his son Harrison to his friend Hannah, fakes his own death, and disappears, seeking to begin a new life as the series ends.

*Flashbacks:* Dexter as a child (Dominic Janes); as a teenager (Devon Graye); age three (Maxwell Huckabee); age seven (Nicholas Vigneau).

## DEBRA CHARLOTTE MORGAN

Debra, nicknamed "Deb," is Dexter's adoptive sister (whom Dexter calls his "foulmouthed foster sister" for her constant use of curse words). She is the daughter of Harry and Doris Morgan and was a tomboy as a child and somewhat jealous that her father spent more time with Dexter than with her. She chose to become a law enforcer and follow in Harry's footsteps. Her mother died from lung cancer when Debra was 16 years old. She began her career as a Miami Police Department patrol officer in 2001 and became a vice squad officer in 2006, a detective with the Homicide Division of the Miami Metro Police Department in 2008, and a lieutenant in the division in 2012. She was also seen as a private investigator and a bail bondswoman for El Way Investigations. Her life changed when she saw Dexter kill Travis Marshall, put the pieces together, and realized her brother was the mass murderer being sought by the police. This caused trauma within Debra, as she felt she could no longer trust him, and she questioned everything she did (as she followed the rules and believed that justice would prevail). As the series progressed, Debra eased her tension toward Dexter and would protect Dexter at any cost to prevent him from being exposed for who he really is (even killing to do so). She later uncovers the fact that Dexter's brother Brian is the notorious Ice Truck Killer (uses the back of an ice truck to kill people). A tragic event occurs for Dexter when Debra is critically shot in the stomach during a case and she lapses into a coma. When Dexter learns that Debra will never regain her brain activity, he unplugs her life support system, telling her as he does so that he loves her (words that she desperately wanted to hear from Dexter for years). She also becomes the last kill for Dexter.

*Flashbacks*: Debra as a child (Laura Marano, then Savannah Paige); as a teenager (Hunter King).

## RITA ANN BENNETT

Rita, age 36, is a former hotel concierge turned real estate agent. She is married to Dexter Morgan and the mother of their son Harrison. Rita (maiden name Brandon) was born in Ashley, Missouri, in April 1973. Her mother is Gail Marie Brandon, but her father is unknown. She lived at 321 Elmview Drive and married John Ackerman, a 21-year-old mechanic, when she was 16 years old in 1989 (they divorced four months later). At an unspecified time after, she had an affair with Paul Bennett and married him when she became pregnant with their daughter (Astor); they had one additional child (Cody), but the marriage ended due to his physical abuse of her (Rita fled to Miami with her children but was followed by Paul, who was then arrested by Debra Morgan during a domestic disturbance call; Dexter met Rita through Debra, and a relationship forms between them, although Rita was unaware of Dexter's secret). Rita and Paul divorce while he is serving time in prison. Rita's favorite sport is hockey, and although she and Dexter have a child together (Harrison), Rita becomes a victim of the Trinity Killer.

## JAMES DOAKES

James is a sergeant with the Homicide Division of the Miami Metro Police Department. He previously served with U.S. Special Forces (the Rangers in the Regimental Reconnaissance Detachment Unit), and the atrocities he witnessed (having to kill innocent people in black operations missions) instilled in him a desire to seek justice however he could—even by killing suspects when alone as opposed to just arresting them. He was one of the few people who knew Dexter's secret (by piecing together clues). Doakes has the ability to pinpoint troublesome situations, and it appeared that he could see the dark side of people (as he could see that Dexter was hiding something, especially since he says he got "the creeps" from Dexter). Doakes rarely interacted with his coworkers and looked on Dexter as a criminal. He was born in 1962 (parents unnamed, although Doakes mentions his father worked in a butcher shop). It is mentioned that he was married (wife not named) to an agent of the Bureau of Alcohol, Tobacco, and Firearms. He also had a close relationship with Maria LaGuerta (full name Maria Esperanza del Alma LaGuerta), the captain of the Homicide Division. She formerly served as a detective, then a lieutenant. Maria is determined and battles for power within the law enforcement system (even breaking protocol to get what she wants). She can be seen as manipulative (intimidates subordinates) and oversees virtually every case that comes before her.

# *Dollhouse*
## (Fox, 2009–2010)

*Cast:* Eliza Dushku (Caroline Farrell/Echo), Olivia Williams (Adelle DeWitt), Summer Glau (Bennett Halverson).

*Basis:* The activities of the Dollhouse, a secretive organization that performs highly questionable assignments through the use of programmed agents called Dolls (also referred to as Actives).

### CAROLINE FARRELL (ECHO)

*Place of Birth:* Los Angeles, California, on June 20, 1980.

*Parents:* Unknown (never seen or mentioned by name).

*Address:* 1653 Orchard Avenue.

*Education:* Fremont College (a high school is not mentioned).

*Measurements:* 34-23-34. She is 5 feet, 5 inches tall and has brown hair and brown eyes.

*Medical Issue:* Due to a prior, unnamed injury, Caroline suffers from headaches; she also wears contact lenses and as a child had the mumps and chickenpox.

*Character:* Caroline appeared to have grown up as a normal, well-adjusted girl, but when she entered college, she became an activist (possibly influenced by a class she took) for human and animal rights.

*The Dollhouse:* A mysterious organization that performs secretive missions for their clients. Once an assignment is accepted, operatives (Actives) do what it takes to resolve the situation with no publicity (headlines mean exposure). Actives are programmed to become the type of person that is needed to resolve a situation for a client. Once the task has been accomplished, the

Active's mind is "wiped clean," and she (most are female) has no memory of what she had become.

*The Rossum Corporation:* A nefarious drug corporation that funds a science lab at Freemont (and other colleges) and secretly runs the Dollhouse (which has 23 branches and created the drugs that make the Dollhouse possible).

*Caroline's Induction:* Two years before becoming an Active, Caroline Farrell was a college student. When she and a classmate (Leo) discover that the nearby drug company (Rossum) is conducting mind control experiments on animals, they decide to expose them. Caroline and Leo successfully break into the lab but are exposed. Leo is killed, and Caroline, who fits a specific profile that Rossum needs, escapes but is later captured. She is sent to the Los Angeles Dollhouse, which is run by Adelle DeWitt, to become an Active for a five-year sentence.

*The Contract:* Persons who are selected to become Actives sign a contract to serve the Dollhouse in whatever capacity is chosen for them. At the end of their internment, their contract expires. Actives' prior lives are erased, and they are given new identities (to protect them from unbearable memories of the past). During her time as a fugitive before being captured, Caroline used whatever means she could to destroy Rossum (including "leaving a trail of bodies behind") and had established a secret retreat in an undisclosed mountainous area of California.

*Caroline's Dollhouse Identity:* Echo.

*Downloads:* Caroline's personality has been downloaded into two females: Wendy (Ashley Johnson), a young woman who works as a waitress, and a 12-year-old girl, Iris Miller (Adair Tishler), each of whom acts as a separate entity from Caroline.

*Echo's Imprinted Personalities:* Eleanor (hostage negotiator), Jordan (backup singer and bodyguard to a rock star), Taffy (safecracker), Rebecca (wife), Roma (investigator), Emily (wife and mother), Bree (escort), and Terry (serial killer). Each personality that is programmed into Echo also gives her the abilities to represent that person. Echo is also the only Active who has become aware of her aliases and soon develops immunity to having her mind wiped.

## ADELLE DEWITT
*Position:* Director of the Los Angeles Dollhouse.

*Duties:* Overseeing (and recruiting) Actives, acting as the main contact for clients who need a specific person for whatever their needs may be, and negotiating the contracts that are required (at substantial fees). Adelle uses her sexuality to form friendly relations and ensure that a client signs on the dotted line.

*Background:* Largely unknown except that before being recruited by Rossum, she worked for a medical facility that experimented with using human stem cells to grow replacement organs.

*Character:* Cold, calculating, and ruthless. The Dollhouse appears to be her life, and if any employee betrays her trust, she deals a harsh punishment: banishment to the prisonlike Attic (a place where Actives remain to regain a sense of who they are and what they have become) or, if she feels it is warranted, to death. Despite what the Dollhouse does, Adelle sees it as providing an essential service and will do whatever it takes to protect its secrecy from the outside world (it is not really explained how clients know about the Dollhouse); as the series progresses, she comes to realize that Rossum is evil, and her personality becomes more passionate toward the Actives (something that does not sit well with Rossum). Adelle has little or no social life, and alcohol appears to be one of the means by which she overcomes this.

## BENNETT HALVERSON

*Occupation:* Chief programmer at the Washington, D.C., Dollhouse.

*Expertise:* Repairing damaged imprint data without corrupting or losing information.

*Character:* Bennett is very smart (perhaps genius level, as Echo calls her "off-the-chart smart"), but she also displays traits (as in speech and mannerisms) that suggest she may have some sort of neural disorder. While gorgeous, she is also very calculating and exceptionally neat and organized (it appears by her office that she can survive on the least amount of "clutter" possible).

*Background:* Bennett was born in California and attended college (Tucson Technical University) in Arizona (acquired a degree in neuroscience; coincidentally, Rossum had also established a science facility at the university). She has no fashion sense, is somewhat nerdy, and speaks in technical "jargon" that no one understands; she has devoted herself to her studies with no social life.

*Measurements:* 33-23-33. She stands 5 feet, 6 inches tall and has brown eyes and brown hair.

*Social Security Number:* 549-24-1889.

# Eight Simple Rules
(ABC, 2002–2005)

*Cast:* John Ritter (Paul Hennessey), Katey Sagal (Cate Hennessey), Kaley Cuoco (Bridget Hennessey), Amy Davidson (Kerry Hennessey), Martin Spanjers (Rory Hennessey), James Garner (Jim Egan), David Spade (C. J. Barnes).

*Basis:* Events in the lives of the Hennessey family: parents Paul and Cate and their children Bridget, Kerry, and Rory. The series was originally titled *Eight Simple Rules for Dating My Teenage Daughter.*

## PAUL HENNESSEY

*Occupation:* Sportswriter for the *Detroit Post.* He first mentions covering the Detroit Tigers baseball games before becoming a columnist in one episode and in another that he worked in a cannery before the newspaper job (exactly what the cannery job entailed is never mentioned). Paul had originally planned on becoming a lawyer but followed his heart's desire to become a sportswriter.

*Address:* Oakdale Street in Michigan.

*Education:* Ohio State University (later mentioned as Michigan State University).

*The Situation:* Two daughters, Bridget and Kerry, who are becoming beautiful young women and Paul's obsession with protecting them from boys (how Paul became so overprotective is not really explained other than he knows what teenage boys are like, as he was once one himself). To hopefully fix the situation, he devised eight simple rules that his daughters' dates must adhere to: (1) "Use your hands on my daughter, and you'll lose them later." (2) "You make her cry—I'll make you cry." (3) "Safe sex is a myth. Anything you try will be hazardous to your health." (4) "Bring her home late, there's no next date." (5) "Only deliverymen honk. Dates ring doorbells." (6) "No complaining while waiting for her; if you're bored, change my oil." (7) "If your pants hang off your hip, I'll gladly secure them with my staple gun." (8) "Dates must be in crowded public places; you want romance—read a book."

*Childhood:* As a kid, Paul would sing to make the thunder stop during storms, played the French horn, and was "yell captain" (cheerleader; "I led cheers") in high school.

*Favorite Movie: Brigadoon.*

*Hope:* To watch a football game when Michigan is playing without interruptions from the family and their problems and, after 20 years of marriage, to be able to discipline his children and not be interrupted by Cate with "not the cannery story."

*Family Meetings:* Called by Paul when he believes there is something important to say. He also insists that the family observe two traditions: the yearly vacation "at the cabin by the lake" and the annual Halloween campout in the backyard tree house (when Paul dresses as "the man with the ax in his head").

*Series Change:* On the morning of November 4, 2003, Cate and the children are about to have breakfast when Cate receives word that Paul, shopping for milk, collapsed in aisle 3 of the supermarket and died of a heart attack (reflecting the real-life passing of John Ritter). Paul's favorite bar, the City Room, paid tribute by introducing "The Paul Hennessey Sandwich." In the fall of 2003 (to 2005), James Garner was brought on as Cate's father, Jim Egan, to help Cate raise the children. He is divorced, served in the Korean War, and previously lived in Florida; he now resides in the basement of Cate's home. C. J. Barnes, Cate's nephew (her sister's son), joined the cast (2004–2005) to complicate life rather than help Cate with the children. He was first a security guard at the local mall and then a schoolteacher (at Liberty High); he shares the basement apartment with Jim. He chases women, smoked marijuana (first saying for two, then five, years), and is rather immature and claims to have served with the army in the Gulf War (where he studied aerial photography).

## CATE HENNESSEY

*Parents:* Jim and Laura Egan (now divorced).

*Place of Birth:* Florida.

*Education:* Garfield High School (where she was on the drill team and recalls herself "as being hot and smart").

*Most Embarrassing Moment:* In high school, Cate was performing in the school Christmas pageant when she fell into the orchestra pit.

*Fantasy:* As a child, Cate dreamed about singing in a smoke-filled bar and wearing a sexy dress. She never pursued it because she thought her father would call it frivolous. In later life, she took the plunge and sang "My Old Man" on Open Mike Night at the Green Bottle Bar.

*Secret:* Hides her old love letters in a box marked "Taxes."

*Occupation:* Nurse (hospital not named), then the nurse at Liberty High School (the school attended by Bridget and Kerry; she is also the PTA recording secretary). She returned to her nursing profession when Paul began working from home.

*Addiction:* Coffee. She doesn't relish cooking and will go on any family vacation as long as she can avoid the kitchen.

## BRIDGET HENNESSEY

*Age:* 16 when the series begins.

*Education:* Liberty High School. She is a "C" student and studies for final exams by reading the first and last lines of a textbook paragraph. When Bridget was in second grade, she drew a picture of a six-legged dog that her parents placed on the refrigerator; her second posting occurred 10 years later when she scored a 92 on her high school aptitude test (beating ultrasmart Kerry, who scored an 88). Bridget is a member of the school drama club (starred in *The Diary of Anne Frank*), the pep squad, the tennis team ("The tennis shorts make me look sexy"), and the chorus.

*Character:* A material girl who believes she can do no wrong ("I'm a winner at everything"). She is obsessed with her looks ("I'm a goddess") and can't resist clothes ("I look good in anything"). Bridget believes she can get by on her looks alone and loves Valentine's Day ("It's a day set aside for beautiful girls"). She wears what she calls "boob dresses, leg dresses, and butt dresses" (she can attempt to wear them, but Paul never lets her leave the house in them). Bridget also wears sexy, cleavage-revealing bras and thong panties—but will not wear such clothes to church. She claims to have "nice bras, but I can never find my respectable panties" (Paul and Cate do not object to Bridget's lingerie and allow her to wear it—as long as she doesn't make it obvious).

*Favorite Dinner:* Macaroni and cheese.

*Dream:* Performing in an all-girl band and playing the drums (she chose the drums because it was the only instrument that came in a color she liked—purple).

*Hope:* To become a beautician; her first job was as a salesgirl at the Strip Rags clothing store (she later worked at the local YMCA/YWCA and as a lifeguard at the local swimming pool).

*Nicknames:* Called "Cup Cake," "Bridge," and "Beej" by Paul.

*Addiction:* Speaking on the telephone and applying makeup (she claims to have great difficulty with this "because of my combination skin").

*Curfew:* 11:30 p.m.

## KERRY HENNESSEY

*Age:* 15 when the series begins.

*Belief:* Not very pretty or as sexy or glamorous as Bridget (whom she calls "Little Miss Blonde Bobble Head: My name is Bridget. I can't believe how much my head shakes when I talk").

*Education:* Liberty High School (an honors student, a member of the Owls cheerleading team, a scenery builder for the drama club, and a debate team member).

*Character:* A bit nasty and very negative about everything. She cares too much about what other people think of her. Thus, Kerry is always hard on herself when she fails at something. She has artistic abilities (the first picture she drew for her father was a giraffe—although Paul thinks it looks like a rabbit). She calls Bridget "Psycho Sister" and made a video for a school project about what life is like for Bridget called "How the Beautiful People Have It So Much Easier."

*Nickname:* Called "Care Bear" by Paul.

*Childhood:* Had a pet rabbit (Mr. Wiggles) and a plush dog (Muttsy). She played soccer in third grade and is very fond of animals.

## RORY HENNESSEY

Thirteen-year-old Rory is mischievous and scheming. He enjoys eavesdropping on Bridget and Kerry and tattles on them. He knows how to get out of doing things because he tells his parents what they want to hear. Kerry feels that Rory gets all the attention "because he's the boy." He attends Liberty Middle School (later Liberty High School) and is a member of the flag football team. "Web Master X" is his internet webcast (where he wears a gorilla mask and reports on school activities). He has a nasty ventriloquist's dummy named "Sheevie" and lives to get his sisters in trouble. He also has a tire under his bed ("It's part of my first car") and enjoys going to the pet shop on feeding day (to see mice being fed to snakes). He also started a car-washing business wherein he charged $10 a car (he called himself "The Car Wash King").

# The George Lopez Show
## (ABC, 2002–2007)

*Cast:* George Lopez (George Lopez), Constance Marie (Angie Lopez), Masiela Lusha (Carmen Lopez), Luis Armando Garcia (Max Lopez), Belita Moreno (Benny Lopez), Valente Rodriquez (Ernie Cardenas).

*Basis:* Events in the lives of a Mexican American family: parents George and Angie and their children Carmen and Max.

### GEORGE LOPEZ

*Parents:* Benita (Benny) and Manny Lopez (Esai Morales, then William Marquez). For many years, Benny was unsure who fathered George (she believed it was a man named Manny, with whom she had an affair). Amaury Nolasco played a young Manny in flashbacks.

*Address:* 3128 Rose Street (near Alan Avenue) in Los Angeles.

*Occupation:* Manager of Power and Sons Aviation (also called Power Brothers Aviation), a company that cannot produce airplane parts as sophisticated as Boeing's "but makes the best knockoffs around." George acquired a job as an assembly line worker for Powers after high school. Although he was good at his job, he was treated a bit unfairly (for the first five years, he was called "Señor Pumpkin Head" by his boss); it took him 12 years to become manager. During high school, George worked as a waiter at Carrello's, a local fast-food burrito store.

*Childhood:* Very difficult for George, as he was raised solely by Benny (who smoked, drank, cursed like a sailor, and had numerous one-night stands). Since Benny was not sure who George's father was, she told him that he had died; it was not until George was an adult that he learned from his Aunt Cecilia (Manny's sister) that Manny, now living in Phoenix, Arizona, was George's father (they did eventually meet each other, but Manny later passed due to kidney failure).

George Lopez, Constance Marie, and Belita Moreno. *ABC/Photofest © ABC*

*Medical Issue:* Dyslexic.

*High School Band:* Dos Bad Asses (George played guitar).

*Pet Dog:* Mr. Needles (diabetic; needs insulation shots).

*Favorite Dinner:* Lasagna.

*Favorite Tavern:* Thirsty's Bar.

*Favorite Drink:* Beer.

*Favorite Sport:* Golf (he practices his golf swing when something bothers him).

*Favorite Sports Teams:* Los Angeles Dodgers, Los Angeles Lakers, and Oakland Raiders.

*Car:* A 4-by-4 with the license plate 4QS W102.

*Award:* The Rising Star Award from the Southern California Minorities and Business Association.

*Catchphrase:* "Esta Loco!"

## ANGELINA "ANGIE" LOPEZ

*Parents:* Vic (Emiliano Díez) and Emilina Palmero (Sonia Braga). Victor, called Vic, is a Cuban immigrant who became rich as a cardiac surgeon.

*Place of Birth:* Originally said to be California, but in dialogue, Vic mentions that Angie was born and raised in Florida.

*Siblings:* Gloria (Jacqueline Obradors) and Ray Palmero.

*Maiden Name:* Angie Palmero (she is Cuban American).

*Occupation:* Sales representative for LaMarie Cosmetics. When she loses her job, she uses her talent for detail and organization to become a wedding planner (she operates Angie's Weddings from the garage, which George renovated as her office).

*Bra Size:* Angie mentions wearing a 34B bra.

*Volunteer Work:* The Allendale High School Library.

*Favorite Activity:* Gardening and helping out wherever she can.

*Family Problems:* Angie blames George's reckless mother for everything that is wrong with George. Angie and George married two years after high school (at which time George was working for Powers Aviation), and Benny has, since day one, interfered in their lives, undermining Angie and trying to control George. Angie is more patient when dealing with Carmen and Max, while George, taking after his mother, flies off the handle when they do something wrong (he often realizes what he is doing is wrong and does blame Benny for his reactions, often calling her "a crazy old bat"). Because of Angie's spoiled upbringing (her father is a wealthy physician), Benny often calls her "Princess."

*High School:* Angie was popular and a member of the cheerleading team. She orchestrated cheers, volunteered for school activities, and was nearly an "A" student (acquired "B's" in some math and science courses). It was said that Angie and George met in high school, but this is not likely, as Angie went to high school in Florida. It could be that the family moved to California, but this is not addressed.

## CARMEN CONSUELA LOPEZ

*Relationship:* George and Angie's eldest child (a teenager when the series begins).

*Character:* A girl who can't wait to become a woman. She is somewhat rebellious and is proud of her Cuban-Mexican heritage. Carmen has always been George's little girl ("like a bud on a flower"). In her seventh-grade school play, she performed as Anna in *The King and I*—and George was there to support her (third seat from the rear and asleep). George spoiled Carmen and was looking forward to her becoming a teenager. He thought she would lock herself in her room and never speak to him again (thus relieving him of the problems of dealing with a teenage daughter). As it turned out, the bud blossomed into a very pretty young woman, and everything in Carmen's life becomes a crisis—and, as George now says, "Trying to solve them is wiping me out."

*Wardrobe:* Very conservative. Carmen would like to wear cleavage-revealing blouses and sexy lingerie like her girlfriends, but George and Angie refuse to let her buy any. George believes that the day Carmen buys a thong will be the day he loses his little girl. In a rather unusual (and strange) situation for a sitcom, Carmen does buy a thong without telling her parents. When George notices that Carmen's panty line is not visible through the back of her jeans, he realizes his worst nightmare has come true. Carmen, noticing a distinct change in George, discards the thong and pleases George when he can again see that her jeans reflect her panty line. Carmen would also like a cell phone, "But that will not happen either," says George (he doesn't fear her getting kidnapped, and thus she doesn't need a phone; "My taxes pay for the Amber Alert"; actually, he is too cheap to buy her a phone).

*Steadfast Rule:* Allowed to have a boy over to do homework (in plain sight) but is not allowed to date until she is 16 years old.

*Education:* Allendale High School (where she is a member of the poetry club). She next attends St. Theresa's High School when she is expelled from Allendale for behavior unbecoming of a student: two violations for showing public affection, six uniform violations (skirt too short), and eight tardiness violations; Angie and George then enroll her in a private school.

*Music Fan:* Alanis Morissette, Linkin Park, 3 Doors Down.

*Hope:* To become a poet.

*Replacement:* As the series came to a conclusion, Carmen was written out when she enrolled in college (in Providence, Rhode Island). She was replaced by Veronica Palmero (Aimee Garcia), her wealthy and snobbish cousin who came to live with George and Angie when her late mother (Emilina) left her trust fund in George's care. Veronica, an expert at poker, uses her sexuality to get men to do what she wants (except George) and caused a problem when Max fell in love with her. (The situation became so bad that George had to warn Max that "she's your first cousin; you have dyslexia. If you have kids with her, your mom and I will have to pay a dollar to visit our grandkids at the carnival.")

*Jobs:* Carmen first earns money by babysitting and then as a waitress on weekends at Carrello's fast-food burrito store.

*Flashbacks:* Young Carmen (Jordan Medina).

## OTHER CHARACTERS

Max, Carmen's younger brother, suffers from a severe case of dyslexia and, like George, had a hard time dealing with schoolwork. His actual name is Maximilian Victor Roberto Magic Johnson Lopez. George wanted to name him after a famous sports figure (Magic Johnson), while Angie was torn between his first three names; they chose to name him after everything they wanted. Max loves to skateboard and is closer to his father than to his mother (Carmen was closer to Angie than to George). Max easily gives into peer pressure and later attends Allendale High School.

Benita "Benny" Diaz Lopez is George's mother. As previously stated, she is reckless and literally unfit to be a mother. Although stories vary about George's biological father, Benny does reveal that George was conceived in the back of a car wash with a man named Manny Lopez. Benny and Manny married shortly after, but Manny, unable to handle the responsibilities of fatherhood, divorced Benny when George was an infant. It is also revealed that George has a sister (Linda) who lived a much happier life when Benny gave her up for adoption. Benny could be seen as a child abuser, as she was cynical and coldhearted and tormented George (not knowing he had dyslexia) and never encouraged him to do anything; she treated him like a burden she couldn't get rid of (thus, George was exposed to the gangs, riots, and other law violations of the crime-ridden neighborhood in which he grew up). Benny, raised in an environment like George's, never considered herself a child abuser; when she was a child, it was called "discipline." She also works the assembly line at Powers Aviation. Maria Beck plays a young Benny in flashbacks, and Rita Moreno appeared as Benny's mother, Luisa Diaz.

Ernest Cardenas, called Ernie, is George's best friend (since the second grade). Their friendship took a turn for the worse when Ernie accidentally saw Angie in her white bra and outraged George (as he knows that Ernie has a huge crush on Angie). He works at Powers Aviation first as an assembly line worker and then as the line's team leader. He is a bit dim-witted and socially awkward and usually does whatever George asks of him. He has a morbidly obese mother and the catchphrase "Golly." It can be seen that Ernie is jealous of George, as he has a good job, a beautiful wife, and two children, while he has nothing after working for 30 years on an assembly line.

# *Ghost Whisperer*
(CBS, 2005–2010)

*Cast:* Jennifer Love Hewitt (Melinda Gordon); David Conrad (Jim Clancy/Sam Lucas); Aisha Tyler (Andrea Moreno); Camryn Manheim (Delia Banks); Tyler Patrick James, then Christoph Sanders (Ned Banks); Jay Mohr (Richard Payne); Jamie Kennedy (Eli James); David Clennon (Carl); Connor Gibbs (Aiden); Joey King (Cassidy).

*Basis:* A beautiful young woman (Melinda) uses her ability to communicate with the spirits of the dead to help them complete unfinished business and see the light.

## MELINDA IRENE GORDON
*Place of Birth:* San Francisco, California, on May 15, 1982.
*Parents:* Beth Gordon (Anne Archer). She raised Melinda as a single mother after Melinda's biological father, Paul Eastman, deserted Beth (she later marries a man named Tom Gordon).

*Husband:* Jim Clancy, a paramedic (they met when Jim was called to battle a fire at Melinda's apartment complex in an unnamed town). They date, marry, and move to Grandview (where Jim becomes a member of the Grandview Fire Department).

*The Change:* Jim is attacked by an intruder while attending a friend's wedding and accidentally shot by a police detective called to the scene (he believed that Jim was the attacker). It appeared that Jim was recovering (shot only in the shoulder), but a blood embolism developed, and he died. Melinda, able to see Jim's ghost, learns that he will not move on (fearing for her safety). In an unusual twist, Jim's spirit possesses the body of a recently deceased man and comes back to life as Sam Lucas; Jim (as Sam) has no memory of Melinda (although Melinda can see that Sam looks just like Jim). In another strange series of events, Sam, who has gotten to know Melinda, almost drowns while attempting to save her life, and Jim's memory of his life with Melinda is restored (although Jim must continue living as Sam Lucas). Melinda and Sam marry and have a son named Aiden (who inherits his mother's powers as well as being an empath [one who shares other people's feelings]). Jim's dream was to become a doctor, and he pursues it by picking up where Sam left off (having completed many of the courses for medical school). They later have another son they name Victor. Aiden, who is advanced in age after his birth, is aided by the ghost of a young girl named Cassidy to help him deal with the spirits he encounters.

*Occupation:* Owner of an antique shop (under her maiden name) called "Same As It Never Was Antiques" in the town of Grandview. Melinda's married name is Melinda Clancy.

*Antique Shop Location:* Grandview Square (a center-of-the-town–like shopping mall).

*Ability:* Sees ghosts and communicates with the dead. Melinda can sense spirits and feel what they are feeling. She believes that spirits contact her so she can help them complete a mission before seeing the light and moving on. For Melinda, it began when she was eight years old and in the fourth grade. After the passing of a classmate, Melinda saw her ghost (who was not aware that she was dead). Melinda's grandmother, Mary Ann, had the ability, but her mother, Beth, does not (it appears to skip a generation).

*Education:* Hillridge High School (where she earned money by babysitting to buy her first car; she was also a member of the hockey team); Washington State University.

*Favorite Fantasy as a Child:* Being a fairy.

*Allergy:* Ho Hos snack cakes (but not any other cake with chocolate or cream filling).

*Greatest Fear:* Being considered an oddity (for her ability) and being studied as such.

*Favorite Fast Food:* Pizza with anchovies.

*Favorite Movies:* Horror films and, as she says, "chick flicks."

*Favorite Holiday:* Christmas.

*Least Favorite Occasion:* Celebrating her birthday.

*Nickname:* "Mel."

*Measurements:* 36-26-38. She stands 5 feet, 3 inches tall.

*Fifth-Anniversary Gift:* On Melinda and Jim's first date, it began to rain, and Melinda's red umbrella was ruined when the wind turned it inside out. Jim replaced it as his gift to her.

*Melinda's Watcher:* Carl, a spirit that guides her.

*Melinda's Partners:* Andrea (killed in a plane crash), then Delia Banks, an agent for Briar Realty, later Banks and Cutler Realty. Ned is Delia's son; Charlie Banks was her late husband. Delia, who is haunted by Charlie's ghost (to protect her), became Melinda's assistant to find relief from the stress of her real estate job.

*Melinda's Associates:* Richard "Rick" Payne and Eli James. Rick is an archaeology professor at Rockland College. He is a widower (late wife Kate) and helped Melinda with his knowledge of the past. He left to pursue an important dig in the Himalayas. Rick mentioned liking the song "The Sound of Silence" and that his hobby was documenting native cultural traditions. Eli James, a therapist at Rockland University, replaced Rick and helped Melinda with his ability to understand ghosts, although he was unable to see them, only sense and hear what they had to say.

*Jim's Family:* Mother, Faith Clancy (Christine Baranski); his father, Aiden Clancy, is deceased.

*Flashbacks:* Melinda, age eight (Grace Fulton, then Abigail Breslin); Melinda, age 10 (Haley Pullos).

# *Gilmore Girls*

## (WB, 2000–2007)

*Cast:* Lauren Graham (Lorelai Gilmore), Alexis Bledel (Rory Gilmore), Liza Weil (Paris Geller), Edward Herrmann (Richard Gilmore), Kelly Bishop (Emily Gilmore), Keiko Agena (Lane Kim), Scott Patterson (Luke Danes), Yanic Truesdale (Michel Gerard), Melissa McCarthy (Sookie St. James).

*Basis:* The tender relationship between a single mother (Lorelai Gilmore) and her daughter, Rory.

Lauren Graham and Alexis Bledel. *The WB/Photofest © The WB; photographer: Lance Staedler*

## LORELAI VICTORIA GILMORE

*Parents:* Richard and Emily Gilmore.

*Place of Birth:* Hartford, Connecticut, in 1968.

*Daughter:* Rory Gilmore.

*Address:* 37 Maple Street, Stars Hollow, Connecticut.

*Belief:* When it snows, wonderful things happen (like her first kiss and the birth of Rory). When it does snow, Lorelai says, "Hey, that's my present." She recalled that when she was five years old and bedridden with an ear infection, she wished for something wonderful to happen. When she awoke the following morning, it had snowed, and everything was better. She now claims she can predict when it is going to snow "by the smell in the air."

*Childhood:* Lorelai had a pet rabbit named Murray and spent her summers at camps. She was expelled from one camp for refusing to call a counselor "Peaches" (the counselors took names after summer fruits) and another (Camp Chatoquoy) for freeing the horses. While she enjoyed it as a child, she now dislikes her mother's concoction of mashed banana on toast. Everything changed for Lorelai when she was 16 years old. She had an affair with her high school boyfriend, Chris Hayden (David Sutcliffe), and became pregnant. Lorelai's strict parents wanted Lorelai to marry Chris, but Lorelai stood her ground. She refused to do so (and become a part of their society world) because she felt they were too young and the marriage would not last. Lorelai's inability to get along with her controlling mother forced her to leave home a year after Rory was born. They found refuge at the Independence Inn in Stars Hollow, Connecticut. The inn's owner, a friend of Emily's, hired Lorelai as a maid and gave her a place to live.

*Nickname:* Called "Lor" by Chris.

*Ability:* Lorelai can take something that is unattractive and make it pretty; for example dressing Rory's bottle of Liquid Paper in a dress. "She's not crazy," says Rory. "She just sounds like it."

*Occupation:* Lorelai first worked one summer as a counselor at the Dean Forrester Hills Inn. She then became a maid and then manager of the Independence Inn in Stars Hollow.

*Dream:* To own her own inn. It becomes a reality when a fire closes the Independence Inn and she and her friend Sookie St. James pool their resources and purchase (and renovate) the abandoned Dragon Fly Inn. Prior to this, Lorelai and Sookie, the Independence Inn chef, became partners in the Independence Catering Company.

*Favorite Flower:* Yellow daisies.

*Favorite Song:* "Shadow Dance."

*Enjoyment:* Watching other people work.

*Favorite All-Girl Singing Group:* The Bangles (she also mentions the Go-Go's).

*Favorite Laundry Detergent:* Dream Fresh.

*Lip Gloss Flavors:* Chocolate, vanilla, strawberry, and marshmallow.

*Cooking:* Lorelai rarely cooks, but when she does, she serves it on her good "china"—a set of *Charlie's Angels* TV series dinner plates. She orders takeout at Al's Pancake World, does her grocery shopping at Doose's Market, and has breakfast at Luke's Diner.

*Member:* Stars Hollow Video Club (card number 6247).

*Favorite Movie:* *Willy Wonka and the Chocolate Factory.*

*Addiction:* Junk food, coffee (she calls herself a "coffee junkie"), and mail-order catalogs (she doesn't know why, but the more she receives, the happier she is; she has made up the names Squeegee Buckingham and Tootie Clothespin to get even more).

*Obsession:* Sweaters and breast size ("An evil, crazed spirit obsessed with breast size takes over my body and makes me go nuts"). While it is a bit odd, she has arguments with Rory over whose breasts are bigger.

*Measurements:* 36-27-36. She stands 5 feet, 9 inches tall and has brown hair and blue eyes.

*Fishing Trip:* She caught her first fish (a large carp), which she named "Jayne Mansfield," and kept it in the bathtub.

*Religion:* Protestant.

*Political Affiliation:* Appears to be a Democrat (just to oppose her parents' affiliation as Republican).

*Pet Dog:* Paul Anka (after the pop recording star).

*Jeep License Plate:* 937 G5R.

*The 2003 Stars Hollow Festival of Living Pictures:* People dress up as famous paintings; Lorelai chose "The Renoir Girl."

*Dislike:* Seeing blood (makes her squeamish).

*Cherished Childhood Memory:* Her dollhouse.

*Tradition:* Almost every episode has Lorelai and Rory visiting Lorelai's parents; it can be seen that a different maid appears in each of these episodes (as explained by Richard's comment to Emily, "You can't hold on to a maid").

*Flashbacks:* Lorelai as a teenager (Chelsea Brummet).

## LORELAI LEIGH "RORY" GILMORE

*Parents:* Lorelai Gilmore and Chris Hayden.

*Place of Birth:* Hartford, Connecticut, during a snowstorm on October 8, 1984 (at 4:03 a.m.).

*Name:* Lorelai named Rory (her nickname) after herself "because I was in the hospital and whacked out on demerole and figured that if boys could be named after their fathers, girls should be named after their mothers." She is 16 years old when the series begins and is the brightness in all the darkness in her mother's life (Lorelai considers Rory "low maintenance like a Honda"). Rory and Lorelai are not only mother and daughter but also best friends. Rory even inherited her mother's addiction to coffee (which they enjoy at Luke's Diner).

*Address:* 37 Maple Drive in Stars Hollow; later with her grandparents in Hartford, Connecticut, when she and her mother have a falling out.

*Childhood:* When Rory was a child and learned that the tree in front of the Independence Inn was a weeping willow, she spent hours trying to cheer it up. She had a dream of marrying Prince Charming ("not the *Snow White* one, the *Sleeping Beauty* one"), had a plush chicken (Colonel Clucker), and was called "Droopy Drawers" by her mother (as her loose-fitting pants kept falling off her hips). Rory played a broccoli in her kindergarten play "A Salute to Vegetables" and learned the seven continents from her Hug-a-World Globe. Rory wears a size 6 coat (but Lorelai buys her size 8 "in case she grows") and had a pet hamster named Skippy (which Lorelai says was vicious—"He laughed at me after he bit me"). She took cheerleading classes at Miss Patty's School of Ballet and had a traumatic experience when she was six years old: she was riding a pony when it suddenly died with her on it. She was fearful of the kitchen stove (which Lorelai told her was "the Devil's Hands") and didn't have the courage to walk on wet grass until she was three years old. It took her more than three months to learn how to ride a bicycle.

*Measurements:* 34-24-34. She stands 5 feet, 7 inches tall and has brown hair and blue eyes.

*Addiction:* Coffee (like her mother).

*Favorite Color:* Blue.

*Favorite Muffin:* Blueberry.

*Favorite Flower:* The sunflower.

*Favorite Activity:* Reading (a trait she inherited from her grandfather, Richard).

*Dream:* To attend Harvard University, study journalism, and become a reporter.

*Collects:* Books, Spice Girls memorabilia, Harvard-related material (which she posts on a bulletin board Lorelai calls "The Obsession Board").

*Memorable Moments:* Works at the Independence Inn after school and on special occasions, was voted "Ice Cream Queen" at the Stars Hollow Ice Cream Shoppe, carries a book with her wherever she goes, and played Anita ("Portrait of a Young Girl Named Anita") in the 2003 Stars Hollow Festival of Living Pictures.

*Education:* Rory first attended Stars Hollow Grammar School, then Stars Hollow High School (she is in the German and French clubs), before transferring to Chilton Prep, a prestigious private school (where she has a 4.0 grade-point average; writes for the school newspaper, *The Franklin*; and is a member of the debate team). She is later her senior class vice president and class valedictorian (she scored 740 in verbal and 760 in math on her PSAT test). Rory likes to get her homework done before Saturday night so she can devote time on Sunday to extra-credit reports. Lorelai is a member of Chilton's Booster Club for parents. Rory was accepted to a number of colleges, including Harvard, but chose to attend Yale University, which is closer to her home and her life with Lorelai. At Yale, which is in New Haven, Connecticut, Rory resides in Durfee Hall (suite 5) and is studying journalism (she wants to be a foreign correspondent and writes for the school newspaper, the *Yale Daily News*). The final episode finds Rory accepting a job as a political reporter for an online magazine. At the time when she lived with her grandparents, Rory worked for the DAR (Daughters of the American Revolution), the organization in which her grandmother, Emily, is president.

*Birthday Tradition:* Lorelai always tells Rory the story of her birth.

## PARIS EUSTACE GELLER

*Place of Birth:* Connecticut on December 7, 1984.

*Pet Dog as a Kid:* Skippy.

*Religion:* Jewish.

*Languages:* English, Portuguese, Farsi, Chinese, and Mandarin.

*Medical Issue:* Anxiety (keeps her bottle of antianxiety pills at the bottom of her purse). She is also lactose intolerant and unable to eat what she once enjoyed: macaroni and cheese.

*Quirk:* She is studying premed, but "sick people freak me out."

*Coffee:* Decaf with soy milk.

*Education:* Chilton Preparatory School, Yale University (double majored in political science and biochemistry), Harvard Medical School.

*After-Graduation Occupation:* Owner of Dynasty Makers; associated with the Surrogacy/Fertility Clinic.

*Character:* A pretty teenage girl with one single-minded ambition: attend Harvard University. She is the classic overachiever, as all her energies are directed to achieving her dream. She "studies, thinks about studying, and studies more," says Rory Gilmore, her rival at Chilton, a school with one of the highest reputations for excellence in the country. Paris has become who she is "because 10 generations of Gellers went to Harvard" (her mother was a top student). Paris has no social life. She is 16 years old (when the series begins) and is editor of the Chilton school newspaper, *The Franklin* (which she runs like a big-city newspaper). She does volunteer work for Rebuilding Together (building homes for charity), trains seeing-eye dogs, manned a suicide hotline, volunteered in a trauma center, worked with dolphins, was a summer camp counselor, taught sign language, and organized a senior citizen center. Paris has been accumulating extracurricular activities since the fourth grade. She feels that a prestigious college requires it. She scored a 750 in math and 730 in verbal on her PSAT test and is the student body president at Chilton. Paris is a straight "A" student and a member of the Chilton debate team (with Rory), but with all her achievements, she was not accepted into Harvard. The rejection literally devastated her and sent her on a downward spiral that Rory helped her overcome (her wealthy parents pay little attention to her). While she could not have her dream, she accepted her invitation to Yale and shared suite 5 in Durfee Hall with Rory; she was also a staff member of the school newspaper, the *Yale Daily News*. In the final episode, Paris's dream is realized when she is accepted into Harvard Medical School.

## RICHARD AND EMILY GILMORE

Richard and Emily are Lorelai's parents and Rory's grandparents. Richard, born in 1943, is a graduate of Yale University (where he was on the fencing team) and was first an executive vice president of the Gehrman and Driscoll Insurance Company before establishing his own insurance company, The Gilmore Group (in 2002). Richard awakes every morning at 5:30 a.m. and has half a grapefruit with his breakfast. He plays golf for relaxation and is a member of the Cigar Club (sits in an enclosed room twice a week with other cigar smokers). He loves to read (especially with a brandy by his side), is stern, and adheres to the high-society life that he and Emily have established. Chuck Berry is his favorite singer. In later episodes, he acquires a job teaching economics at Yale University but also suffers from angina and a serious heart attack (2006) that leaves him incapable of returning to his job. Restoring antique cars appears to be his hobby, and as a child he apparently lived in New York, as he mentions enjoying riding the roller coaster at Coney Island (at which time he also mentions loving turtleneck soup). Marion Ross plays Richard's mother, Lorelai "Trixie" Gilmore; she also plays Marilyn Gilmore, Trixie's niece.

Emily is a socialite who lives for charity functions. She is a member of the DAR, the Edward R. Wardus Rare Manuscript Foundation, the Philharmonic Club, the Historical Society, and the Hospital Committee. She is president of the Horticultural Society and cochair of the Starlight Foundation. Emily is also a perfectionist and, as Richard says, "can't hold on to a maid" (she is always replacing them when she finds the slightest fault). She was born in 1942, attended Smith College (majored in history), and met Richard at a Yale college party (they married when Emily was 23 years old). She is Protestant and had Lorelai when she was 26 years old (she was in labor for 14 hours). She has a sister (Hope, who lives in Paris), takes water aerobics classes, and loves shopping (Bloomingdale's is her favorite department store). She is rather fearful of appearing nude (e.g., she wore a raincoat when she and Richard went skinny-dipping) and was on the field hockey team in college.

## SOOKIE ST. JAMES

Sookie, Lorelai's friend and chef at the Independence Inn, is a perfectionist when it comes to meal preparations but is a bit accident prone outside the kitchen. She is later co-owner of the Dragonfly Inn when she and Lorelai pool their resources to purchase their own inn. As the series progresses, she develops a romantic interest in Jackson Belleville (Jackson Douglas), the produce supplier for the Independence Inn, and the two eventually marry (with Jackson stating that he wants four children in four years; two are born during the course of the series: Martha and Davey; the series ends with Sookie revealing she is pregnant with their third child).

## LANE KIM

Lane, born in Stars Hollow in 1984, is Rory's best friend (they met in kindergarten). She attends Stars Hollow High School (where she is a cheerleader) and later Adventist College and works as a waitress at Luke's Diner. She is a member of the band Hep Alien (plays drums) and is considered the town's resident music adviser. Her mother, called Mrs. Kim (Emily Kuroda), is very strict, but her father is rather mysterious (called Mr. Kim but never seen). Mrs. Kim strongly adheres to her Korean upbringing and is trying to pass that on to Lane (who has to devise ways of keeping her love of the American way of life secret from her mother). She drinks soda (but it has to be flat—no carbonation) and dislikes eating meals at home (as her mother is on a health food kick and Lane finds the meals she prepares rather tasteless and disgusting). She later marries (Zack) and gives birth to twins she names Kwan and Steve.

## MICHEL GERARD

Michel is first the assistant manager of the Independence Inn and then of the Dragonfly Inn. He is not the most hospitable of people and is often grumpy, sarcastic, and rather unpleasant. He is a health food nut and had two dogs: Chin-Chin and Paw-Paw. He began working at the Independence Inn in 1998 and enjoys accompanying Lorelai and the inn's cook, Sookie, on their business ventures. He is not fond of swans (attacked by one as a child living in France) or children. Celine Dion appears to be his favorite singer (attended six of her concerts). He lived in France until he was 18 years old, but a reason for leaving is not stated. He is very particular about what foods he eats (e.g., he counts the blueberries in his waffles, won't eat omelets if they are made from egg whites, and will not touch fat-free milk, as it is actually only 2 percent fat free). He is enthused about dancing, but his personality makes it difficult to determine if he is straight, bisexual, or gay (although in the 2016 update, it is revealed that he is married).

## LUCAS "LUKE" DANES

Luke is the owner (and chief chef) at his place of business, Luke's Diner (Lorelai and Rory's favorite hangout). The store originally housed William's Hardware, which was owned by Luke's late father (Luke changed it to a diner after his father [William Dane] passed). He carries on the traditions that his father started (e.g., Founder's Day reenactments and town hall meetings). At Star Hollows High

School, Luke was on the track team and now lives above the diner. It can be seen throughout the series that Luke has romantic feelings toward Lorelai. His signature look is plaid or flannel shirts (with first a brown and then a blue baseball cap), and he can be seen as a health nut, as he shows concern over Lorelai and Rory's poor eating habits. Luke, a Scorpio, loves fishing and camping but dislikes coffee and champagne. He has a steadfast rule that cell phones are not permitted in the diner (which annoys Lorelai), and as a kid he was a "Trekkie" (*Star Trek* fanatic) and was called "Butch" in high school. His phone number is (860) 294-1986. April Nardini (Vanessa Marano), a student at Martin Van Buren Middle School, is Luke's daughter (from an affair with a woman named Anna Nardini [Sherilyn Fenn]), who later comes to live with Luke after Anna's mother becomes ill and Anna leaves to care for her.

**UPDATE**

*Gilmore Girls: A Year in the Life* is a 2016 Netflix miniseries that reunites the cast of *Gilmore Girls* to explore what has happened since the series ended. Lorelai, still the owner of the Dragonfly Inn, has now been dating Luke Danes for 10 years and has accepted his proposal of marriage (they marry in the final episode). Rory, working as a freelance journalist, takes the advice of her boyfriend Jess Mariano (Milo Ventimglia) to write a book about her experiences with her mother. She also reveals to Lorelai in the final episode that she is pregnant. Richard, Lorelai's father, has since passed away, and Emily, his wife, is seen as a woman desperately trying to cope with the loss of her husband (it is seen that after Emily accepts what happens, she sells her home, resigns from the DAR, and moves to Nantucket). It is also learned that Chris allowed Lorelai to raise Rory alone (never petitioning the court for parental custody) because it was best for Rory.

# *Girlfriends*
## (UPN, 2000–2008)

*Principal Cast:* Tracee Ellis Ross (Joan Clayton), Persia White (Lynn Searcy), Golden Brooks (Maya Wilkes), Jill Marie Jones (Toni Childs).
*Basis:* Events in the lives four African American women who are also best friends: Joan, Lynn, Maya, and Toni.

**JOAN CAROL CLAYTON**

*Place of Birth:* Fresno, California, in 1971. She is 29 years old when the series begins and claims she is 26 but realizes she is nearing 30 and has no man in her life.

Jill Marie Jones, Tracee Ellis Ross, Golden Brooks, and Persia White. *UPN/Photofest © UPN*

*Address:* The North 700 Block at Wilton Place (in the historic Wilton District of Los Angeles).

*Education:* The Fresno Dance Academy for Girls; University of California, Los Angeles (UCLA) (acquired her degree in contract law).

*Occupation:* Originally a junior partner with the law firm of Goldstein, Swedleson and Lee (she has an office on the twenty-seventh floor). When Joan sees no chance for advancement (becoming a full partner), she quits to open her own restaurant, The J Spot (originally called Joan's Place). Her first job was as a salesgirl at The Gap (where she invented a method of folding clothes that shaved three seconds off the official Gap folding time).

*Background:* As a child, her father called her "Baby Girl." She was a Girl Scout, and she mentioned that she "hustled cookies from Kmart." At her high school prom, she flashed her breasts to motorists as she rode in the limo. She has been a bridesmaid 14 times but never a bride.

*Meeting:* Maya is Joan's assistant at the law firm, Joan and Toni were friends as children, and Joan befriended Lynn in college.

*Wardrobe:* Extremely sexy. She loves to wear see-through blouses that reveal her sexy bras (and not wear a bra under silky dresses).

*Measurements:* 34-22-36; she stands 5 feet, 7 inches tall.

*Character:* Caring, very sweet, and friendly but sometimes wishes "I could be a bitch" like Toni Childs but realizes she can't "because I'm too kind."

*Thirtieth-Birthday Treat:* Joan decided to change her dull and boring life by doing something outrageous and exciting: she spent the day at a nude beach.

*Favorite Drink:* Vodka martini.

*Favorite Restaurant:* Skia's (originally called 847).

*Steadfast Rule:* She will not have sex unless she has been in relationship with a man for at least three months.

## LYNN SEARCY

*Place of Birth:* Charlottesville, Virginia, on February 9, 1971 (later said to be in 1970). It was first said that Lynn was abandoned by her black parents and raised by a white family. It is later revealed that Lynn's mother, Sandy, was white and had an affair with a black man (Ken). Lynn was given up for adoption and raised by a black family (Ed and Beth). This second version appears more credible when Lynn is reunited with her white birth mother, Sandy (Karen Austin) in 2003. To further complicate matters, it was also said that Sandy's parents paid Lynn's father (Ken) a considerable amount of money to disappear because they did not want Lynn to marry a black man.

*Character:* Lynn, beautiful as she is, is not one to use her looks to accomplish things but is highly unmotivated to do anything. She is not very responsible and appears to be a permanent graduate student at UCLA. She has five degrees and owes more than $200,000 in student loans. She has no money and no job and lives with Joan Clayton. Although she has degrees, she has not followed through on them with a job. She takes whatever odd jobs she can find (like waitress at Amy's Diner); when she is desperately in need of money, she sells her blood: "I like to do it before 4 p.m. before all the good cookies are gone."

*Measurements:* 34-24-35; she stands 5 feet, 8 inches tall.

*Degrees:* "Geology, anthropology, psychiatry, science, and I can't remember the fifth one."

*Career:* In 2001, Lynn completed her college education, but it was not until 2003 that she found her calling: documentary filmmaker. She later gave this up "to find myself." She became a tour guide, a street-performing robot ("like a mime but dressed in silver"), host of a public access cable show called *Ambush* (wherein she degrades guests), a celebrity photographer, and finally an artist (singer/guitarist) with Dirty Girl Records.

*Her Films: Lives in the Balance: The African American Woman and the AIDs Crisis* and *Life in the Balance: Single Mothers.*

*Film Funding:* The Thompson Foundation.

*Living on Her Own:* A converted garage on Florence Street.

*Pet Dog:* Vosco.

*Volunteer Work:* The South Side Free Clinic; a telephone hotline service.

*Writing Career:* Earns money by writing trashy, soft-porn stories for Climaxxx Publishing.

*Allergy:* Cashew nuts.

*Favorite Restaurant:* Skia's (originally called 847).

*Food Preference:* Vegan.

*Her Band:* Indigo Style.

*Meeting:* Lynn was Joan and Toni's roommate at UCLA.

*Dating:* Lynn, famous for what she calls "The Lynn Spin" during sex, dates frequently (mostly one-night stands); she is attracted to artistic and spiritual men.

## MAYA DENISE WILKES

*Place of Birth:* A farm in Fresno, California, in 1971.

*Education:* UCLA (for two years). She later enrolled at the City of Industry School of Life Science at the Monrovian School of Psychology.

*Occupation:* Legal secretary to Joan Clayton at the Los Angeles law firm of Goldberg, Swedleson and Donaldson (later called McDonald, Swedleson and Goldstein, then Goldberg, Swedleson and Lee).

*Address:* Unit 8 at the Landmark Park Village.

*Family:* Mother of Jabari (Kendre Berry); her husband, Darnell Wilkes (Khalil Kain, then Flex Alexander), is in the air force.

*Claim to Fame:* Her cousin is Bern Nadette Stanis (the actress who played Thelma on the TV series *Good Times*).

*Favorite Magazine: Black Detective* (she is hoping to stumble across a crime and write an article).

*Religion:* Baptist. She put her religious beliefs in a book she wrote called *Oh Hell, Yes* (published by Inner Vision Press).

*Political Affiliation:* Democrat.

*Fear:* Gaining weight.

*Measurements:* Wears a 36B bra and stands 5 feet, 6 inches tall.

*Belief:* "I am not only gorgeous but brilliant."

*Dislike:* Cars.

*Favorite Restaurant:* Skia's (originally called 847).

## ANTOINETTE "TONI" MARIE CHILDS

*Parents:* Eugene (Isaac Hayes) and Veretta Childs (Jenifer Lewis).

*Place of Birth:* Fresno, California, in 1971.

*Siblings:* Sherri Childs (Yvette Nicole Brown), Melanie Childs (Karimah Westbrook), and Antoine Childs (Russell Hornsby).

*Address:* Apartment 303 at the Royale Apartments in Larchmont Village.

*Occupation:* Real estate broker (she first worked for Colonoda Realty before starting her own business—Toni Childs Realty ["I specialize in class"]).

*Office Location:* Sunset Plaza.

*Dream:* Marrying a millionaire.

*Wardrobe:* Very sexy. She loves to show ample cleavage in low-cut blouses and her legs in short dresses and skirts.

*Measurements:* 34-25-36; she stands 5 feet, 6 inches tall.

*Character:* Toni is, as Maya says, "a gold digger who dates rich men for what monetary gifts they can give her." Toni is attracted to rich men but backs down when situations become too serious (she grew up in a poor family and doesn't want to be poor again). She is self-centered and hates to be told she is not the youngest at the bars she frequents. Toni sizes a man up by the clothes he wears; if they are not expensive, that fixation is over. She also believes that other women are jealous of her looks, style, and sex appeal. When she is depressed, eating a Nutty Buddy ice cream cone raises her spirits.

*Favorite Magazine:* Forbes.

*Religion:* Catholic.

*Good-Luck Charm:* A "Li'l Jesus" statue (which she carries with her everywhere she goes).

*Good-Luck Food:* Mini kasha's.

*Favorite Restaurant:* Skia's (originally called 847).

*Change:* While Toni did date a lot, she married Todd Garrett (Jason Pace), a white Jewish plastic surgeon. A year later, they have a daughter (Morgan) and move to New York City (thus allowing Jill Marie Jones to leave the series during season 6).

# *Grounded for Life*
## (Fox, 2001–2002; WB, 2002–2005)

*Cast:* Donal Logue (Sean Finnerty), Megyn Price (Claudia Finnerty), Lynsey Bartilson (Lily Finnerty), Griffin Frazen (Jimmy Finnerty), Jake Burbage (Henry Finnerty), Kevin Corrigan (Eddie Finnerty).

*Basis:* A look at an American family where it appears that the children (Lily, Henry, and Jimmy) are raising their parents (Sean and Claudia), high school sweethearts who act more like teenagers than adults. In the final episode, Claudia and Sean become the parents of a fourth child, Rose (also called Gracie).

## SEAN FINNERTY
Sean, 32 years old when the series begins, believes he is "a cool, young-thinking father" (he became a parent at the age of 18 when Lily was born). He lives with his family at 856 Winslow Place on Staten Island in New York. The family also has a pet dog named Murphy.

Sean, a graduate of St. Finian's High School, married Claudia, a classmate, after graduating. He first worked "in a dump" as a sanitation landfill supervisor. He is next an electrician and then construction supervisor for the New York Subway System (actually, in real life, the Metropolitan Transit Authority). He found the subway job too dirty and noisy (working in tunnels all day) and quit to join his brother, Eddie, in opening a bar called the Red Boot Pub.

When Sean makes homemade pizza, he does so with ketchup on pita bread. He drives a car with the license plate CQP 293 (later STY 293) and believes his New York Knicks basketball team jersey is lucky (as the team always wins when he wears it). Sean can play the guitar and was in a band with Eddie when they were teenagers. Richard Riehle appeared as Sean's father, Walt Finnerty.

## CLAUDIA FINNERTY
Claudia (maiden name Claudia Bustamonte) became pregnant with Lily when she was 17 and a senior at St. Finian's High School. Claudia was very immature in high school and childlike through most of her marriage (her character matured when the series switched networks). Claudia worked as "a hostess at a very popular Soho restaurant" (in Manhattan). It is said that Claudia married Sean after the birth of Lily.

Claudia hates cell phones ("They annoy me"). She is a very sexy woman who relishes in the fact that she can still turn men's heads after having three children. Her flamboyant style earned her the nickname "The Neighborhood Hot Mom." Claudia measures 39-26-36 and stands 5 feet, 6 inches tall.

Claudia is taking classes at Wadsworth College "to improve my mind" and uses, according to Sean, "embarrassing Raggedy Ann checks" (as Claudia says, "The bank sent them, so I use them"). In her youth, Claudia as well as Sean were heavy smokers (have since quit), and even though she and Sean earn a salary, Claudia claims they cannot afford to take a decent vacation and always wind up at the Jersey Shore.

## LILLIAN "LILY" FINNERTY
Lily, the 14-year-old daughter of Sean and Claudia, attends St. Finian's High School on Staten Island. Lily, as she is called, wears her plaid school skirts much

too short, shows cleavage (doesn't seem to bother her parents), and is a cheerleader. Lily is also a member of the dance squad and the Science Nauts, the school science club.

Lily has a sign posted on her bedroom door that reads, "Stop! Keep Out! Trespassers Will Be Shot." She treasures her privacy and reads *Tres Chic* magazine. She has a fake ID card under the name "Lillian Winterhaven" and a tattoo on her lower back of a golden sprite (how she acquired it, being under 18, and without her parents' permission is not revealed, as it is a "tramp stamp"). Lily Fin is her computer screen name.

Lily believes that "my father lives to humiliate me." As a young girl, Lily put a cigarette in her mouth and pretended to smoke, copying what she saw her parents do (this prompted Sean and Claudia to quit smoking). Lily also observed how her mother flaunted her breasts to get attention and copied this when she got older, but Claudia has not stopped her from doing it. At the age of 13, Lily had the nickname "Freckle Monster," loves the music from her favorite movie (*Grease*), and hangs out at Mocha Joe's. Fiddle Faddle and Fruit Rings cereal (which she eats dry from the box) are her favorite snacks.

Lily's sexuality becomes apparent when she performs a racy version of the song "Big Spender" in a 10th-grade school play. Lily had her first job sweeping up in a butcher shop. Mike Vogen played Lily's boyfriend, Dean Peramotti.

## JAMES AND HENRY FINNERTY

James Francis "Jimmy" Finnerty and Henry Finnerty are Lily's younger brothers. Jimmy and Henry attend St. Finian's Grammar School and are as different as night and day. Jimmy admires his unethical uncle, Eddie (who, by dialogue, appears to be involved in everything that is illegal, but he is cunning enough to avoid being arrested). He is the most intelligent and sensible member of the family and gets little attention, as he causes the least amount of trouble. Henry, the younger brother, is very impressionable, and his curiosity always gets him into trouble. When Jake Burbage, the actor who plays Henry, left the series to be with his family back east, Henry was seen at the beginning of season 5 and then totally disappeared; he was referenced to several times, but a physical character did not appear.

# Hannah Montana

(Disney Channel, 2006–2011)

*Cast:* Miley Cyrus (Miley Stewart/Hannah Montana), Billy Ray Cyrus (Robby Ray Stewart), Emily Osment (Lilly Truscott), Jason Earles (Jackson Stewart), Mitchel Musso (Oliver Oken).

*Basis:* To live her dream of becoming a pop star yet retain her life as a normal girl, 12-year-old Miley Stewart creates Hannah Montana, the girl who performs onstage while she lives her normal life. Final-season episodes are titled *Hannah Montana Forever.*

## MILEY STEWART/HANNAH MONTANA

*Parents:* Robby Ray and Susan Stewart. Susan (Brooke Shields in flashbacks) died in an automobile accident when Miley was 11.

*Place of Birth:* Crowley Corners, Tennessee (also said to be Nashville), on November 23, 1994.

*Brother:* Jackson Stewart.

*Astrological Sign:* Sagittarius.

*As a Child:* Miley had a plush bear she called "Berry Bear" and would put a diaper on her head and call herself "Captain Diaper." Miley had a pet goldfish (Scaly Joe), a hamster (Mr. Squeakers), a pig (Rainbow Piggy), and a favorite doll (Daisy Diaper).

*Background:* Miley and Jackson grew up on a farm and were typical children living a typical life with their mother and father. When Miley turned nine, she received a guitar for Christmas, and it changed the course of her life. She learned to play it from her father, a musician, and it instilled in her the desire to become a singer. Shortly after her mother's passing, Robby used his connections in the music industry to jump-start Miley's singing career and moved the family to California. Miley chose not to perform as herself so that she could live the life of a normal teenage girl. To accomplish this, she chose to disguise herself (with a blonde wig [over her brunette hair] and makeup and chose the name Hannah Montana for its rhyming sound). She can now attend school and not fear being recognized as her alter ego. Miley keeps "an emergency Hannah Montana kit" in the back of the family car for quick access when she needs to be Hannah.

*Concert Trait:* Before each performance, Miley has what she calls "Hannah Berry Milk" (a strawberry/banana shake).

*Reveal:* After six years living the life of two people, Hannah appears on *The Tonight Show with Jay Leno* and reveals to the world that Hannah and Miley are the same person. She first appeared as herself on her Aunt Dolly Parton's TV special, *Dolly from Dollywood* (where she sang the song "Kiss It Goodbye").

*Character:* Stylish, witty, and somewhat nervous, especially when she gets herself into a predicament that places her true identity in jeopardy. She can also be seen concocting elaborate ruses to help someone or get herself out of a jam.

*Education:* Seaview Middle School (where she was the bicycle-riding mascot, a pirate, for the school basketball team), Seaview High School, and Stanford University (at which time the series ends).

*Home:* A beach house in Malibu, California; later a ranch-style home a short distance away (at 451 Destiny Drive, Malibu Beach, California 90250).

*Miley's Catchphrase:* "Sweet niblets" (which she says when something goes wrong). She also has a tendency to say, "Say what?" and "Ya think?"

*Nickname:* Called "Mile" by her father.

*Horse:* Blue Jeans (which she boards at the Malibu Horse Stables).

*Radio Show:* Hannah hosted *The K-Team Radio Hotline* (for teenagers).

*TV Roles:* Judged the TV talent competition on *America's Top Talent*; guest starred as Zaronda, Princess of the Undead, on the mythical teen series *Zombie High*.

*TV Commercial:* Spokesgirl for Magic Glow Skin Cleanser (a zit remover).

*Hannah's Movie Roles:* The voice of Dink in the animated feature film *Dink the Determined Duck*; the adventuress Joanie in *Indiana Joanie and the Curse of the Golden Cobra* (produced by Rob Reiner). Hannah was also pranked on the TV series *Gotcha!*

*Favorite Breakfast Cereal:* Family Cereal (as seen on the box).

*Dislike:* Raspberries. In 1999, Miley won the County Fair Pie Eating Contest by eating five raspberry pies in 10 minutes (she became ill and has since disliked raspberries).

*Favorite Food:* Curly fries. (She also mentions liking cheese, and when she becomes nervous over meeting a boy, she often says, "Do you like cheese? I like cheese. Will you go out with me?")

*Injury:* Miley broke her right arm while skiing.

*Unusual Habit:* If she is upset about something, Miley will suck her thumb in her sleep.

*Makeup Choice:* Smudge-free lipstick and waterproof mascara.

*About Her Adolescence:* "Both a blessing and a curse."

*Relaxation:* Enjoys knitting.

*Hannah's Autograph Catchphrase:* "Rock on."

*Hannah's Awards:* Most notably "The Silver Boot Booty" for her crossover song (country and western to pop), "True Friend" (which earned her a diamond on the "Hollywood Parade of Diamonds" Walk of Fame), and the International Music Award for "Female Artist of the Year." Hannah has also sung for the queen of England and the president of the United States. The Sunshine Girls have named her "Role Model of the Year."

*Hannah's Hit Songs:* "Super Girl," "Nobody's Perfect," "We Were in the Mood," "The Best of Both Worlds," "Just Like You," "Rock Star," "Old Blue Jeans," and "Ordinary Girl."

*Rival:* Mikayla (Selena Gomez), the pop star who is determined to win over Hannah's fans.

*Godmother:* Actress/singer Dolly Parton (who Miley calls "Aunt Dolly").

*Twin Cousin:* Luanne (Miley Cyrus), who Miley believes is nothing like her for all the "evil" things Luanne does (like trying to undermine her or blaming her for something she did). Miley contradicts herself when she says she named her pet pig "Luanne" because Luanne snorts like a pig when she laughs; she previously called the pig "Rainbow Piggy" (as stated above).

*Secret Uncovered:* Miley's friends Lilly and Oliver (see below) uncover but promise to keep her secret.

*Driver's License:* Class C (#PO 3096 086890); expires on November 23, 2013.

*Principal Boyfriend:* Jake Ryan (Cody Linley), a teen actor.

*Miley's Nemesis:* Amber Addison (Shanica Knowles) and Ashley DeWitt (Anne Marie Perez de Tagle), Seaview High's "queen bees."

*Flashbacks:* Young Miley (Mary-Charles Jones, then Ryan Newman).

## ROBERT "ROBBY" RAY STEWART

Robby, Miley's father, is a former singer and musician (guitar), known as Robby Ray, who now acts as Hannah Montana's manager, agent, and songwriter. He is a widower (late wife named Susan) and is also the father of Jackson, Miley's older brother. He was born in Buford County, Tennessee, in 1968 and moved to Crowley Corners, Tennessee, before relocating to California after the death of his wife. Before retiring, he had 14 number 1 hit singles. He won a Music Video of the Year Award and International Music Award for his country-and-western–themed albums; he was also awarded a diamond on the "Hollywood Parade of

Diamonds" Walk of Fame. In his disguise as Hannah's manager, Robby wears a fake mustache to hide his real identity. As a kid, he had a dog named Banjo and is an expert horseshoe pitcher and enjoys fishing.

Robby is left-handed and made a comeback on Dolly Parton's TV special *Dolly from Dollywood.* "Robby Ray Does Ragee" is the title of his never-released album; *Dr. Love Will See You Now* was his first hit album. Loco Hot Cocoa is the drink he devised (that, unfortunately, gives drinkers strange dreams). Robby was raised in a family with seven siblings and only one outhouse; he is now very reluctant to let anyone use his private bathroom. It can be seen that Robby is afraid to see Miley grow up, and for a keepsake he has a keychain made from Miley's first haircut. Although it is said that Robby writes Hannah's songs, it can be seen that Miley also writes them. Robby is a fanatic about his hair and uses the Limited Edition Jet Stream with Ion Diffuser—"the most powerful hair dryer known to man." Vicki Lawrence appears as Ruthie Ray Stewart, Robby's mother, whom Miley and Jackson call "Memaw" (it can also be seen that Ruthie and Dolly Parton simply do not get along and are always at odds with each other).

## LILLY ANN TRUSCOTT
Lilly, Miley's best friend, was born in California on October 22, 1992. She is aware of Miley's secret alias and helps her by portraying Lola Huftnagle, a flashy girl who sports more than 80 different wigs to conceal her true identity (she says, "I dress like a Japanese cartoon character when I'm Lola"); she is most often seen in a blue, white, pink, or purple wig. She befriended Miley when she first moved to California. She attends Seaview Middle School, Seaview High School, and finally Stanford University with Miley. Her favorite band is Radiohead, and in high school she was a cheerleader and member of the volleyball team and the skateboard and surf clubs. Lilly worked as a waitress at the Smilin' Sub (fast food) and at the concession stand at Outlane's Funtopia (at the Malibu Pier on the Seaview Boardwalk). Lilly discovers that Miley is Hannah when she meets Hannah and sees that she is wearing the bracelet that she gave to Miley. Lilly is a neat freak, hates buttered popcorn and muffin crumbs, and eats Sugar Crunchies cereal for breakfast; she also has a poodle-shaped birthmark on her butt. Jon Cryer played her father, Ken Truscott.

## OLIVER OKEN
Oliver is best friends with Lilly (who he has known since kindergarten) and Miley (whom he first met in the sixth grade at Seaview Middle School). He was born in 1992 and is the son of a police officer (Nancy Oken) and an unnamed father, a judge. He attended Seaview High School, chose not to attend college, and tours with his band. He is Jewish, suffers from type 1 diabetes, and, when

first introduced, had an unrelenting crush on Hannah Montana (unaware at first that Miley was Hannah). He believes that Hannah is a goddess and relentlessly stalks her, hoping to one day marry her (Miley reveals her secret to Oliver to put an end to his obsession). To be with Miley when attending Hannah's concerts, he uses the alias Mike Standley III. Oliver is a talented singer (although he was first shown with an inability to sing) and most likes rap music (in his songs, the words "fricky, fricky fresh" can often be heard). At school, he is known as "The Locker Doctor" (for his uncanny ability to unlock jammed lockers). He becomes close to Lilly (after his Hannah infatuation) and begins to share her interests in surfing, ice hockey, and skating. In one episode, he claims to be afraid of gum; in another, he is seen chewing it. It is seen that Lilly was not Oliver's first girlfriend; he dated Joanne Palumbo (Hayley Chase) for 12 episodes. His favorite band is Coldplay, and he enjoys reading his mother's "chick magazines." Although a bit unflattering, when Lilly broke out in pimples, Oliver was inspired to write the song "Lilly Pop" (it became his nickname for Lilly; Lilly called him "Ollie Pop"). Oliver also attended Seaview High School, but after entering and winning the singing competition on the TV show *America's Top Talent*, he begins a tour, leaving school in his senior year (but being taught by a tutor while on the road). He is sometimes called "Ollie," and, according to Miley, one of his nostrils is bigger than the other. His only sibling is Penny, who lives in Europe (for her job).

## JACKSON ROD STEWART

Jackson, Miley's older brother (born in 1990), is lazy, not as academically inclined as Miley, and loves to pull pranks. He attends Seaview High School and is more interested in girls, video games, and sports than he is in schoolwork (he is on the school's volleyball team). He works at the beach store (Rico's Surf Shop), drives a red car, and has the catchphrase "I said good day!" Jackson, whose middle name is a reference to singer Rod Stewart, is very untidy and the reason why the housekeepers that Robby hires quit. He is dating a girl name Serena (Tammin Surock), a model for Ba-Ba-Ba Bikinis, and buys his clothes at Dicky Roy's Clothes for Boys. Jackson later attends Malibu Junior College and acquires a job as a video game tester (at Rec Pizza) as the series ends.

# *Hope and Faith*
## (ABC, 2003–2006)

*Principal Cast:* Faith Ford (Hope Shanowski), Kelly Ripa (Faith Fairfield).
*Basis:* The relationship between two sisters (Hope and Faith) who are as different as night and day.

## HOPE MARIE SHANOWSKI

*Place of Birth:* Glen Falls, Ohio, in 1968 (she is 35 years old when the series begins).

*Maiden Name:* Hope Fairfield.

*Hope and Faith's Father:* Jack Fairfield (Robert Wagner); their mother, Mary Jo, is deceased.

*Husband:* Charlie Shanowski (Ted McGinley), an orthodontist. Edward (Hal Holbrook) and Joyce Shanowski (Dixie Carter) are Charlie's parents.

*Children:* Sydney (Nicole Paggi, then Megan Fox), Hayley (Macey Cruthird), and Justin (Jansen Panettiere, then Paulie Litt).

*Sister:* Faith Fairfield (see below).

*Education:* U.S. Grant High School; Ohio State University (studied journalism).

*Occupation:* Housewife and mother. As the series progressed, Hope took a job with the *Glen Falls Gazette* as a columnist (writes "Life in the Carpool Lane") and had previously turned down a reporting position with the *Chicago Tribune* to marry Charlie.

*Character:* Hope is a simple girl who likes life to be as uncomplicated as possible. She is a bit of a control freak and loves to go shopping. She always buckles her seat belt, always reports for jury duty ("It's a civic responsibility"), and enjoys celebrating special occasions (like birthdays and anniversaries).

*Activities:* President of the Grant High School PTA, chair of the Glen Falls Hospital and Volunteer Committee, and hostess for her weekly book club meetings.

*Quirks:* Hope admits to doing strange things such as, "I found a broken egg in a carton and replaced it with another egg from another carton before buying it," and she stands by the fact that the strongest drug she has ever taken is Ibuprofen ("Aspirin upsets my stomach").

*Dog as a Child:* Pickles.

*Childhood Nickname:* Called "Sunshine" by her father.

*Breast Issues:* Hope measures 35-24-35 and stands 5 feet, 2 inches tall. Faith's measurements are 32-24-33, and she stands 5 feet, 3 inches tall. Hope mentions that in high school she was virtually flat chested and worried about her developing figure (so much so that she would shower in a two-piece bathing suit after gym class just to prevent other girls from seeing her nude). Faith would flaunt her much fuller figure, and Hope became jealous, wanting larger breasts to impress boys. At some point, perhaps when Faith started acting, she had breast implants (as Hope says, "Her breasts are bigger because she had a boob job"). While Faith's after-implant size is not mentioned, Faith believes that Hope's breasts are larger than hers and is mystified as to why Hope is so jealous of her figure, especially when she points out that Hope wears a bra to bed (and Hope responds with, "I need the support"). The issue is mostly dropped as the series progresses, although Faith continually shows cleavage while Hope wears more conservative clothes.

## FAITH FAIRFIELD

*Place of Birth:* Glen Falls, Ohio, in 1969 (she is 33 years old when the series begins).

*Address:* 22 Cherry Lane in Glen Falls (lives with her sister Faith and her family [husband Charlie and their children Sydney, Hayley, and Justin]).

*Education:* U.S. Grant High School.

*Childhood:* Unlike the levelheaded Hope, Faith had her head in the clouds and was irresponsible from the beginning. When she was 13, for example, she used her father's coin collection to pay for the invitations to her upcoming birthday party and then mailed them with stamps from his stamp collection.

*Ability:* Acting (which she first showed when she played a pirate in her third-grade play *The Pirates of Penzance*). Her mother encouraged her, and her first professional job was in a TV commercial for a cold medicine. She next appeared on the talent program *Star Search* but lost.

*TV Roles:* With the great body she thinks she has, Faith became the star of a sexy and steamy cable movie called *Weapons of Mass Seduction* (wherein she had her first nude scene—she had to remove her bra and use it as a tourniquet to stop the bleeding when her partner was shot). She next starred on the mythical ABC soap opera *The Sacred and the Sinful* as April Storm and her twin sister Ashley. After a 10-year run, Faith was written out when April shot Ashley and then killed herself. With no money, no house, and no place to live, Faith left Hollywood and returned to Glen Falls and moved in with Hope.

*Faith Now:* Faith has every episode of her soap opera on tape. She cherishes her one Daytime Emmy Award and claims, "For the first time in my life, I have no role. I just don't know who to be." She relates incidents about life she thinks are real but are actually scenes from her series. She claims that her greatest talent is her ability to cry on cue (Hope calls her "a famous star with a Daytime Emmy and fake boobs").

*Local Jobs:* TV commercials for Handsome Hal's Used Cars, wearing a red bikini to model jackhammers at a local trade show, and columnist ("Life in the Star Pool Lane") for the *Glen Falls Gazette*.

*Agent:* Animal and Artists Talent Agency.

*Nickname as a Child:* Called "My Little TV Star" by her father.

*Nickname for Her Breasts:* Faith calls them "The Girls."

*Life with Faith:* Faith lives in the glory of her past and hopes to one day return to New York (where her soap was taped) and once again make her mark on the world. In the meantime, she is struggling to adjust to a much simpler life—and in doing so causes numerous problems for the family, especially for Hope, who always becomes the innocent victim in her harebrained schemes to make money. Charlie also feels his life is plagued by Faith, as he is always the one who has to step in and get them out of trouble (often involving himself in their silliness).

## THE CHILDREN

Sydney is the eldest child, a sophomore in high school. She is very pretty and totally devoted to looking the best she can. While smart, she is not addicted to schoolwork and believes she can get by on her physical assets. Younger sister Hayley is pretty and very smart. Her life revolves around her ability to improve her mind, and while she could be very attractive, she doesn't dress to impress boys. Justin, the youngest, is smart but not as intellectual as Hayley. He is easily impressed by others and often takes on different personas to impress people (e.g., several episodes portray him as imitating Frank Sinatra).

# *House, M.D.*
## (Fox, 2004–2012)

*Cast:* Hugh Laurie (Gregory House), Jennifer Morrison (Allison Cameron), Omar Epps (Eric Foreman), Olivia Wilder (Remy Hadley), Lisa Edelstein (Lisa Cuddy), Robert Sean Leonard (James Wilson).

*Basis:* A brilliant but maverick antisocial doctor (Gregory House) treats patients afflicted with baffling or mysterious illnesses.

## DR. GREGORY HOUSE

*Date of Birth:* 1959 (seen as May 15 on his driver's license but mentioned as June 11).

*Mother:* Blythe House. His father is unknown. Blythe had an affair with a marine pilot (John House) and an affair with Thomas Bell while John was stationed overseas. Gregory believes that Thomas was his father because they share the same characteristics.

*Childhood Interests:* Chemistry, music, and playing both piano and guitar. He also spent time in various foreign countries, as John was constantly transferred from base to base.

*Wife:* Dominika (Kardina Wydra), whom Gregory married in season 8 after his breakup with Lisa Cuddy (see below). He originally married Dominika as a means for her to get her green card (which forced them to live together to prove to the Immigration and Naturalization Service that their marriage was legitimate).

Hugh Laurie. *Fox Broadcasting/Photofest © 2004 Fox Broadcasting; photographer: Justin Stephens*

*Education:* Johns Hopkins University (in Baltimore; enrolled in a premed program); University of Michigan Medical School. He obtained degrees in infectious diseases, pathology, and nephrology.

*Address:* 221-B Baker Street (the same as Sherlock Holmes, implying that House is the Holmes of the medical profession) in New Jersey.

*Position:* Doctor of diagnostic medicine at the Princeton-Plainsboro Teaching Hospital in New Jersey. He also works in the hospital's clinic and prefers to treat the illness, not the patient.

*Philosophy:* "Treating illness is why I became a doctor. Treating patients is what makes doctors miserable." He also says, "We treat. If the patient gets better, we're right; if not, we learn something else."

*Character:* Smug ("Smugness is easy to maintain"), rude, and no bedside manner. House does not dress like a typical doctor (he refuses to wear hospital whites or greens). He also does not believe in pretense: he says what he thinks. If a case intrigues House, he will break his rule and speak to the patient. He has a degree in infectious diseases and balks at having to work the common areas of the hospital clinic (he is six years behind on his obligation to the clinic and says, "I'm here from nine to five"). He calls himself "a lonely infectious disease guy." Dr. Lisa Cuddy, the hospital administrator, will not fire him because "the son of a bitch is the best doctor we have." House will steal, lie, and cheat to get what he needs if it means helping a patient. His "insane diagnosis and treatment procedures are usually right," says Lisa.

*The Limp:* House can be seen walking with a cane (which he calls "The Flame Cane," as it makes him appear to walk fast) and taking medication to relieve the intense pain he suffers in his leg. Two versions are given as to how the condition arose. It is first mentioned that House suffered a heart attack that left him with a partially crippled right leg. It is next said that he suffered an infarction in his leg while playing golf. The condition worsened to the point where a leg muscle stopped working and amputation was suggested as the only cure. House opposed this, but when the pain became so intense, he was put in a medically induced coma (if not, the pain would cause heart failure). It was decided to remove the damaged muscle, saving his life but leaving him with a nasty scar and constant pain. While Vicodin is the drug he takes for pain, he also uses himself as a guinea pig to test experimental drugs and procedures in the hope of finding a cure for his pain.

*Favorite TV Show:* General Hospital (which he tries to watch while on call at the hospital).

*Inspiration:* Video games.

*Ability:* Encyclopedic knowledge of medicine and best when faced with a baffling medical condition.

*Dislike:* Pickles.

*The House Fund:* Dr. Cuddy has a special medical fund where she keeps $50,000 for lawsuits brought by patients who face Gregory's treatment (Cuddy estimates that 40 percent of all legal issues can be attributed to House).

*Blood Type:* AB.

## DR. LISA CUDDY

Lisa, the hospital administrator and dean of medicine, was born in 1968. She is single (although she was married for six days and had the marriage annulled) and is the adoptive mother of a daughter named Rachel; Arlene is her mother (her father, not named, is deceased), and Julia Cuddy is her sister. Lisa was editor of her high school yearbook and since the age of 12 had always wanted to become a doctor (following in a family tradition). Her major problem is House, who defies authority, is abusive to staff and patients, and doesn't comply with his obligation to perform clinic duty (which he has avoided for six years until Lisa forces him to make up for all that lost time by assisting patients four hours a week). Lisa met Gregory at the University of Michigan (she was an undergraduate, and he was in medical school; he first saw her in the school's library), where they developed a romantic interest in each other (and had a one-night stand). Lisa admires House for his ability to ignore emotional attachments when a patient's life is on the line. Although he has known Lisa for many years, he describes her as "a control-seeking narcissist," something that also defines himself.

## DR. ALLISON CAMERON

Allison, age 38, was born in Illinois. She was first married to Bob (divorced), then Robert Morse (deceased), and then an unnamed third husband. She is first a doctor and a member of Gregory's diagnostic team and then the emergency room attending physician. House claims he hired Allison because she is pretty ("It's like having a nice piece of art in the lobby"). Allison was not at the top of her class and did her internship at the Mayo Clinic. She is sweet, trusting, and compassionate and even had romantic feelings for House. Unlike House, she has sympathy for patients but takes too personal an interest in their problems.

## DR. ERIC FOREMAN

Eric, a diagnostician, is a member of House's team (he is later the dean of medicine at the Princeton-Plainsboro Teaching Hospital; he is also a neurologist). He was born in 1973 and is closest to House (although more outgoing). Eric is the son of Alicia and Rodney Foreman (deceased) and was born in an unnamed borough of New York City. Crime, poverty, homeless people, and gangs were mentioned as being prevalent in his neighborhood. He has a younger brother, Marcus, and, although raised in a very religious family, his environment led him to be arrested as a juvenile delinquent for petty crimes; he was also a gang member and still carries a tattoo from that time. While the advice from his mother, "I'll pray for you," made Eric see the light, Marcus continued his life of crime, only to be captured and sentenced to prison. Eric revealed that as a teenager he was overweight and a bed wetter (this last fact is something Dr. House holds over Eric to embarrass him when he needs Eric to side with him on a medical issue). Eric attended Columbia University (on a full scholarship) and studied biochemistry; he next attended Johns Hopkins Medical School (where he later did his internship).

## REMY BEAUREGARD HADLEY

Remy was born in New York City (possibly in 1981) and is the daughter of John and Anne Hadley. She has a sister (Amy) and an unnamed brother (deceased). Remy is suffering from the early stages of Huntington's disease (inherited from her mother; it also affected her brother). She fears losing control over her emotions and movements but tries not to let it interfere with her work as a specialist in internal medicine at Princeton-Plainsboro Teaching Hospital. Remy's schooling is a bit of a mystery, as nothing is explained to clarify things (other than her family moved several times). In Massachusetts she attended Newton North High School (possibly only as a freshman and sophomore); in West Virginia she was a junior at an unnamed high school. She next attended Sarah Lawrence College in Yonkers, New York (where she was a student in residence taking premed courses), but her medical college is not revealed (only that she did her internship in Miami).

Remy, called "Thirteen," received the nickname when she was classified applicant 13 of the 39 applicants who were chosen for an interview with Gregory House for acceptance into the hospital. Remy is bisexual (while attending medical school, she had intimate relations with her roommate, a girl from Iowa, but also dated men and women). She served time in prison (for euthanizing her mother when she became institutionalized and no longer wanted to live). Remy is caring and compassionate toward her patients but has a very difficult time dealing with the death of a patient.

## JAMES EVAN WILSON

James is an oncologist and head of the Department of Oncology at Princeton-Plainsboro Teaching Hospital. He was born in New Jersey and is the son of a Protestant father (Henry) and a Jewish mother (Sophie); he followed in the religion of his mother. Sophie was a nurse; Henry taught wood shop in a high school. James has been married and divorced three times (Samantha was his first wife; Bonnie, his second; and Julie, his third). He has degrees from the University of Pennsylvania, Columbia University, and McGill University. He loves monster trucks, has a good bedside manner, and cares about his patients. James, later diagnosed with cancer, is allergic to dandelions and ragweed and first drives a Volvo, then a Ford Taurus.

# *How I Met Your Mother*
## (CBS, 2005–2014)

*Cast:* Josh Radnor (Ted Mosby), Neil Patrick Harris (Barney Stinson), Cobie Smulders (Robin Scherbatsky), Alyson Hannigan (Lily Aldrin), Jason Segel (Marshall Eriksen), Lyndsy Fonesca (Penny Mosby), David Henrie (Luke Mosby), Cristin Milioti (Tracy McConnell).

*Basis:* Ted Mosby, a 26-year-old New York City architect, begins a quest to find the perfect girl and begin a family. A futuristic Ted (voiced by Bob Saget) is heard as he speaks to his children (Penny and Luke) in the year 2030 to relate the story of "How I Met Your Mother" (Tracy). Josh Radnor provides the voice of future Ted in the final two episodes.

## THEODORE "TED" EVELYN MOSBY

*Place of Birth:* Shaker Heights, Ohio, on April 25, 1978.
*Parents:* Virginia (Cristine Rose) and Alfred Mosby (Michael Gross).
*Sister:* Heather Mosby (Erin Cahill).
*Wife:* Tracy McConnell (deceased; seen in flashbacks). It is mentioned that Ted dated 65 women before finding Tracy.

Alyson Hannigan, Jason Segel, Josh Radnor, Cobie Smulders, and Neil Patrick Harris. *CBS/Photofest © CBS; photographer: Monty Brinton*

*Children:* Luke and Penny Mosby.

*Education:* Wesleyan University (degree in architecture).

*Occupation:* Professor of architecture at Columbia University in Manhattan (also said to be New York University).

*Buildings Designed:* The Spokane National Bank; Manhattan headquarters of GNB (Goliath National Bank).

*Languages:* English, American Sign, Italian, French, and (poor) Spanish.

*Religion:* Catholic.

*Nervous Habit:* Peels labels off beer bottles; forgetting people's names after meeting them.

*Favorite Bar:* MacLaren's Pub (which is below his apartment on Amsterdam Avenue).

*Favorite 1970s Movies: Star Wars* and *Annie Hall.*

*Favorite Baseball Team:* The Cleveland Indians.

*Childhood Obsession:* Collecting Jedi Knights (from *Star Wars*).

*Musical Ability:* Plays the piano.

*Unusual Quirk:* Believes the women he dates were all previously men.

*Address:* First lived in Manhattan in what was called "The Apartment" and later in a house in Westchester, New York (where he created the plans for its restoration).

*Future Ted:* In his youth, Ted went to great lengths to find his perfect mate. He dated many women and relates his experiences with one woman in particular, Robin, to his children in the year 2030 (his children, Luke and Penny, are normally seen seated on a sofa, facing the camera, while Ted's narration is heard in each flashback).

## ROBIN CHARLES SCHERBATSKY JR.

*Place of Birth:* Vancouver, Canada, on July 23, 1980.

*Parents:* Robin (Eric Braden then Ray Wise) and Genevieve Scherbatsky (Tracey Ullman); they are divorced. Robin Sr. gave his daughter a male middle name, as he wanted a boy.

*Sister:* Katie Scherbatsky (Lucy Hale, Stacy Keibler, and Hallie Lambert).

*Husband:* Barney Stinson (see below).

*Pet Dog as a Child:* Sir Scratchewan. When the dog passed, her father replaced it with a turtle and told Robin her dog was transformed into a turtle through a medical procedure called "canine testudine cerebra engraft."

*Occupation:* As a teenager, Robin became a pop singing sensation under the name Robin Sparkles (her one hit song was "Let's Go to the Mall"). "Sandcastles in the Sand" and "P.S., I Love You" were her less successful songs. Robin then costarred on the Canadian TV series *Space Teens* (about outerspace crime fighters) with her girlfriend Jessica Glitter (Nicole Scherzinger).

Robin next ventured into journalism, where she became a cub reporter for Channel 22, a TV station in Red Deer (in Alberta, Canada). Hoping for bigger and better things, she moved to New York City, where she acquired a job as a field reporter for *Metro News 1* (but only wrote fluff stories). When she became bored with the job, she became a foreign correspondent (stationed in Japan). After one week, she returned to New York, where she became the host of the early morning TV series *Come On, Get Up New York*. She then worked as a researcher for *World Wide News* (before accepting the job, she was offered but rejected the position of currency rotation specialist on the game show *Million Dollar Heads or Tails*; Ted called the job "coin flip specialist").

*Bad Habit:* Including the word "literally" too often in conversations and using "but . . . um" on her live TV reports.

*Favorite Hockey Team:* The Vancouver Canucks.

*Favorite Pastime:* Drinking scotch and smoking cigars (also said to be cigarettes).

*Favorite Bar:* MacLaren's Pub.

*Character:* A tomboy at heart (as her father raised her as the son he never had). She is sarcastic and very secretive about herself. To please her father as a teenager, she joined the school hockey team but disappointed her father when he caught her kissing a teammate; she was no longer that boy he wanted (it was at this time that she moved in with her mother).

*Revelation:* Robin never had children (unable to conceive).

*Hobby:* Guns. She carries a handgun in her purse, owns a number of firearms, and enjoys frequenting a firing range.

*Dislike:* Nicknames.

*Address:* An apartment in Park Slope, Brooklyn, New York.

*Allergy:* Lobster.

*Flashbacks:* Robin, age six (Shelby Zemanek); age 11 (Olivia Howard Bagg).

## BARNABAS "BARNEY" STINSON

*Place of Birth:* Staten Island, New York, in 1976.

*Mother:* Loretta Stinson (a single mother; his biological father is Jerome Whittaker, whom Loretta said was his Uncle Jerry; she also told him that TV game show host Bob Barker was his father).

*Maternal Half Brother:* James Stinson.

*Paternal Half Sister:* Carly Whittaker (Ashley Benson).

*Paternal Half Brother:* Jerome "J. J." Whittaker Jr.

*Birth Sign:* Scorpio.

*Wife:* Robin Scherbatsky. Barney proposed to Robin in December 2012, and they married in May 2013, but the marriage ends in 2016.

*Daughter:* Ellie Stinson.

*Occupation:* Worker in an unnamed coffee shop, then for the AltruCell Corporation, "a company that makes the fuzzy yellow stuff on the surface of tennis balls"; he later works for GNB.

*Favorite Bar:* MacLaren's Pub.

*Quirks:* Talks in nonsensical catchphrases; uses an unusual high-pitched voice; before watching a movie, he picks the protagonist based on the film's title; treats his clothes as if they were like living people; and imagines he is being interviewed by CBS newscaster Jim Nantz when he is nervous.

*Twitter Account:* @broslife.

*Obsession:* His own appearance.

*Favorite Rock Band:* Van Halen.

*Medical Issue:* Painful eyes (caused by watching his 100-inch flat-screen TV at too close a distance). He also claims to have a learning disorder, although he was a straight "A" student in school.

*Fears:* Commitment and abandonment issues.

*Character:* A playboy who sees women as sex objects. He is stylish, loyal to his friends and family, but somewhat ignorant when it comes to pop culture. He loves magic (which he uses to impress women) and the game of laser tag (but gets carried away and becomes too aggressive). He enjoys being a blogger, but a somewhat childlike personality can also be seen at times. One of his biggest challenges was to get his friend Lily (see below) to show him her breasts.

*Apartment Feature:* A Storm Trooper and a Clone Trooper costume from the movie *Star Wars*.

*Quirk:* When Barney uses statistics, he often mentions the number 83 (or a variation of it, like 38, 8, or 3).

*Catchphrase:* "Suit up" (referring to what to wear from his elaborate and expensive wardrobe of suits).

*Flashbacks:* Young Barney (Tanner Maguire, then Riley Thomas Stewart).

## LILY ALDRIN

*Place of Birth:* Park Slope, Brooklyn, New York, on March 22, 1978.

*Parents:* Mickey (Chris Elliott) and Janice Aldrin (Meagan Fay). Mickey practically raised Lily, a stay-at-home father who was obsessed with creating the next great board game. Janice, an extreme feminist, devoted her time to two jobs and was very strict with her (not even allowing Lily to have what she wanted most—an Easy Bake Oven).

*Childhood:* Lily took ballet and gymnastics and had a dog named Bean. In high school, she was out of control (defiant, drinking under age, and terrorizing her neighborhood). At one point, she studied abroad in Paris for one semester.

*Occupation:* Kindergarten teacher; waitress (at the Big Wave Luau, a Hawaiian restaurant); Ted's office assistant; art consultant (for "The Captain").

*Husband:* Marshall Eriksen (see below).

*Children:* Marvin and Daisy Eriksen (and a third, unnamed child).

*Address:* An apartment in Manhattan on Amsterdam Avenue at 75th Street (which she shares with Marshall and her children).

*Education:* Wesleyan University (majored in art).

*Favorite Song:* "Good Feelings" by the Violent Femmes.

*Favorite Bar:* MacLaren's Pub.

*Valentine's Day Tradition:* Watching the movie *Predator* with Marshall.

*Dream:* To become an artist.

*Character:* Selfish, cannot keep a secret (loves to gossip), is very caring, and cannot control her spending habits (she impulsively buys and is in debt). Despite her girl-next-door appearance, she (like Barney) is a very sexual person. She is also very manipulative and must have things her way (even if it means ignoring what someone else may want).

*Quirk:* Is curious about other people's romantic and sex lives. She fantasizes about making love to Robin (also said that when she has a martini her desire for Robin becomes overwhelming).

*Medical Issue:* Lactose intolerant.

*Habit:* Peeling labels off of bottles (much like Ted); chews loudly (even soft foods like bread).

*Dislike:* The word "moist. "

*Pet Names:* Lily calls Marshall "Marshmallow"; he calls her "Lily Pad."

*Flashbacks:* Lily, age seven (Francesca Capaldi); age 11 (Piper Mackenzie Harris).

## MARSHALL ERIKSEN

*Place of Birth:* St. Cloud, Minnesota, in 1978.

*Wife:* Lily Aldrin (see above).

*Children:* Marvin, Daisy, and an unnamed, third child.

*Occupation:* Corporate lawyer with the Manhattan firm of Nicholson, Hewitt & West; then a lawyer for GNB and environmental lawyer for Honeywell & Cootes; New York State Supreme Court judge in 2020 (as stated in Ted's narration).

*Education:* Wesleyan University (where he met Lily); Columbia Law School.

*Background:* Marshall has two brothers (Marvin Jr. and Marcus); his parents (Marvin Sr. and Judy) taught him to respect others (which can be seen in the politeness his character displays as an adult). His favorite sport was "baskiceball" (basketball combined with ice skating) that his father invented. His skills at basketball earned him the title of "Slam Dunk Champion of Nicollet County" (in Minnesota) and the nickname "Vanilla Thunder" (he called his skill at dunking "The White Windmill"). He is also interested in wrestling and at the age of 13 smoked his first cigarette. Although he stands 6 feet, 4 inches tall, he is the shortest male member of his family.

*Favorite Bar:* MacLaren's Pub.

*Habit:* Using the nonsense word "lawyered" when speaking of cases and often sings what he is doing (as opposed to just normal talking).

*Belief:* Anything supernatural (like ghosts) and unexplained phenomena (like Bigfoot)—traits he shares with Lily.

*Favorite Movies: Field of Dreams* and *Star Wars.*

*Obsession:* Food and its origins.

*Ability:* Very good at playing video games; can create websites (such as he did when he and Lily chose to sell items they had accumulated with the site Lilyandmarshallselltheirstuff.com.

*Favorite Sports Team:* The Minnesota Vikings.

*High School Band:* "The Funk, the Whole Funk, and Nothing but the Funk."

*Flashbacks:* Marshall, age three (Koby Rouviere); age 10 (Tyler Peterson).

# *Joan of Arcadia*

(CBS, 2003–2005)

*Cast:* Amber Tamblyn (Joan Girardi), Joe Mantegna (Will Girardi), Mary Steenburgen (Helen Girardi), Jason Ritter (Kevin Girardi), Michael Welsh (Luke Girardi).

*Basis:* A 16-year-old girl (Joan Girardi) performs special missions for God when He chooses her as His earthbound helper.

## JOAN AGNES GIRARDI

*Place of Birth:* Chicago, Illinois, on November 24, 1987.

*Parents:* William and Helen Girardi.

*Brothers:* Kevin and Luke Girardi.

*Address:* 2320 Euclid Avenue, Arcadia, Maryland.

*Social Security Number:* 507-07-1113.

*Driver's License Number:* G-726 1871 73 136 (expires on December 6, 2006).

*Education:* Arcadia High School (a C-plus student).

*School Activities:* Member of the debate team, the chess club, the band (playing drums), and the cheerleader team (the Eaglettes).

*Favorite Color:* Green.

*Favorite Melon:* Cantaloupe with a dash of salt.

*Background:* Joan grew up as a typical girl, enjoying life and getting into all kinds of mischief. She broke her arm roller-skating, she chipped a tooth when the training wheels were taken off her bicycle and she fell, and she pulled a groin muscle when she attempted to snowboard.

*Character:* Joan is very pretty but believes she is not as pretty as other people see her. She is shy, has few friends, and cherishes those who are close to her. She is always willing to give of herself to help others, but her most unusual characteristic has not manifested itself: her ability to talk to God.

*The Change:* Joan is a sophomore in high school when God first appears to her. Joan is unbelieving until God reminds her that if her brother (Kevin) survived a car crash (that crippled him), she would do anything God asked. God, who appears to Joan in various human forms (from the school janitor to a young girl), needs her help in resolving small problems that arise. Joan accepts what is happening and performs her first mission: acquiring a job at the Starlight Book Store to help its owner overcome a minor crisis. When Joan sees that she successfully helps the store owner, she believes that she actually talked to God and will do what He asks.

*The Complication:* Joan's missions often place her in awkward positions and make her appear strange at times. She explains this as, "I'm an adolescent girl searching for my mission in life." It is also not obvious to Joan what God intends her to do when he assigns her a mission (e.g., building a boat in her basement to bring her father and Kevin closer together when they take over the project). Each mission that Joan takes makes her learn that she is capable of doing something that she never knew she could (like cutting wood and fitting pieces together for the boat).

*The Night of Kevin's Accident:* It is first seen that Joan was watching the movie *The Nutty Professor* when Kevin was injured; later, it is seen as Joan (and Luke) watching the Three Stooges.

*Revelation:* During a history class lesson on Joan of Arc, Joan realizes that she is unique and, in a way, a modern reincarnation of her. It is known that God talked to Joan of Arc and that she was a female warrior who carried out missions in His name. It is also uncanny that Joan Girardi resembles Joan of Arc.

*God's Appearances to Joan:* These include Candice Azzara (as "Housewife God"), Susan Sullivan ("Rich Woman God"), Allyce Beasley ("Cat Woman God"), Christy Carlson Romano ("Hall Monitor God"), Anastasia Baranova ("Exchange Student God"), Curtis Armstrong ("Security Guard God"), John Kissir ("Mime God"), Adam Richman ("Butcher God"), and Russ Tamblyn (Amber's real-life father as "Dog Walking God").

## WILLIAM AND HELEN GIRARDI

William and Helen originally lived in Chicago, where Will was a police detective. He moved his family to Arcadia, Maryland, when he was offered the job of police chief of the Arcadia Police Department "to get the kinks out of the system." The department disbands when Will uncovers internal corruption in the town's infrastructure, and he becomes the chief of detectives of the Hogan County Sheriff's Department (which assumes the duties of the Arcadia Police Department). A differing story line claims that Will relied on a false tip to bust a drug dealer and was demoted from police chief to detective when the tip didn't stand up under scrutiny. He served for several years in this position and eventually worked his way back to captain (at which time the infrastructure scandal hit the department). Will was born on September 5, 1955, and attended Mother Cabrini High School then Morton Junior College. His car license plate reads PRZ 3S5, and L-100 is his police car code. He was never in the delivery room with Helen for his children's births "because I can't see my wife in pain." It can be seen that Will always drinks from a cup with a picture of Joan, Kevin, and Luke on it.

Helen (maiden name Helen Brody) is an artist (paints landscapes). She first worked in the administrative office of Arcadia High School, then as the school's art teacher. She is a caring mother who loves her very different children with equal devotion but with different approaches. Joan is pretty, insecure, and not easily motivated. Kevin is handicapped (injured his spine in a car accident and must now use a wheelchair) and also self-pitying. Luke, the youngest child, is a brilliant student who shelters himself and stays mostly to himself.

Helen's artwork reflects a dark side in her that resulted from an incident in her past: a man broke into her college dorm and raped her; to this day, he remains at large. Red wine makes Helen tipsy, and she insists that she do the family laundry. She was raised Catholic but never received Confirmation.

## KEVIN AND LUKE GIRARDI
Kevin was crippled in a car accident while a student in high school (he failed to stop a fellow student from driving drunk after a party; in the pilot episode, it is mentioned as having happened a year and a half ago, making it the spring of 2002, but it is later mentioned as happening on November 9, 2002). Kevin attended Jefferson High School (seen on his yearbook but mentioned as Staten High School) and played on the school's basketball team (which earned him a scholarship to the University of Arizona). Unable to attend college due to his accident, Kevin acquired a job as a fact-checker for the local newspaper, the *Herald*, then as a journalist, and as the series ends, he pursued a career as a local TV news anchor.

Luke, the youngest child (born on November 19, 1988), devotes much of his time to science (hoping to become a scientist when he grows up). He is a straight "A" student in school and keeps mostly to himself until he meets Grace Polk (Becky Wahlstrom), a girl also interested in science but an activist who is opposed to any kind of authority. She is the daughter of Sarah and Rabbi Polanski.

# Malcolm in the Middle
(Fox, 2000–2006)

*Cast:* Jane Kaczmarek (Lois Wilkerson), Bryan Cranston (Hal Wilkerson), Frankie Muniz (Malcolm Wilkerson), Christopher Masterson (Francis Wilkerson), Justin Berfield (Reese Wilkerson), Erik Per Sullivan (Dewey Wilkerson).

*Basis:* Life with a not-so-typical American family: parents Lois and Hal and their children, Malcolm, Francis, Reese, and Dewey.

## LOIS WILKERSON
*Place of Birth:* Manitoba, Canada, in 1962.
*Parents:* Victor (stepfather, Robert Loggia) and Ida Welker (Cloris Leachman); her biological father is Radu Gogorsky.
*Sister:* Susan Welker (Laurie Metcalf, then Bonita Friedericy).
*Maiden Name:* Lois Welker.
*Address:* 123341 Maple Road. The family has been voted "The Most Hated Family in the Neighborhood."
*Medical Issue:* Asymmetrical shoulders (her third and fourth vertebrae become unaligned if she gets upset).
*Character:* Lois is abrupt, short-tempered, and rude (in high school, she was called "The Mouth") for taking her frustrations out on other people. She finds that she must always be right even if she is wrong. She is so overpowering that Hal is terrified of her (rather than create an argument, he always agrees with her). She is totally stressed out by her kids and cares little about modesty. She walks around the house in her bra and sometimes without a bra (but nudity is obstructed by something, or she is seen from the back). She is very strict when it comes to disciplining her children, especially Reese, who is the most troublesome. Sleep is the only escape Lois has from the responsibilities of motherhood.

*Dream:* Having a family of obedient girls. In a dream sequence, she is seen as the mother of three daughters: Mallory (Lisa Foiles), Renee (Mimi Paley), and Daisy (Jennette McCurdy). She hopes to one day give birth to a girl. It failed to happen when she gave birth to another boy, Jamie (James and Lukas Rodriquez), in 2003.

*Occupation:* Salesgirl at the Lucky Aide department store (where she has the nickname "Beans"; the store's slogan is "The 'L' Stands for Value"). Lois once thought of becoming a blackjack dealer on an Indian reservation, "but stubby thumbs stopped me."

*Birthday Presents:* On her birthday, Lois gives each of her children $10 to buy her a present.

*Favorite Song:* "Tears of a Clown."

## HAL WILKERSON

*Parents:* Walter (Christopher Lloyd) and Sharon Wilkerson (who are wealthy). They despised Lois and her family because they were lower class.

*Place of Birth:* California in 1956.

*Sisters:* Claire (Jeanine Jackson) and Amelia (Brenda Strong).

*Occupation:* Hal originally worked as a systems supervisor at G.N. Industries ("Making the World Safe with Our Products" and "We've Got the Solution if You've Got the Problem"). He is later laid off when the company CEO uses funds to buy his wife a recording studio. He then works at various jobs, including salesman at a store called "U Buy It."

*Character:* Lois's total opposite and rather lenient when it comes to punishing the children (he seems to not like Lois's punishment of having the children stare at the wall). He is somewhat immature and confessed that certain cartoon characters frighten him. He is so afraid of Lois that he actually bribes his children to take the fall for something he has done. His midlife crisis led to his becoming an artist.

*Addiction:* Roller-skating (he calls it "The Brotherhood of the Wheel"). He also claims to be addicted to coffee (so much so that he drinks three pots a day).

*Skills:* Shown to be a skilled bowler (makes a strike each time) and a talented hairdresser.

*Fetish:* It can be seen that he may have an obsession with women's feet.

*Celebrity Crush:* When Hal was 15 years old, he had an unrelenting crush on Farrah Fawcett and bought her an engagement ring, hoping that she would marry him.

*Radio Host:* Hal was "Kid Charlemagne, the Voice of the Little Man" on a pirate radio station when he was in college.

*Favorite Drink:* A vodka martini.

*Fears:* Monkeys, snakes, and clowns.

*Flashbacks:* Young Hal (Dean Bates, then Robert Thomas Preston).

## FRANCIS WILKERSON

Francis, the firstborn child, is so mischievous that his parents were forced to send him to the Marlin Military Academy for rehabilitation (it is under the iron-fist rule of Edwin Spangler [Daniel von Bergen], who has a hook for a hand). Francis believes his mother is a domineering control freak and has made it his goal to one day stand up to her. After graduating from the academy, Francis marries Piama Tananakaakna (Emy Coligado) and held several jobs: band manager, children's book author, waiter in an Alaskan diner (where he met Piama), logger at a logging camp (where he was a member of the Logs Ice Skating Team), foreman of the Grotto Ranch in New Mexico, and finally data processor at Amerisys Industries (where he enjoys sitting in a cubicle all day). Piama also worked briefly at a snow globe factory. As a kid, Francis had a pet snake named Otis and is the only child in the family who can claim to have beaten his mother at what he calls "Lois's Punch-Out Tactics" (her way of getting the kids to tell who did something bad by threatening them). Despite his bad reputation, his younger siblings look up to him as their hero.

*Flashbacks:* Young Francis (Tyler Ryan, Easton Gage, and Scott Berkhausen).

## REESE WILKERSON

Reese, the second-born child, is following in Francis's footsteps and solves all his problems by fighting. He attends North High School and is a straight "D" student (but he uses the same shade of ink that his teacher uses to change the grades on his report card). Reese is quite naive and easily taken advantage of and has "a shiny box" under his bed "for shiny things I find." He likes to stare at clouds ("for the sky kittens I see") and has what he calls a "wishing hole" (a tree on Jefferson Street with a hole on which he makes wishes). Reese believes he is a ladies' man (but can't get a date), and his only talent appears to be making gourmet meals. To impress "the ladies," Reese became a member of the Wildcats Cheerleading Team at school. It can be seen that Lois appears to dislike Reese the most, as she considers him an absolute moron with no potential. The most outrageous thing Reese did was to lie about his age (saying he was 18 when he was 17) to enlist in the army under the fake name Reese Jetson (he was heartbroken when a girl he loved, Beth [Molly Orr], broke up with him and he needed to find a new life). He passed basic training, was sent to Afghanistan, and obtained the rank of private first class before he was rescued by Lois (who revealed his true age) and discharged. He later acquires a job as the janitor at a college.

*Flashbacks:* Young Reese (Connor M. Morrison, Dillon John Dailidonis, Jay Collette, and Austin Wolff).

## MALCOLM WILKERSON

Malcolm, the third-born child, is the genius of the family (and, besides Hal, the only stable one). He has an IQ of 165 and excels at math at North High School (where he is a member of the gifted class, Krelboyne). Malcolm is the only family member who is aware of a viewing audience and speaks directly to them. His first job was as a babysitter, and he later worked with his mother at Lucky Aide (store 167). He is also the only family member who does something good: volunteers at Memorial Hospital three times a week. It can be seen that Malcolm harbors a deep resentment for Lois as she attempts to control him in any manner and never allows him any freedom. Hal, a NASCAR fan, named Malcolm after his favorite racer, Rusty Malcolm.

*Flashbacks:* Young Malcolm (Noah Matthews, then Cody Estes).

### DEWEY WILKERSON

Dewey, the youngest child before the birth of Jamie, is the most conniving of the children (he uses what he calls "turning on the cute" to get things from people). He is a musical prodigy, attends Grace Elementary School, and has a plush teddy bear (Domingo), an adopted dog he found (Marshmallow), and a grossly overweight white rabbit (Gordo). To make money, Dewey cuts school to perform as "Le Great El Foldo" (squeezes himself into a box for money). He believes he has the ability to understand what dogs are saying when they bark, and when he becomes upset, he hides in the crawl space under the house.

*Flashbacks:* Young Dewey (Matthew Dunn).

*Note:* The family's last name of Wilkerson was revealed in the pilot episode (as seen on Francis's Marlin Academy uniform tag), but due to the unrealistic portrayal of characters, it was decided that the family should not have a last name. "No-last-name" became an inside joke, and every attempt to reveal the family's last name in an episode is always obstructed by something to prevent it from happening. The locale also remained anonymous but was revealed to be Star City, California.

# *The Mentalist*
## (CBS, 2008–2015)

*Cast:* Simon Baker (Patrick Jane), Robin Tunney (Teresa Lisbon), Xander Berkeley (Red John), Tim Kang (Kimball Cho), Owain Yeoman (Wayne Rigsby), Amanda Righetti (Grace Van Pelt).

*Basis:* A man (Patrick Jane) who pretends to be a psychic helps the police solve puzzling crimes. *The Mentalist* could be considered a copy of *Psych* (see title), which aired beginning in 2006 and used the same premise.

Robin Tunney and Simon Baker. *CBS/Photofest © CBS; photographer: Cliff Lipson*

## PATRICK JANE

*Place of Birth:* California. His actual birth date is unclear (shown as July 30, 1969, on his driver's license, then September 16, 1974, on his marriage license when he married Teresa Lisbon).

*Father:* Alex Jane (his mother is not named).

*Wives:* Angela Ruskin Jane (with whom he had a daughter named Charlotte Anne [Dove Cameron]); Teresa Lisbon (with whom he had an unnamed child).

*Background:* Patrick attended an unnamed grammar school, but anything further appears unlikely. He developed a keen sense of observation and deduction while growing up and became a part of a carnival sideshow run by his father when he was a teenager (presumably after graduating from grammar school). Alex, somewhat abusive to Patrick, raised him alone and billed him as "The Psychic Boy," a scam conceived by Alex to use Patrick's observational abilities to bilk carnival goers. It is revealed that Alex's grandparents came from Ireland and that Alex simply preyed on innocent people, as clairvoyant powers did not run in his family.

*Life Changer:* When Alex forced Patrick to use his abilities to scam a dying girl and her grandmother, Patrick, now about 17 years old, knew that what he was doing was dishonest and deserted Alex and the carnival life. Since Patrick's mother is not mentioned or named, it is suggested that she most likely died when Patrick was young, and, before Alex could care for him, Patrick spent time in a foster home. Since Patrick's past is conveyed through flashbacks, it is also a bit inconsistent (as with his birth date). But it is also seen that while working at the carnival, Patrick met a fellow worker (Angela Ruskin) whose mother and father also ran a sideshow. Angela knew that Patrick and his father were pulling a scam, and she begged Patrick to give it up. He did, and the two ran away together (this causing his split with Alex) and later married.

*Occupation:* At some point after his marriage, Patrick appears to have returned to "the psychic game" to earn money (he, Angela, and their daughter, Charlotte Anne, now live in a house in Malibu, California). His act consisted of reading minds and, on television appearances, contacting the deceased relatives of audience members. On one such telecast, it is shown that Patrick has been assisting the police as a psychic consultant to help them catch a serial killer known as Red John. When questioned about the killer on a TV broadcast, Patrick belittled him by calling him "an ugly, tormented little man. A lonely soul. Sad, very sad."

*The Consequences:* Red John did not take the comment well and sought revenge by killing Angela and Charlotte Anne. Before discovering the murders, Patrick found a note on his bedroom door from Red John. ("I do not like to be slandered in the media, especially by a dirty money-grubbing fraud. If you were a real psychic instead of a dishonest little worm, you wouldn't need to open the door to see what I've done to your lovely wife and child.") The murders caused Patrick to have a mental breakdown (blaming himself for what he did), and he spent six months in a institution. During this time he vowed to find and capture Red John.

*The Redemption:* A year after the murders, Patrick approaches Teresa Lisbon, head of the CBI (California Bureau of Investigation), asking for information regarding Red John. His arrival coincides with the police hunt for a killer. Not aware that Patrick pretends to be a mentalist, she asks for his help. Patrick agrees, and with his "abilities," the killer is caught. Patrick realizes that what he pretends to be is also his saving grace, as he can help bring criminals to justice. The CBI hires Patrick as a consultant, but as the series concludes, Patrick leaves the unit to become a consultant for the FBI (see Teresa Lisbon, below).

*Character:* Patrick is skilled at playing mind games and is a master manipulator but is averse to confrontation and carrying a gun (even in his pursuit of Red John). He almost always dresses in a three-piece suit (sometimes with a mismatched vest) and has a Cockney-like attitude with a tendency to avoid authority. His mentalist act is so convincing that people actually believe he can read minds (so much so that he has been labeled "the finest detective in California"). Although it appears that Patrick has not attended high school or college, he has an appreciation of the arts and music and presents himself as well read and educated. He appears to have a photographic memory, as he can recall things no ordinary person can from his past (he claims to store such information in "The Memory Palace" of his brain). He pays attention to details at a crime scene and notices the little things that can easily be overlooked.

*The Fear:* That Red John will target Teresa as his next victim. Red John is driven to destroy anyone close to Patrick, while Patrick is as driven to end Red John's killing spree.

*Home:* Patrick maintains the Malibu beach house he shared with his family before their murders (when he visits it, the smiley-face image of Red John, drawn with his wife and daughter's blood, can be seen). Patrick now lives somewhat in the CBI building (sleeping on Teresa's office couch and adapting an unfinished part of the building as his "lair") but officially resides in a motel close to CBI headquarters.

*Car:* A blue Citroën DS 21 Pallas (manufactured in France).

*Favorite Beverage:* Black Chinese tea.

*Habit:* Constantly eating (even helping himself to food at suspects' homes).

*Medical Issue:* Lactose intolerant (although he can't drink it, he hates warm milk).

*Non-Fake Expertise:* Poker player, performing sleight-of-hand magic, and the ability to hypnotize people. He also feels more confident using his wits rather than relying on the latest forensic methods to solve crimes.

*Religion:* Atheist.

*Musical Tastes:* Light classical and opera. He can also carry a tune.

*Hobby:* Solving mysteries and puzzles.

*Favorite TV Shows:* Nature documentaries.

*Interests:* Horses, motorcycles, and airplanes (especially remote control ones; he even makes paper planes).

*Dislike:* Doctors (believing they are cold and lack compassion).

*Values Most:* Trust from other people in what he does.

*Introduction:* When meeting a crime victim, Patrick often says, "My name is Patrick Jane. I'm here to help you."

*CBI Case Closure:* At the conclusion of each crime that is solved, Patrick brings food into the squad room to celebrate. It began with donuts but evolved into pizza.

*Flashbacks:* Teenage Patrick (Chris Brochu).

## TERESA LISBON

*Parents:* Not named; her siblings are Tommy, Jimmy (Robert Belushi), and Stan Lisbon (Derek Phillips).

*Husband:* Patrick Jane (see above).

*Occupation:* Detective with the San Francisco Police Department; special agent in charge of the CBI; police chief; FBI special agent.

*Background:* Teresa was born in Chicago to a mother who worked as a nurse and a father who was a firefighter. At the age of three, Teresa "decorated" her bedroom closet with a crayon drawing of her family. The family appeared to suffer from financial difficulties (as Teresa recalls, the sewing machine her mother owned was constantly finding a new home in a pawnshop). While not specifically mentioned, Teresa and her brothers, being raised Catholic, most likely attended Catholic grammar and high schools. Her life changed dramatically at the age of 12 when her mother was killed by a drunk driver. Her father became a heavy drinker after the incident, and the responsibility of raising her brothers fell on her shoulders (making her education beyond grammar school a mystery). A short time after, her father committed suicide. In her teenage years, Teresa worked as a waitress to support herself and her brothers. It is revealed that Tommy later became an electrician (for Town and County Electrical) and worked as a bounty hunter on the side. Stan, a housing contractor, has money problems (being in debt to loan sharks), and Jimmy, whose profession is not mentioned, is involved in nefarious activities (at one point, he was wanted as a material witness in a murder investigation). As Teresa says about Tommy, "I practically raised that punk and his brothers."

*Adult Life:* At some point, Teresa left Chicago for the West Coast (where she joined the San Francisco Police Department's rookie school). After serving time as a beat cop, she was promoted to detective (and received the nickname "St. Teresa" for capturing a serial child rapist), then appointed to the CBI. Later, after the CBI is dismantled, Teresa accepts the job as police chief in Cannon River, a small town in Washington State. She resigns from the job a short time later to join Patrick (now a consultant for the FBI) as an FBI special agent.

*Character:* A strict professional who adheres to the letter of the law and keeps her personal life just that: personal.

*The Relationship:* Although Teresa is constantly annoyed by Patrick's unorthodox methods, she eventually falls in love with him, and the two marry. Prior to this, Teresa rarely showed any affection toward Patrick (although he could sense her feelings about him). Patrick also became overly protective of Teresa and resented the fact that she must deal with danger and not be rescued from it.

*The Marriage:* Patrick and Teresa wed in the series finale (Teresa is pregnant at the time, but the sex of their unborn child is not revealed). Patrick gave Teresa the wedding ring of his first wife, which Teresa now wears as a necklace with a cross that her mother had given her. Patrick purchased land in Texas and plans to remodel the cabin where they will now live.

*Favorite Music:* Jazz.

## RED JOHN

Red John, the alias of Thomas McAllister, is the elusive serial killer sought by Patrick Jane. He often uses the alias Roy Tagliaferro and began his "career" in 1988 (Patrick ended it in 2013 when he killed him by strangulation after a arduous foot chase).

Red John, listed in the CBI case files as just "R.J." or "R.J.K." (Red John Killer), was revealed to be California's worst and most elusive serial killer (even more so than the real-life Zodiac Killer [whose identity is still unknown]). The CBI has associated 41 murders with Red John and has revealed that Red John founded the Blake Association, a secret criminal organization of law enforcement officials who are linked to Red John and manipulate the system to cover up his crimes (thus, the murder count may be higher). It was Red John's killing of Patrick's wife and child five years earlier that led Patrick on a never-ending quest to find him. It became a game of matching wits until Patrick won six years later. Patrick's frustration can be seen, as Red John always appears to be one step ahead of him and always manages to escape from Patrick no matter how foolproof Patrick thought his plans were (it can be seen as a Sherlock Holmes vs. Professor Moriarty situation).

Red John's trademark is a red-painted smiley face that he leaves behind at each crime scene. He is a psychopath and takes great pleasure inflicting pain (then death) on his victims. He is seen mostly in shadows as himself but also in full view when he pretends to be someone else (Sheriff McAllister is a second repeated alias). Patrick's investigations have revealed that Red John is a master manipulator, highly intelligent, and cultured (seen enjoying classical music and tea and admiring the work of poet, composer, and painter

William Blake, after whom he named his association and after whom he took his nickname [from Blake's series of paintings called *The Great Red Dragon*]). While Red John's actual appearance is unknown, clues to his identity indicate that he is a white male, somewhere between 40 and 45 years of age and distinguished by a tattoo of three dots on his left shoulder. He also speaks in a nonrealistic high-pitched voice (most likely using a voice-altering device).

Information regarding Red John's prior life is virtually unknown. Through dialogue, it is learned that he most likely has no living family members and that he drew his first smiley face while working as a farmhand for a church in the town of Elliston (where he committed his first two killings, those of his coworkers). It is known only that he next moved to Napa County, California, where he took on the guise of Sheriff Thomas McAllister. Before becoming known as "Red John," the newspapers dubbed him "The Smiley Face Killer," as his signature was a smiley face drawn in a victim's blood.

### GRACE VAN PELT RIGSBY

Grace is a CBI special agent who worked with Patrick and Teresa. She was born in Iowa and is the daughter of Amos Van Pelt (mother not named), the local high school football coach. She is married to Wayne Rigsby, a fellow agent with the CBI, and the mother of Madeline (with Wayne) and his son, Benjamin, from his prior marriage to Sarah Harrington. Wayne, the team's arson specialist (also helps with interrogations), met Grace when she joined the team and eventually began a romantic relationship with her (something that is against CBI regulations). While they eventually married, they were not allowed to work together, and it was Wayne who chose to leave the unit by accepting a transfer to the CBI San Francisco office. Grace's specialty is computers and hacking. When the CBI was dismantled in 2013, Grace and Wayne opened a private investigative firm dealing with computer fraud. She is religious and believes in psychics, ghosts, and other supernatural-related entities.

### KIMBALL CHO

Cho is a CBI special agent who works with Patrick and Teresa. He was formerly a member of the U.S. Army's Special Forces. Because of his army experiences, he takes case investigations seriously and follows the letter of the law in his role as the unit's interrogator. He is somewhat superstitious, careful with his money (although not cheap), and a ladies' man. He is also very stubborn and most always follows Patrick's or Teresa's lead. Little is revealed about Cho's past other than that he grew up in a tough neighborhood and, before joining the army, was a member of a gang called "The Avon Park Playboys" (where he had the street name "The Iceman"). He was eventually caught and spent time in juvenile detention. When the CBI was dismantled, Cho joined the FBI and, after completing his training at Quantico, became a supervisory special agent. Cho dislikes pineapple and is averse to most alcoholic beverages.

*Series Note:* Two of Red John's accomplices, Rebecca Anderson (Shauna Bloom) and Oscar Cordero (Joe Nievens), are the only characters where "Red" can be seen in their names spelled backward (Rebecca An*der*son and Oscar Cor*der*o). It can also be seen that Xander Berkeley, who plays Red John, also has "Red" in his first name (Xan*der*).

# The Middle
## (ABC, 2009–2018)

*Cast:* Patricia Heaton (Frankie Heck), Neil Flynn (Mike Heck), Eden Sher (Sue Heck), Charlie McDermott (Axl Heck), Atticus Shaffer (Brick Heck).
*Basis:* Life with a family of five (parents Frankie and Mike) and their children (Sue, Axl, and Brick) living in Orson, Indiana.

### FRANCES "FRANKIE" HECK

Frances, called Frankie, is the daughter of Pat (Marsha Mason) and Tag Spence (Jerry Van Dyke). She was born in Indiana in 1965 and has a sister named Janet (Molly Shannon). She lives at 427 Birchwood Avenue and first worked as a salesgirl for Ehlert Motors (a used-car lot). When she is fired due to downsizing, she attends school to become a dental assistant (she acquires a hygienist position with Dr. Ted Goodwin [Jack McBrayer]). She is somewhat neurotic, struggling to pay bills and dealing with an uncooperative and seemingly dysfunctional family. Frankie doesn't become overly involved in her children's lives and sort of lets them take care of their own problems (due to her job or other day-to-day concerns). Frankie is often forgetful, and one of her most noticeable traits is always leaving behind the blue bag of snacks when the family goes on an outing. Chicken is her favorite dinner, and donut holes are her favorite snack.

Frankie is optimistic about everything (no matter how grim things look) but does not like certain occasions, like Mother's Day (for all the fuss involved). She hates all televised awards shows except the Oscars and knows that she neglects her children but is most happy when Axl hugs her (she also covers for Brick, who is forgetful, by doing or finishing up his homework assignments; she also tries to encourage Sue to have a better outlook on life, but her advice usually backfires, and Sue reverts back into her "nobody knows I'm alive" shell). Frankie likes grilled cheese sandwiches but is very particular as to how they are served: cut into a triangle and with potato chips placed in the middle. Colin Firth is her favorite celebrity

Eden Sher, Patricia Heaton, Atticus Shaffer, Neil Flynn, and Charlie McDermott. ABC/Photofest © ABC

(so much so that she named her dog Colin and uses the computer password Mrs. Frankie Firth). While she is not the greatest parent in the world, she has a unique talent to hold off creditors when money is short and bills cannot be paid. Frankie is able to multitask (like listening to a conversation while doing something else; she claims she can listen to four conversations at once) and has the uncanny ability to change clothes within 20 seconds and pull what she needs from her handbag without looking. Dick Van Dyke plays Tag Spence's brother, Dutch.

### MICHAEL "MIKE" HECK
Mike, the son of "Big" Mike Heck, was born in Indiana in 1963 (his mother died of lung cancer when he was a teenager). He has a brother named Rusty (who lives in a tent in Orson, played by Norm MacDonald) and works as the manager of the Orson Lime Quarry; he also held a job as a deliveryman for Little Betty Snack Cakes. Mike can simply be described as blunt, tall, and somewhat boring. He is practical and straightforward but hides his emotional side. It is revealed that when Mike first met Frankie, she did not like him (in fact, she did everything to avoid him, even using a fake name). Mike did persist and won Frankie over, and they eventually married (although Frankie was not too pleased that their honeymoon was a camping trip). Frankie is very attractive now, but Mike believes that she lost what he was attracted to: her youth "and shiny-looking appearance."

Mike's favorite movie is *Reservoir Dogs*, and it can be seen that he and Frankie bicker often about money, about their position in life, and, most important, about their children and the paths in life they are taking. Mike favors Axl the most (because of his love of sports) and almost always forgets Sue, which makes her feel out of place. Brick has the unique distinction of almost always being forgotten by both parents. Mike's typical wardrobe is a checkered shirt and jeans, and he is very fond of cats (he named a stray cat at the quarry "Limestone").

## SUE HECK

Sue, born on February 29, 1996, is the middle child of Frankie and Mike. She is socially awkward but appears as a nerd, as she fails at virtually everything she does. Her official name is Sue Sue Heck (her parents accidentally wrote her first name as her middle name on her birth certificate). Sue is overemotional and often saddened by all the bad luck she has but maintains a positive attitude. Although she is here and there, no one ever remembers her name or notices her. She loves Selena Gomez (and her TV series *The Wizards of Waverly Place*), Taylor Swift, Justin Bieber, and the group One Direction. Being that her birthday falls on a leap year, her birthday is celebrated only once every four years. Sue attends Orson High School (where she called herself "Frosh" and is ignored by students), then East Indiana State University. In high school, she was a member of the cross-country team and suffered a fainting spell when she wore her team sweatshirt (number 10) everywhere. Sue was also a cheerleader for the Orson High wrestling team (she created the name "The Wrestlettes" for the cheerleading team) and a cheerleader for the volleyball team. Sue held a job at The Potato Place at the mall and was a member of the JPLA (Junior Peer Leadership Advisor). Sue is on Facebook and has an Instagram account (@sueheckwins) and a Twitter account (@SueHeckWins); her phone password is Sue Heck Wins. Although "Sue Sue" bothered her at first (and she thought of changing her middle name to Lily), she overcame it when someone mentioned that "Sue Sue was a unique name."

Although Sue wears horrible, visible braces, she also wears a retainer at night while sleeping (it appears that Sue originally had a normal overbite cross bite, but when her dentist attempted to fix it, he "overcorrected it with a rare overbite under bite." Sue is left-handed, loves peaches (and peach scent), and created her own alter ego, Suki (who was right-handed). She loves waffles, gets along with Brick, but often fights with Axl.

## AXL HECK

Axl, middle name Redford, is 15 years old when the series begins and the oldest of Frankie and Mike's children. He first attended Orson High School, then East

Indiana State University (studying business on a football scholarship). He is the only one of the children to marry (April, played by Greer Grammer), which they did in haste and then quickly annulled the marriage when they realized that none of their parents approved.

Axl enjoys raiding the refrigerator and walking around the house in his boxer shorts. He is very lazy and sloppy and expects other people to pick up after him. He could be seen as a "momma's boy" and often refers to himself as "Awesome." He wore jersey 32 as a member of the Orson High football team and, like his mother, loves donut holes. His high school grades were not good (although he was proficient on the football team). Green is his favorite color, and he mentions that pizza is his favorite dinner and bananas his favorite fruit. He held a job as a lifeguard during the summer (and walked barefoot everywhere). Watching TV is his favorite activity, and he had a band called Axl and the Ax Men. Frankie claims that Axl is an expert on astronomy because he watched the movie *Hot Tub Time Machine* numerous times (Charlie McDermott, who plays Axl, played Chaz in the movie).

### BRICK HECK

Brick, whose middle name is Ishmael, is the youngest of the children (born in November 2001). He loves to read (takes a book wherever he goes) and has a bad habit of whispering to himself (explained that when he hears certain words and wants to hear them again, it must be in a quiet mode). While he is academically smart, he is very lazy and constantly forgets things (like doing his homework). He attends Orson Elementary School (later Orson High) and is a loner (he tends to isolate himself from his classmates, and his only friend is his backpack). Brick has an eidetic memory (remembers virtually everything he reads) and enjoys competing in school spelling bees (although he loses by spelling a word but saying the last letter in a whisper). Like his mother, Brick loves donuts (prefers donut holes) and had been "the family snitch" (Frankie "paid" him with candy cigarettes to spy on the rest of the family). Yellow is his favorite color, and while he has an obsession for joining school activities, he has a short attention span and never follows through on anything. He also has an uncanny interest in words with three syllables and type fonts, and, being that Brick was an accident (Frankie and Mike did not intend for a third child), his parents called him "Oops" for the first three years of his life.

Excessive amounts of sugar make Brick appear normal, and no matter what, he must say the Pledge of Allegiance 20 times before bedtime. Brick did not live with Frankie and Mike for the first month of his life (Mike became so engrossed with a football game that he accidentally wheeled the baby of the Ferguson family out of the nursery). While most people put dressing on their salad, Brick will eat his salad only with lime Jell-O. "Planet Nowhere" is his favorite book series, and fearing he will trip in his dreams, he rolls up the bottoms of his pajama legs to make sure he is safe. His biggest fear is crossing the covered bridge that is near his home (he eventually overcomes it—but only by walking across it, not by being in a car). He plays the French horn, and while the family is seen attending church, Brick does not believe in God (strongly opposing Sue, who has a very strong belief). It is intimated that Brick has Asperger's syndrome as well as type 2 ontogenesis imperfect (a condition that causes bones to break easily).

# Modern Family
## (ABC, 2009–)

*Cast:* Ed O'Neill (Jay Pritchett), Sofia Vergara (Gloria Pritchett), Julie Bowen (Claire Dunphy), Ty Burrell (Phil Dunphy), Sarah Hyland (Haley Dunphy), Ariel Winter (Alex Dunphy), Jesse Tyler Ferguson (Mitchell Pritchett), Rick Rodriquez (Manny Delgado), Nolan Gould (Luke Dunphy).
*Basis:* Life with a dysfunctional family of five living in Los Angeles: parents Jay and Gloria Pritchett and their children Claire, Mitchell, and Manny.

## JASON "JAY" FRANCIS PRITCHETT
*Place of Birth:* Youngstown, Ohio, on May 23, 1947 (his parents are not named).
*Siblings:* Donnie and Becky Pritchett.
*Wife:* De De Pritchett (first wife; divorced; her maiden name is De De Williams); Gloria Pritchett (current wife; her maiden name is Gloria Ramirez).
*Children:* Mitchell and Claire (with De De). He is the stepfather of Manny (Gloria's son from a prior marriage to Javier Delgado) and Joe (natural child with Gloria).
*Grandchildren:* Haley, Alex, and Luke Dunphy (from Claire's marriage to Phil Dunphy).
*Occupation:* Owner of a closet store called Closet Fornia, then Pritchett Closets and Blinds (where Claire works and became the owner when Jay handed the business over to her).
*Military Service:* Served with the navy during the Vietnam War (he did his training in Pensacola, Florida). Jay, 18 at the time, had his first sexual experience with a 31-year-old woman named Charlotte.
*First Crush:* As a child, Jay fell in love with actress Gina Lollabrigida and vowed to one day marry her.
*Character:* Charismatic, strict (from his navy training), and a bit manipulative. He is a caring father but, because of his age, finds that he cannot enjoy what they enjoy (finds it to be boring). He is most uncomfortable with Mitchell, who is openly gay and in a relationship with Cameron "Cam" Tucker (Eric

Stronestreet); they later marry and adopt a Vietnamese girl named Lilly (who then becomes Lillian Elizabeth "Lilly" Tucker-Pritchett). First played by twins Ella and Jaden Hiller, then Aubrey Anderson-Emmons. Lily was born in Vietnam in 2008 and cared for by a group of Asian women while living in an orphanage; she now attends Watson Elementary School.

*Catchphrase:* "Oh, jeez."

*Hobby:* Building model airplanes.

*Favorite Sport:* Fishing (although he is seen enjoying sports like football).

*Quirk:* Sleeps with a butter knife under his pillow for protection (having grown up during the Cuban missile crisis as a child).

## GLORIA PRITCHETT

*Parents:* Fulgencio (father) and Pilar (mother) Ramirez.

*Siblings:* A sister, Sonia (Stephanie Beatriz), and two unnamed brothers.

*Full Name:* Gloria Marie Ramirez Delgado-Pritchett.

*Place of Birth:* Barranquilla, Colombia, South America, on May 10, 1971.

*Husband:* Jay Pritchett (she is 24 years younger).

*Ex-Husband:* Javier Delgado (Benjamin Bratt).

*Children:* Joe (with Jay); Manny with ex-husband Javier; she is the stepmother of Jay's children (from his prior marriage to De De) Claire and Mitchell.

*Occupation:* Housewife (current); she previously worked as a hairstylist, then a taxicab driver.

*Background:* Gloria grew up in a poor, crime-ridden village in Colombia. She experienced violence in her youth and worked various manual labor jobs to help support her family. She had her own machete for protection and has become used to killing animals (as her relatives owned a butcher shop). She believes in the supernatural and that her family is cursed with bad luck (being thrown in jail) due to her great-great grandfather, who made "a deal with the Devil." Although her adolescent years were tough, she found enjoyment in entering and winning beauty pageants (where her talent segment consisted of a ventriloquist act with her dummy, Uncle Grumpy; when the dummy is later seen, Jay notices a considerable likeness to himself). Gloria's entrance to the United States came in a sneaky way: she intercepted a letter meant for her sister, Sonia, to come to the country and used it for herself, leaving Sonia behind. Gloria is also not the sweet and innocent woman she appears to be. She has been deported twice and is wanted by authorities in Florida for subletting an apartment that her roommate turned into a brothel. She married Javier in the mid-1990s and gave birth to their son, Manny, in 1999. After divorcing Javier shortly thereafter, Gloria began raising Manny alone. It was at this time that she began working as a hairstylist and cab driver but could afford only an apartment in the slums. Apparently,

Jay frequented a diner in this area and first saw Gloria there. The two became friendly and began dating (Jay would always complain that climbing the stairs to Gloria's third-floor apartment was exhausting for him).

*Character:* Other than her beauty, the most noticeable thing about Gloria is the loud, high-pitched voice she uses when she gets upset (neighbors think the Pritchetts own a parrot; it was said that Gloria's voice can set off a car alarm and that it drove a neighbor's dog mad). Because of her upbringing, she has an unstable attitude and no hesitance about stating her opinions. Her temper is quite explosive, and she rants and raves in Spanish when she gets upset. She becomes extremely jealous if another woman is perceived to be prettier or better dressed than her.

*Religion:* Catholic.

*Expertise:* At some point, Gloria became familiar with guns and is now an excellent shot; she is also proficient at playing chess.

*Fear:* Spiders.

*Dream Car:* A Rolls-Royce.

## OTHER CHARACTERS

Claire Melinda Dunphy, Jay's daughter by his first wife, De De, is married to Phil Dunphy and the mother of Haley, Alex, and Luke. She currently oversees her father's business, Pritchett Closets and Blinds, and previously worked as the account manager for Starcrest Hotels. She was born in 1970, and, unlike her older brother Mitchell, who is gay, Claire is straight. As a 12-year-old girl, Claire became hooked on the just-released video game "Pac-Man" and was not the perfect daughter. She was a wild child and constantly getting into trouble (one related incident is Claire being arrested and returned to Jay and De De clad only in her bra and panties). She is known to have dated older men and met future husband Phil when she was attending an unnamed college. It was also at this time that Claire became pregnant (with their first child, Haley) and the two eloped. To make it legal, they married four months later. Claire considers herself a perfectionist and is quite capable (more so than Phil) of running a household and caring for children. Claire is also very competitive and claims that her favorite holiday is Halloween (for the death and the macabre it represents). Claire is afraid of flying, has a tendency to drink too much red wine, loves crafting, and has a strange (and illegal) habit of stalking children on Facebook under her false account "Brody Kendall."

Philip "Phil" Humphrey Dunphy, born in Florida on April 30, 1969 (also implied as April 3), is married to Claire and is the father of Haley, Alex, and Luke. He is the son of Frank and Grace Dunphy and works as a real estate agent. While good at sports (especially baseball), he devoted his high school and college years to the school's cheerleading teams. He is horrified by clowns (having stumbled across a dead one in the woods as a child), has a fear of small places, and considers himself "the coolest of dads," although he acts childlike and can be a bit awkward at times (Claire can be heard referring to him as "the kid I married"). He is a science-fiction fan and embraces the theory that robots will one day rule. Phil keeps fit by walking and using a treadmill. He appears to like music by Hall and Oates, is a fan of magic, enjoys computers and technology, and embarrasses himself in front of others (but is not aware of it) by bragging that he was a male cheerleader (thinking it is cool). His and Claire's song is "If You Leave" (which was playing when they first kissed). Phil mentions he plays the flute (started in his school) and has an undisclosed respiratory condition.

Haley Gwendolyn Dunphy, born in Los Angeles in 1993, is the daughter of Claire and Phil Dunphy. She currently works as a social media club promoter; she was formally a college student (University of California, Los Angeles), an assistant fashion designer, makeup artist, and assistant TV weather girl at KJQS, Channel 12. She was rebellious and in her teen years a party girl. Haley is a bit dense and considers her beauty the key to her success. She is lactose intolerant and has an eating disorder (anorexia) that makes her appear mean when she is hungry (as she says, "My whole life is a hunger game"); she can be seen toying with food but not actually eating it; she is not a model but feels she must maintain a model's look. As the series progresses, Haley's rebellious ways gradually cease, but she develops a liking for alcoholic beverages.

Alexandria "Alex" Anastasia Dunphy is the second-born child of Claire and Phil Dunphy; she has an older sister (Haley) and a younger brother (Luke). She was born in Los Angeles in 1997 and is the smartest of the children. She is an overachiever and believes she is above most people (especially her family, whom she taunts when they are rude to her). Although she most often gets along with her family, she and Haley are total opposites and constantly bicker over everything, including appearance (Alex is not fashion conscious), boys, and dating. Alex is also a bit hard on herself, as she feels the only way she can win her mother's approval is by maintaining a straight "A" grade average. In her unnamed high school, she is a member of the French club, the debate team, and the lacrosse team. She plays the cello and sings backup vocals for her band, Electric Light Dorkestra (slang for a combination of "dork" and "orchestra"). She graduates as valedictorian and next attends Cal Tech, majoring in biochemistry (although Harvard was her dream school, she was rejected for entry). She feels that using blue index cards relaxes her and makes studying more efficient.

Lucas "Luke" Philip Dunphy is the youngest child of Claire and Phil Dunphy. He was born in Los Angeles in 1998 and has two sisters: Haley and Alex. He is not the brightest of teenagers (actually a vacuous dullard) who does questionable things and has a very short attention span (somewhat like his father). While Luke has a lot in common with his father, he is just the opposite when it comes to clowns (likes them) and magic (hates it). He is allergic to foods that contain soy and likes adding salt to hot chocolate (makes it taste better?).

Manuel Alberto Javier Alejandro Ramirez Delgado, better known as Manny, was born in Florida in 1999 to Javier Delgado and his now ex-wife, Gloria Pritchett (Jay Pritchett is his stepfather); Claire, Mitchell, and Cameron are his step-siblings. Although he is only 10 years old when the series begins, he is quite mature (relates well to adults) and has a keen interest in music, the arts, and literature (he is even quite a chef). But, by observing his family, he has become scheming and sneaky. He is a preteen ladies' man but quite ignorant on how to impress girls and is always hurt in the end. He attended Walgrove Elementary School and Palisades High School (graduated in 2017) but has not yet chosen which college to attend. He likes jazz, Frank Sinatra (copies Frank's taste in Fedora hats), and is proud of his Latin heritage. Strange as it may seem, Manny is afraid of butterflies, is an expert at chess, and was shocked to learn that as a baby his mother dressed him as a little girl.

*Series Note:* Although it is stated that "*Modern Family* is the first show in history to have a gay couple," it is simply not true. The series *Hot L Baltimore* and *Soap* did so in the 1970s, and in the 1980s it was the series *Brothers* that featured TV's first gay couples.

# *Monk*
## (USA, 2002–2009)

*Cast:* Tony Shalhoub (Adrian Monk), Bitty Schram (Sharona Fleming), Traylor Howard (Natalie Teeger), Ted Levine (Leland Stottlemeyer), Emmy Clarke (Julie Teeger), Jason Gray-Stanford (Lieutenant Randall Disher).
*Basis:* A brilliant but neurosis-plagued detective (Adrian Monk) uses unusual methods to help the police solve crimes.

### ADRIAN MONK
*Parents:* Jack Monk (Dan Hedaya), a textbook writer (he abandoned the family in 1972 when he went out for Chinese food and never returned; he now works as a big-rig driver for Tiger Bay Trucking); his mother is not named (played by Rose Abdoo in flashbacks).
*Place of Birth:* Marin County, California, on October 17, 1959.
*Brother:* Ambrose Monk (John Turturro); he has a half brother named Jack Monk Jr. (Steve Aahn). Ambrose is an instruction manual writer; Jack tells

people that Jack Jr. is an orthopedic surgeon; in reality, he is jobless and living in Jack's basement.

*Dislike:* Christmas. Adrian was raised by very strict parents. During Christmas 1964, his mother became very ill, and Ambrose locked himself in the basement to avoid the holiday. Jack presented Adrian with his only gift—one-half of a walkie-talkie set (as Jack stated, Monk didn't have any friends and did not need a set). When Jack left, Adrian became the man of the house, caring for his mother (who died in 1994) and Ambrose, cooking, cleaning, and doing the grocery shopping. Adrian's favorite hangout was a store called The Cave.

*Favorite TV Series as a Child: The Patty Duke Show* (he has a picture of Patty Duke on the inside of his school locker door). He later mentions the mythical series *The Cooper Clan.*

*Education:* Westover Junior High School; Virginia High School (a member of the track team); California's Berkeley University (class of 1981; he showed compulsive behavior and acquired the nickname "Captain Cool" for his weekly habit of defrosting the student lounge refrigerator; it is here that he met his future wife, Trudy, and lived in dorm room 303). In high school, Adrian was a member of the track team but quit after he bent down to tie his shoelace and missed the starting gun.

*Occupation:* Consulting detective (originally a detective with the 14th Precinct of the San Francisco Police Department [SFPD]). Since he began his career, he has solved 105 murders—except that of his wife, Trudy. With the help of his first nurse, Sharona Fleming, Adrian establishes a private consulting business to help people in trouble (and the police when a crime stumps them). When Sharona leaves, his new assistant, Natalie Teeger, assists him in becoming a private detective and opening a business: A. Monk, Private Investigations (located in the Arcade Building on Sunpile Road).

*Late Wife:* Trudy (Stellina Ruisch, then Melora Hardin), an investigative reporter for the *San Francisco Examiner* who was killed in 1997 by a car bomb. Was she working on a story? Did she get too close to something? These are the questions that plague Adrian as he desperately attempts to solve the mystery of her murder. He often returns to the scene of the bombing (parking space 5-B) in a building garage for inspiration. Trudy's death also affected Adrian in a most unusual way. It trigged a rare anxiety disorder that makes him a germophobe and afraid of virtually everything. The condition immediately interferes with Adrian's work, and he is given a 325 temporary suspension from the police department (a psychological discharge). He is ordered to see a psychologist (Dr. Charles Kroger [Stanley Kamel], later replaced by Dr. Neven Bell [Hector Elizondo]); his appointments are on Mondays and Fridays and every other Wednesday. He then hires a full-time nurse (Sharona Fleming) to assist him; when Sharona leaves, Natalie Teeger replaces her.

*Trudy Ellison:* It is first mentioned that Trudy met Adrian at Berkeley College when he was working at the school's library; it is later stated that Trudy met Adrian when he was a detective with the SFPD. Trudy, the only child of Dwight and Marcia Ellison, was born in Los Angeles in 1962. She attended the Ashton Preparatory School and graduated at the age of 15 in 1977. She and Adrian had a tradition: when walking hand in hand and they had to let go, Trudy always said "Bread and butter" as a means of separating. Trudy was allergic to fish, wore a perfume scent called Shalimar, and used a cinnamon stick to sweeten her coffee.

*Police Badge Number:* 8396.

*Water Preference:* Adrian is first seen drinking only Sierra Springs bottled water (he will even become dehydrated if he can't have this brand); he is later seen drinking Summit Creek bottled water. Adrian deviates from his water tradition once a year on his and Trudy's anniversary to have a sip of wine (Trudy's favorite drink). That one sip is enough to give Adrian a hangover.

*Favorite Number:* 10 (his name also has 10 letters).

*Favorite Musical: The Music Man.*

*Fee:* $500 a day plus expenses. He assists the police on an observer basis only.

*Wardrobe:* Adrian claims that his outerwear is brown (although various shades of the color are seen in his suits, vests, and sweaters).

*Fears:* Heights, germs, cars, spiders, insects, bugs, the dark, "and even milk" (as Sharona says, "He's making good progress on the milk"). The dentist is his greatest fear (so much so that he won't have a chipped tooth fixed).

*Character:* Adrian is a compulsive cleaner and dislikes being touched. If he must shake someone's hand, Sharona gives him a Lever Brothers 2000 Moist Towelette. He is superstitious, and when he must ride in a car, he prefers that Sharona do the driving. Adrian is a constant worrier and often has great difficulty thinking because he is always worrying (e.g., did he leave the coffeepot on before leaving the house?). Adrian needs to have a five-watt night-light on in order to sleep (Trudy's picture can be seen on his nightstand). He is allergic to tomatoes (although he is seen eating them) and is used to certain meals on certain days (e.g., chicken pot pie on Tuesday); he becomes upset if Sharona changes the menu. He must have the crust cut off his bread "to create a sense of symmetry." He places everyday clothes in plastic bags, fixes pillows on couches (even in suspects' homes), straightens hanging pictures, and makes sure that any desk or bulletin board he sees is in perfect order. He also feels compelled to touch things as he walks along a street (e.g., a mailbox, a fire hydrant, or a fence rail, which contradicts his phobia about germs). He has an encyclopedic knowledge of strange and obscure facts. He cleans to think and notices everything about people. He has a photographic memory and the deductive skills of Sherlock Holmes. He is capable of spotting evidence at a crime scene that even the most highly trained investigators overlook. He can tell a cigarette brand simply by the odor; he can deduce, from a crime scene, the height, weight, and gender of the killer. He can rearrange shredded documents, and everything must make sense to him in order for him to function properly. A person who is neat and tidy impresses Adrian. When he goes to a restaurant, he orders separate plates for his various foods (foods that touch upset him), and he brings his own silverware.

*Household Disinfectant:* Lysol.

*Quirks:* When he is with his psychiatrist, he refuses to respond to any questions about his and Trudy's sex life (he sings show tunes instead to avoid the questions). He sleeps only on dark pillowcases and must have a star-shaped nozzle on his showerhead; he takes three showers a day. Although it is believed that the human brain starts recording memories beginning only at age three, Monk claims to remember his own birth. Crime scenes, no matter how gruesome they are, do not upset Adrian, but his phobias often manifest themselves during these times. He mentions taking a correspondence swimming course, polishes lightbulbs, has seven fire extinguishers under his kitchen sink, and has a color-coded guide to the contents of his refrigerator on the inside door. When investigating a crime scene, Monk uses a gesture similar to jazz hands to scope out the scene.

*Comfort Zone:* The pillow Trudy slept on. She used strawberry shampoo and a lilac perfume, and her scent still lingers on it. When Adrian hugs the pillow, the audience sees what Monk sees—a vision of Trudy that helps Adrian solve a problem.

*First Meetings:* After people meet Adrian for the first time, their reaction is, "That's the famous Adrian Monk, the living legend? He's nuts!" Sharona assures them that he's not.

*Musical Ability:* Playing the clarinet.

*Favorite Singer:* Willie Nelson (with whom he played clarinet).

*Good-Luck Charm:* A key chain given to him by Trudy.

*Catchphrase:* When Adrian uncovers the culprit, he says, "He's the guy!"

*Address:* 1740 Oak View Drive (as a child; Ambrose still lives there); Adrian now lives in Apartment 2G at an unnamed location.

*The Change:* When his psychiatrist, Dr. Kroger, recommended that Adrian try a new drug (Doxinae) to suppress his condition, Adrian became a totally different person, and everything he feared was now commonplace to him. He lost his deductive abilities and called himself "The Monk" (when the pill's effects wore off, he became his "normal" self).

*Monk Finds Trudy's Killer:* In 1982, 15 years before she met Adrian, Trudy was a student at Berkeley. She had an affair with her law professor (Ethan Rickover) and became pregnant. To avoid publicity, Ethan hired a midwife (Wendy) to deliver the baby. The baby girl was placed with an adoptive family, but Trudy, who never saw the baby, was told she lived for only nine minutes. Twelve years later, when Ethan is appointed as a judge, Wendy attempts to blackmail him. Ethan kills her and buries her in the backyard of his home next to a sundial. He then arranges to have Trudy killed via the car explosion. Adrian learns, through a videotape he found that Trudy made days before she was killed, that she was working on a story about Ethan. Adrian, however, hasn't enough evidence to nab Ethan—until he uncovers a newspaper story about Ethan's appointment as a judge. The article, accompanied by a picture of Ethan standing by that sundial and a statement that he would never sell his house, intrigues Adrian. Armed with a gun, Adrian approaches Ethan and orders him to dig up the ground surrounding the sundial. Leland (see below), tipped off by Natalie that Monk has gone after Ethan, arrives just in time to see Monk nail Trudy's killer. Wendy's skeletal remains are found, and the telltale clue was the tree that overshadowed the sundial—"Who would place a sundial under a tree?" Later, Leland has good news for Adrian: he tracked down Trudy's daughter, Molly Evans, a movie reviewer for the *East Bay Chronicle*, in nearby Monterey. Adrian and Molly immediately bond. Molly and Adrian will now be a part of each other's lives, and Adrian and Natalie continue in their capacity as special consultants for the police department.

*Flashbacks*: Adrian as a child (Grant Rosenmeyer); young Trudy (Lindy Newton).

## SHARONA FLEMING

*Parents:* Douglas and Cheryl Fleming. Douglas owned a hardware store in New Jersey (where Sharona was born) and later died (when Sharona was 12) from dementia.

*Husband:* Randy Disher (see below).

*Ex-Husband:* Trevor Howe (Frank John Hughes); their marriage ended when Trevor, addicted to alcohol and gambling, cheated on her.

*Son:* Benjy Fleming (Max Morrow, then Kane Ritchote); he was born when Sharona was 18 years old.

*Sister:* Gail Fleming (Amy Sedaris).

*Occupation:* Nurse (and Adrian's personal assistant). Sharona and Trevor lived in Atlantic City, New Jersey, and to support herself after Trevor left, Sharona held a variety of jobs, including posing nude for men's magazines and as a ballroom dancer. She had moved to San Francisco and was working as a nurse when Adrian found her. She interned at Modesto General Hospital.

*Character:* When Adrian studies a crime scene, Sharona says, "He's doing the Zen Sherlock Holmes thing" (referring to his and Holmes's method of deductive reasoning). Sharona is very devoted to Adrian, but his disorder sometimes gets to her, and she exclaims, "I quit!" (but always comes back "because I miss Monk"). When asked why she works for Adrian, she says, "It's the worst job I ever had, but it's also the best job I ever had. I'm having adventures; I'm putting bad guys behind bars. I feel like Lois Lane [from Superman]. How many practical nurses can say that? Not many!" Sharona does act like Lois Lane and puts her life on the line to help Adrian—who becomes her Superman when he overcomes a fear only momentarily to save her life. Sharona took a creative writing course where she wrote the murder mystery *Fatal Recipe*.

*Address:* 308 Valencia at 28th Street (where she lives with Benjy, who is in the sixth grade and loves to draw comics).

*Drawback:* Sharona cannot take a vacation because Adrian cannot live without her.

*Station Wagon License Plate:* 4GB1 462; later 4PC 1357.

*Bank:* North California Bank.

*Belief:* Sharona believes in psychics ("I can't tell you how much money I wasted on those TV psychics"). Adrian, on the other hand, does not believe in psychics—"Only in what I can see." Sharona believes that "Monk is a psychic who doesn't believe in psychics."

*Departure:* Sharona leaves Adrian and moves back to New Jersey in season 3 to remarry her ex-husband (a contract dispute between Bitty Schram and the show's producers could not be resolved).

## NATALIE JANE TEEGER

*Parents:* Robert (Michael Cavanaugh) and Peggy Davenport (Holland Taylor); they own the Davenport Toothpaste Company.

*Full Name:* Natalie Jane Davenport Teeger.

*Brother:* Jonathan Davenport (Rob Benedict).

*Late Husband:* Mitch Teeger (a U.S. Navy pilot who was killed in a plane crash six years ago).

*Daughter:* Juliet "Julie" Teeger (she has a pet Crimson Marble fish named Mr. Henry, given to her by her father). She compares Adrian to the TV series *Scooby-Doo, Where Are You?*, claiming, "He's like Velma" (the brainy girl of the team). Julie attends Astoria Elementary School.

*Background:* Born into a wealthy family but became estranged from her parents when she married Mitch (who her parents considered "a common man" and not suited for their daughter). Before Mitch's passing, she lived (with Julie) in Las Vegas, where Natalie worked as a blackjack dealer (and where she also became addicted to gambling). She later worked in an office (but quit when she was unable to adjust to the routine). She next moved to San Francisco and earned money as a bartender (she refused to go crawling back to her parents for help). One night, an intruder broke into her home and, in self-defense, Natalie killed him. With suspicion lingering over Natalie that she may have deliberately killed the man, she seeks the help of Adrian to clear her (as the intruder took nothing but only grabbed her). Intrigued by the case, Adrian takes on the assignment. He is without Sharona at this time but finds assistance on the case from Natalie, whom Adrian considers the perfect replacement, and he hires her after solving the case (a stolen moon rock that was placed in an aquarium kit that Julie had purchased and that was sought by the intruder). At one point before meeting Adrian, Natalie was an exchange student in Greece.

*Temporary Job:* The Lotto Girl for the TV drawings of the Pick Six Gold Rush lottery game.

*Cars:* Jeep Grand Cherokee; Buick Lucerne; Ford Escape; Audi A-3; Nissan Sentra; and, finally, a Hyundai Genesis.

*Address:* 304 Downey Road.

## LELAND STOTTLEMEYER

Leland, a captain with the Homicide Division of the SFPD, is the youngest officer to have been promoted to detective, then captain. He originally worked with Adrian, but their partnership ended when Leland accepted a promotion while Adrian chose to remain a homicide detective to investigate cases (Adrian met Leland two weeks after he became a detective; Leland was his fourth partner, as the previous three "just didn't click" with Adrian). It was Leland, worried about Monk after Trudy's death, who found Sharona and sent her to Monk (as Adrian says, "She showed up one day and never left"). Leland is often amazed by Adrian's abilities: "How does he see what he sees? I have two eyes and see everything he sees, but I don't see what he sees."

Leland is currently married to T. K. Jensen (Virginia Madsen), a reporter. He has two children (Jared and Max) with his second ex-wife Karen (Glenne Headly), a documentary filmmaker (he had a first wife but information is not given). Leland mentions a brother (who served during the Vietnam War) and an aggravating sister (whom he would like to strangle at times).

Leland first drove a 2002 Ford Crown Victoria (departmental issue), then a 2007 black Dodge Charger (something he babies, but it is always put in harm's way). Leland can play the guitar, hates port wine, and, when he gets upset over a case and can't sleep, goes to his favorite bar, orders a shot, watches the goldfish in its tank at the back of the bar, drinks his shot, and is finally able to sleep when he goes home.

## RANDALL "RANDY" DISHER

Randy is a lieutenant with the SFPD and Leland's second in command. In the last episode he marries Sharona Fleming, Adrian's former nurse. In 2009, Randy and Sharona had been dating long distance (he in San Francisco, she in New Jersey) and leaves Leland for the job of police chief in Summit, New Jersey, to be with Sharona. Randy becomes Benjy's (Sharona's son from a first marriage) stepfather.

Randy was born in San Diego, California, on July 19, 1959. At some point, his family moved to Pennsylvania, where Randy attended Temple High School (he formed a band called the Randy Disher Project; he also suffered from an extreme case of acne). Randy is loyal but a bit naive (and overambitious) when it comes to police matters. He first drives the department-issued Ford Crown Victoria (tan), then a Ford Festiva (although not as fussy about cars as Leland). His mother is named Maria (father not mentioned), and although Randy states that he has no relatives, one episode ("Mr. Monk Visits the Farm") reveals that Randy does have an Uncle Harvey. In the pilot episode, Randy's last name is credited as "Lieutenant Deacon."

# Numb3rs

(CBS, 2005–2010)

*Cast:* Rob Morrow (Don Eppes), David Krumholtz (Charlie Eppes), Judd Hirsch (Alan Eppes), Peter MacNichol (Larry Fleinhardt), Alimi Ballard (David Sinclair), Sabrina Lloyd (Terry Lake), Diane Farr (Megan Reeves), Navi Rawat (Amita Ramanujan).

*Basis:* An FBI agent (Don Eppes) receives help in solving crimes from his brother Charlie, a mathematical genius who believes that numbers can be used to capture criminals.

## DONALD "DON" EPPES

*Parents:* Alan and Margaret Eppes (Margaret is deceased; she was an attorney and a composer; died of cancer).

*Place of Birth:* Los Angeles (at St. Vincent's Hospital) on July 15, 1967.

*Brother:* Charlie (born in 1975).

*Education:* Don attended high school and college (although not named). He played baseball in high school and was awarded a baseball scholarship to college, where he contemplated a career in the major leagues. After graduating, he joined a local team, the Stockton Rangers (as a utility player), but became dismayed when teammates began using steroids and he felt he had no chance for advancement. He quit and joined the FBI Training Academy at Quantico.

*Occupation:* FBI special agent with the Metro Bureau in Los Angeles; his official title is supervisor of the FBI's Violent Crime Squad. Following his graduation from the academy, Don taught unstated classes before becoming an agent in fugitive recovery. He was next assigned to the Albuquerque field office before requesting a transfer to his hometown of Los Angeles.

Seated: David Krumholtz and Diane Farr; standing: Alimi Ballard and Rob Morrow. *CBS/Photofest © CBS; photographer: Monty Brinton*

*Character:* Often skeptical that numbers can be used to solve crimes (although Charlie proves they always do). He is totally devoted to his job (hence, he has a very limited social life). He is also a perfectionist and not too kind to agents who make mistakes. He likes watching baseball and hockey games on TV. In addition to playing baseball, Don enjoyed playing hockey, but it was a present his father gave him as a child (a toy gun) that played a role in his later life: when he quit the Rangers minor league ball team, he recalled the fun he had with the toy gun and turned his attention to law enforcement.

*Address:* 8111 Aquacade in Los Angeles.

*Car:* A silver Mitsubishi four-door sedan.

*License Plate:* 4Q 49902.

*Car Code:* 3695.

*Computer Type:* Dell.

*Favorite Breakfast:* Pancakes (something Charlie doesn't like).

*Principal Partner:* Megan Reeves. Megan is an FBI profiler who doubles as Don's replacement team leader when he is away on an assignment; she later leaves the FBI when she receives an assignment with the U.S. Department of Justice (she was originally brought on to replace Don's original partner, Terry Lake). Megan teaches Krav Maga (a form of self-defense developed by the Israeli army in the 1940s) at the local YMCA. She is an expert shot, can speak French, and worked with the Behavioral Analysis Unit of the FBI. She drives an Acura and left home when she was 16 years old (due to an uneasy relationship with her father, from whom she is now estranged).

*Flashbacks:* Margaret Eppes (JoBeth Williams).

## CHARLES "CHARLIE" EDWARD EPPES

*Parents:* Alan and Margaret Eppes.

*Place of Birth:* Los Angeles on September 5, 1975.

*Home:* Charlie lives with his father in a historic two-story home that he later purchased when Alan, a retired city planner, wanted to downsize to a condo. Before and after the house purchase, Charlie and Alan (with Don visiting) continue their tradition of the family gathering for beers and watching a baseball game on TV.

*Background:* Charlie was discovered to be a mathematical genius at the age of three (at which time he could multiply four-digit numbers in his head). His education became a top priority, and his parents hired tutors to further advance his ability. As he grew, he developed an uncanny interest in numbers and believed they could solve a number of problems, including crimes. His one chance to prove it was when Don returned to Los Angeles and he convinced Don that his theory can work.

*Education:* An unnamed high school (although eight years younger than Don, he graduated at the same time). He next attended Princeton University (acquiring degrees in math).

*Occupation:* Professor of applied mathematics at CalSci (a mythical variation on Cal Tech); Mathematical consultant to the FBI and National Security Agency.

*Book: The Attraction Equation: The Power of Pi.*

*Award:* Recipient of the Milton Award for Combinatory (a mathematical branch "that combines objects belonging to a finite set in accordance with certain constraints, such as those of graph theory").

*Character:* Cares about the victims of crimes but tries not to let it interfere with his job.

*Sport:* Golf (plays it only to please his father).

*Member:* The American Sundial Association.

*Romantic Interest:* Amita Ramanujan, a computer programmer and astrophysicist who works alongside Charlie at school (later becoming a professor at CalSci) and with the FBI. She has a very high IQ and built her first computer when she was 13 years old. She also won the 2006 Milton Award for Combinatory a year after Charlie's win (it was he who was chosen to present it to her). Amita, whose grandparents come from southern India, was born in Los Angeles (at Cedars-Sinai Hospital) on June 1, 1975. At the end of season 5, Charlie proposes to Amita; in season 6, they marry. Brian George plays her father Sanjay Ramanujan, and Gita Reddy plays her mother Tapti Ramanujan.

*Best Friend:* Lawrence "Larry" Fleinhardt. Larry, a PhD, is intrigued by life and all its permutations. He is a professor at CalSci with Charlie (although working there for a much longer time). He delights in helping Charlie with his numbers solutions for crimes. He holds the Walter T. Merrick Chair in Theoretical Physics and is a theoretical physicist researching black holes, gravitational waves, and various aspects of string theory ("a cosmological theory based on the existence of cosmic strings"). He wrote the books *Quantum Cosmology* and *Zero Point Energy* and is fascinated by the night skies (his obsession with stars began at age three when his parents gave him a telescope). Larry recalls his father wanting him to follow in his footsteps and become an artist, but he could never master it. He is a rather boring teacher and offers very little outside help to his students. He loves antique cars and first drove a 1944 Volvo, then a 1931 Ford Model A. He likes jazz and treasures his first award, the Newton Lacy Pierce Prize in Astronomy from the American Astronomical Society.

# The Office
## (NBC, 2005–2013)

*Principal Cast:* Steve Carell (Michael Scott), Rainn Wilson (Dwight Schrute), Jenna Fischer (Pamela Halpert), John Krasinski (Jim Halpert), Ellie Kemper (Kelly Erin Hannon), Mindy Kaling (Kelly Kapoor), Amy Ryan (Holly Flax), Angela Kinsey (Angela Martin).

*Basis:* A tongue-in-cheek look at the nine-to-five white-collar world as seen through the antics of the employees of a paper distribution company in Pennsylvania (located at 1725 Slough Avenue).

## MICHAEL GARY SCOTT

*Place of Birth:* Scranton, Pennsylvania, on March 15, 1964.

*Ancestry:* Mixed (English, Scottish, and German; he also claims to be part Native American).

*Childhood:* Michael claims to have been a lonely child. At some point (not specified), Michael was a star of a local Philadelphia kids' show called *Fundle Bundle*. His unnamed parents had put money aside for college, but when Michael acquired it, he lost it in a Ponzi-like scheme.

*Wife:* Holly Scott (maiden name Holly Flax).

*Education:* Scranton Elementary School and Scranton High School.

*Occupation:* Salesman, then branch manager of the Scranton Division of the Dunder Mifflin Paper Company; owner of his own business, the Michael Scott Paper Company, Inc. (bought out by Dunder Mifflin); branch manager when Dunder Mifflin merged with Sabre, a printer company based in Tallahassee, Florida, to form Dunder Mifflin-Sabre. Michael later moves to Colorado when the governor appoints him as the director of paper distribution for the Department of Natural Resources (where, because of his aversion to work and knack for screwing things up, he has been nicknamed "Dennis the Menace").

Steve Carell, John Krasinski, and Rainn Wilson. *NBC/Photofest © NBC; photographer: Justin Lubin*

*Awards:* "Best Salesman" at Dunder Mifflin.

*Character:* Michael is awkward, lives in his own dream world, and appears to be unable to separate his personal life from his work life (he has no management skills and does work "really, really hard" for about 1 percent of each day). He is loyal and will do what he believes is best for the company (not what the company believes is best). He feels he has to be the center of attention, tries to impress potential buyers with his self-purchased coffee mug that reads "World's Best Boss," and is not quite familiar with pop culture icons and phrases.

*Catchphrase:* "That's what she said!" (most often used).

*Hobby:* Composing parodies of famous songs.

*Second Career?:* Michael is attending acting classes (specifically improv) but is seen quite incapable of mastering it.

*Alter Ego:* Michael has numerous "characters" that he adapts to enable him to face situations and entertain his staff. He is most famous for "Agent Michael Scarn," a spy, but he is also known to use the names "Carnac" (a rip-off of Johnny Carson's *Tonight Show* character "Carnac the Magnificent," who "can read" letters before he opens them), the overweight "Michael Scotch," and "Date Mike," an obnoxious guy that is despised by the women he tries to date.

*Clothing:* Not-so-typical office dress, as he prefers jeans (he calls his favorite pair "Fun Jeans").

*Cars:* Michael first drove a Sebring convertible, then a Porsche, and finally a PT Cruiser convertible.

*ATM PIN:* 9622.

*Favorite Movies:* Varies from filmed to animated movies: *Toy Story, Finding Nemo, Scream 2,* and *The Devil Wears Prada.*

*Favorite TV Series: Entourage.*

*Favorite Sport:* Looks to be basketball, although he is hopeless at playing it.

*Favorite Ice Cream Flavor:* Mint chocolate chip.

*Stock:* Owns shares in Blockbuster Video.

*Favorite Bar:* Poor Richard's Pub.

*Favorite Radio Station:* Froggy 101 FM (an actual country-and-western radio station in Pennsylvania).

## DWIGHT KURT SCHRUTE III

*Occupation:* Salesman for Dunder Mifflin. He was previously a salesman at Staples, security supervisor, assistant to the regional manager, and finally vice president of sales at Dunder Mifflin. He also owns and operates his family's business, Schrute Farms (which produces table beets that he sells to stores, restaurants, and roadside beet stands). To make extra money, Dwight has converted part of the farmhouse into a very dilapidated bed-and-breakfast. He was also a volunteer sheriff's deputy in the Lackawanna County Sheriff's Office (apparently where he learned his mentioned surveillance, tactical, and martial arts skills) before venturing into sales.

*Place of Birth:* Pennsylvania in 1977.

*Parents:* Heda and Dwight Schrute II.

*Siblings:* Frannie and Jeb.

*Wife:* Angela Martin.

*Ancestry:* Apparently German by his references to the past (his ancestors came to the United States by U-boat; his grandfather fought in World War II and was held in a German prisoner-of-war camp; had an uncle named Gunter, who worked a goat farm before the Allied invasion of Germany).

*Background:* Dwight was born on the family's 60-acre farm and claims to remember his birth (his father delivering him and his mother severing the umbilical cord by biting through it; he also remembers having a twin, but he absorbed it in his mother's womb). The only other TV character to claim that he remembers his birth is Adrian Monk (see *Monk*). His formative years were quite horrific, especially between the ages of four and six, when he was ignored by his family (he opened a can of tuna fish and neglected to save the oil). In seventh grade, he embarrassed his parents by misspelling the word "failure" and losing a spelling bee. He also played "Mutey the Mailman," a made-up character in his school's production of *Oklahoma*. Dwight grew up in a dysfunctional family, and while his religion is not really mentioned, it can be seen through his cousin Mose, who claims to be Amish (and dresses as one), that many family members were Amish. As a child, Dwight's father would take him and his siblings to the local swimming hole, where they played until 10 in the morning—and then worked the farm until midnight.

*Belief:* The supernatural exists (like vampires).

*Favorite Movie and TV Genre:* Science fiction (he mentions the film *The Crow* as his favorite) and TV shows *Battlestar Galactica* and *Lost*. This is later contradicted when he says reality shows like *The Apprentice* and *Survivor* are his favorites.

*Car:* A 1987 Pontiac Trans-Am.

*Secret Office Stash:* An alarming amount of weapons (from guns to swords) that he concealed in his office when he was named the Scranton branch "official security supervisor."

*Skill:* A wildlife survivalist (apparently learned from his father, who took him hunting when he was a child).

## PAMELA "PAM" MORGAN HALPERT

*Occupation:* The office administrator. She worked previously as the secret assistant to the regional manager, then as a receptionist and a sales representative.

*Husband:* Jim Halpert, a paper salesman at Dunder Mifflin (formally a regional manager).

*Infant Children:* Cecelia and Phillip Halpert.

*Maiden Name:* Purposely (?) misspelled several ways: "Pam Beesly," "Pam Beasley," "Pam Beesley," and "Pam Beasly."

*Character:* Blessed with a good sense of humor but also shy and hesitant to approach something she feels uncomfortable about. It appears she has taken jobs with Dunder Mifflin only as a stepping-stone to a career as an artist (it can be seen that she has very little enthusiasm for her job). Her dream appears to become a reality when she is accepted into the Pratt Institute of Design in Manhattan. She also makes a difficult decision: quit her job and leave Jim Halpert, whom she had been dating, and move to Manhattan, where she acquires a job at Dunder Mifflin's corporate headquarters; six months later, she fails one of her art classes. When she discovers that she must remain in New York for another three months to retake the course, she returns home to Scranton to be with Jim and is rehired as the Scranton branch receptionist. Shortly thereafter, when Pam discovers she is pregnant, she and Jim decide to marry (in Niagara Falls). Two years later, after the birth of their second child (Phillip), Jim quits Dunder Mifflin to join a friend in opening Athlead, a sports marketing business (that is later renamed Athleap).

*Education:* Schools are not named, but Pam was a semipro volleyball player in college.

*Likes:* Chicken wings; mixed berry yogurt; French onion–flavored Sun Chips.

*Dislikes:* People speaking pig Latin; Frisbee competitions.

*Favorite Coffee:* Black with a sprinkle of cinnamon.

*Medical Issue:* Very nearsighted (her vision is 20/400); she wears contacts and has a backup pair of eyeglasses.

*Hobby:* Sudoku.

*Religion:* Presbyterian.

*Jim's Family:* Parents Gerald and Betsy Halpert; brothers Tom and Pete Halpert; sister Larissa Halpert.

## KELLY ERIN HANNON

*Background:* Very little revealed. She does not know who her parents are, only that she is an orphan and spent her formative years in several foster homes. Life in such homes toughened her but also made her quite ignorant when it comes to dealing with certain situations.

*Occupation:* Receptionist at the Scranton office of Dunder Mifflin. She previously worked at Taco Bell Express (but when the name was changed to Taco Bell, she felt it would be too much work and quit).

*Office Name:* Erin Hannon (she uses her middle name as her first name to avoid confusion with office worker Kelly Kapoor [Mindy Kaling], a Hindu who knows very little about her religion; her full name is Kelly Ranigandha Kapoor, and she works at the Scranton Dunder Mifflin as the customer service representative).

*Character:* Erin is naive, easily impressed, and very competitive; she hates to lose at anything. When it comes to dating, Erin is fine; it is a breakup that causes stressful situations for her. She cares deeply about what people think of her and fears someone saying something negative about her (like dressing up as a cute puppy for Halloween but fearing that people will think she is a dog and not a puppy).

*Medical Issue:* Epilepsy. She was born at five months and as a result could eat only soft babylike foods until she was six years old. Erin mentions that she had to spend three years in a hospital (for undisclosed reasons).

*Education:* Keystone College (prior education not mentioned).

*Singing Group:* Subtle Sexuality (formed with Kelly); they made the music videos "Male Prima Donna" and "The Girl Next Door."

*The Movie:* In an internet-produced episode, Erin and Kelly, eager to break into show business, write a horror movie and convince their friend, Ryan (B. J. Novak), to produce it. The story, titled "The 3rd Floor," begins when a woman approaches Erin and asks to buy some paper. When Erin finds that the woman has no money, she refuses to serve her. Angered, the woman (dressed like a Gypsy) places a curse on her—to become all the serial killers that ever existed. Erin shrugs it off, but slowly she begins to change. She develops the right arm of Lizzie Borden, the left arm of Jeffrey Dahmer, the heart of Jack the Ripper, and the legs of all the serial killers who escaped the law. Now, wielding an ax, Erin begins her rampage, killing all the third-floor employees—or at least attempting to do so.

## ANGELA NOELLE MARTIN

*Parents:* Sean and Anne Marie Martin.

*Sister:* Rachel Martin.

*Husband:* Dwight Schrute (see above).

*Ex-Husband:* Robert Lipton.

*Son:* Phillip Schrute.

*Occupation:* Senior accountant and safety officer at Dunder Mifflin. She is also head of the company's Party Planning Committee.

*Pet Cats:* Angela loves cats and had many; these include Sprinkles (her favorite), Princess Lady, Bandit, and Milky Way. She is so obsessed with cats that she dresses as a feline at office Halloween parties.

*Character:* Strict, stubborn, and rather unpleasant to her fellow workers, as she often belittles them. She is homophobic, gets highly emotional over trivial matters, and needlessly bottles up her emotions, causing outbursts when she becomes stressed. As a child, Angela entered beauty pageants and enjoyed being judged. She judges other women by the color of the clothes they wear (she believes orange and green indicate that a girl "is a whore") and dislikes mystery novels ("I hate being titillated"). While religious (Christian), she disapproves of other religions, especially Hinduism.

*Medical Issues:* Sleep apnea and germophobia.

*Food Preference:* Vegetarian (she especially hates seafood).

*Car:* A Ford Focus, then a Saturn.

*Physical Issues:* Angela claims to weigh 90 pounds (then 82 pounds) and stands 4 feet, 10 inches tall. She wears child size 10 clothes and thus cannot shop at normal stores. Her stores of choice are Gap Kids (but she often finds them too childlike for her) and the more conservative styling of the American Girls store. Because of her height, Michael calls her "Booster Seat" (referring to small children who must sit in a booster seat in restaurants).

*Sports:* Angela appears not to be a sports fan but enjoys playing games with her cats. She is the only employee who does not participate in the company's "Office Olympics."

*Favorite Song:* "Little Drummer Boy."

# Parks and Recreation
(NBC, 2009–2015)

*Principal Cast:* Amy Poehler (Leslie Knope), Nick Offerman (Ron Swanson), Chris Pratt (Andy Dwyer), Aubrey Plaza (April Ludgate), Aziz Ansari (Tom Haverford).

*Basis:* An idealistic young woman (Leslie Knope) battles the red tape of the bureaucratic system as an employee of the Pawnee, Indiana, Department of Parks and Recreation.

### LESLIE BARBARA KNOPE

*Parents:* Marlene (Pamela Reed) and Robert Knope (deceased).

*Place of Birth:* Eagleton, Indiana, in 1975.

*Husband:* Ben Wyatt (Adam Scott).

*Children:* Sonia (Chloe Ewing), Stephen (Jonathan Banks), and Wesley (Harrison Schick).

*Occupation:* Deputy director of the Parks and Recreation Department of fictional Pawnee, Indiana. She also created Camp Athena, a retreat for troubled girls.

*Education:* Pawnee High School (student body vice president; founder of the Young Independents [while also a member of the Young Republicans and Young Democrats] and a member of the debate team, the school orchestra, and the drama club; because of her haircut that resembled that of Angela Lansbury in the series *Murder, She Wrote*, Leslie was called "Angela Lansbury"); Indiana University's School of Public and Environmental Affairs (she believed that the government should be for the people; it was also here that she kissed another girl).

*Dream:* To become the country's first female president (which, in a flash-forward, suggests that she becomes president in 2048; it is also revealed that she became Indiana's governor in 2025, the regional director of the Mid-

Paul Schneider, Aziz Ansari, Amy Poehler, Rashida Jones, and Nick Offerman. *NBC/Photofest © NBC; photographer: Mitchell Haaseth*

western National Park Service, and the deputy director of operations for the Department of the Interior).

*Affiliation:* The Indiana Organization of Women, the Equal Opportunity Committee, and various committees associated with bathrooms (e.g., the Clean Restroom Task Force and the Handicapped Restroom Task Force).

*Idol:* Secretary of State Hillary Clinton.

*Favorite Movie Series: Harry Potter.*

*Likes:* Cute animals (owls being her favorite) and scrapbooking.

*Dislikes:* Salad, turtles, and "disgusting things."

*Favorite Music Group:* R.E.M.

*Favorite Sport:* Bowling.

*Favorite Eatery:* J.J.'s Diner (where she enjoys Belgian waffles).

*Flashbacks:* Young Leslie (Audrey P. Scott).


## RON ULYSSES SWANSON

*Mother:* Tamara Swanson (father not named).

*Brothers:* Don (Matt Offerman), Lon (Herbert Russell), and Vaughn Swanson (Michael Strassner).

*Wives:* Tammy 1 (Patricia Clarkson), Tammy 2 (Megan Mullally), and Diane Lewis (Lucy Lawless). Diane has two children from a prior marriage: Ivy (Rylan Lee) and Zoe Lewis (Sadie Salazar).

*Occupation:* Head of the Parks and Recreation Department (Leslie's superior) and owner of his own business, Very Good Building and Development Company, Inc.

*Unusual Childhood:* Was hit by a bus at the age of seven; went to work in a sheet metal factory (age seven); worked with leather at a tannery (age 11); attended his middle school prom at the age of 12; worked at a metal factory at the age of 18.

*Hates:* Hugging in public, banks (has his money in the form of gold), skim milk, and lying (but likes fatty, high-cholesterol foods and alcohol).

*Desk Signature:* A shotgun (that he hopes will intimidate people who ask him for favors); a green U.S. military land mine.

*Interest:* Mysteries, riddles, puzzles, and aviation.

*Awards:* The first man to receive the Dorothy Everton Smythe Female Empowerment Award (seen in a newspaper clipping as "Woman of the Year Crowned"; he won by taking credit for Leslie's Camp Athena for troubled girls); the Indiana Fine Woodworking Association Award for Best Chair (Ron enjoys making furniture); Pawnee Employee of the Month.

*Alter Ego:* Duke Silver, a saxophonist who plays in Eagleton at Cozy's Bar.

*Car:* A Buick Park Avenue Ultra.

*Favorite Eatery:* J.J.'s Diner (where he enjoys a breakfast called "Four Horsemeals of the Eggporkalypse"). He shops at Food 'n' Stuff. He also has a stash of bacon in his office ceiling.

*Dislikes:* Birthdays (he has been able to delete all references to his birth date except from files at Baskin-Robbins); Canada and Europe (especially France).

*Allergy:* Hazelnuts.

## APRIL ROBERTA LUDGATE

*Place of Birth:* Pawnee, Indiana, in 1989.

*Parents:* Larry (John Ellison Conley) and Rita Ludgate (Terri Hoyos). They called her "ZuZu."

*Sister:* Natalie Ludgate (Minni Jo Mazzola).

*Husband:* Andy Dwyer (see below).

*Child:* Jack Dwyer (from a flash-forward in 2023).

*Obsession:* The occult, the macabre, and Halloween.

*Education:* Pawnee High School (where she created her own course, Halloween Studies; dressed as a goth girl; played softball); Pawnee Community College.

*Occupation:* Pawnee Parks and Recreation Department intern (then assistant to its director and deputy director of animal control). She also served as the assistant to the Pawnee city manager and the manager of a band called Mouse Rat. She later works at the American Service Foundation.

*Favorite Band:* Neutral Milk Hotel.


## THOMAS "TOM" MONTGOMERY HAVERFORD

Tom, born in Bennettsville, South Carolina, in 1985, is the son of parents who were born in India (his real birth name is Darwish Sabir Ismael Gani; he changed it "for political reasons"). He originally worked as Leslie's right-hand man, then as the Parks and Recreation Department administrator (where he had authority over the tennis court renovation). He quit to open two companies (Entertainment 720, a party service, and the clothing store Rent-A-Swag, where Tom rents his own high-end clothing to middle school boys whose mothers refuse to buy them fashionable outfits; the business folds due to competition at Tommy's Closet). He next establishes the successful Tom's Bistro eatery. He was also bartender at the Snakehole Lounge. He is divorced from Wendy (Jamie Williamson), a Canadian he married to help her get U.S. citizenship, and is now married to Lucy Santo Domingo (Natalie Morales). Tom abuses power, is lazy, is often ineffectual, and, even though married to Wendy, pursues other women.

Tom created his own holiday ("Treat Yo' Self") as well as a knockoff of the TV game show *The Newlywed Game* called "Know Ya Boo." He has 26 internet dating profiles (from "Tom A" to "Tom Z") and constantly uses the term "Boo" when talking to girls. His favorite alcoholic drink is what he calls "Snake Juice."

*Note:* Pawnee has its own gay bar (The Bulge), strip club (The Glitter Factory), and newspaper (the *Pawnee Journal*); its sister city is Braque, Venezuela. There are no wanted criminals, only the most wanted mischievous animals: Vlad (a bat); Zorro, Poopy, Nutz, and Paw Papa (raccoons); Jangle Bo Jingles (feral cat);

Leanor (crow); Spyke (porcupine); and Fairway Frank (possum). When the map of Pawnee is seen, it is actually a flipped version of Muncie, Indiana. The air in neighboring Eagleton smells like vanilla (from the cupcake factory).

## ANDREW "ANDY" MAXWELL DWYER

Andy is married to April (see above) and lead guitarist in a band called Mouse Rat. He was born in Pawnee, Indiana, in 1981 and previously worked at the shoe shine stand in front of Pawnee City Hall (also its weekend security guard) and assistant at the Sweetums Charity Foundation. When Andy discovered that he had a talent for writing and performing children's songs, he changed his name to Johnny Karate and performed on his own TV series (*Johnny Karate's Super Awesome Musical Explosion Show*). His parents are not named, but he has six brothers: Aaron, Adam, Alan, Albert, Alex, and Anthony.

Andy attempted to become a policeman but failed the personality test (he scored 100 on the written exam). Andy has a dream of becoming a rock star, and before he devised Mouse Rat as his band, he used numerous other names, including The Andy Dwyer Experience, Scarecrow Boat, The Artist Formerly Known as the Lead Singer of Mouse Rat, Puppy Pendulum, Nothing Rhymes with Orange, and Department of Homeland Obscurity.

Skittles placed between two Starburst candies is Andy's favorite food (which he calls "Andy's Mouth Surprise"). He spoils movies by trying to predict the end, played baseball in high school, has difficulty telling when a woman is pregnant, and questions 2 percent fat-free milk (wondering what the other 98 percent is). He is intelligent but lacks common sense (like naming his and April's son Jack—standing for "Burt Snakehole Ludgate Karate Dracula Macklin Demon Jack-O-Lantern Dwyer"), forgetting to brush his teeth, losing cars (forgetting where he parks them), and wishing to work for Chuck E. Cheese's. After befriending a British businessman (Eddy), Andy is knighted as "Sir Andrew" by him during the finale of his TV series.

# *Psych*
## (USA, 2006–2014)

*Cast:* James Roday (Shawn Spencer), Dulé Hill (Burton Guster), Corbin Bernsen (Henry Spencer), Maggie Lawson (Juliet O'Hara), Timothy Omundson (Carlton Lassiter), Kirsten Nelson (Karen Vick).

*Basis:* Shawn Spencer, a man with phenomenal powers of observation, helps the police solve baffling crimes by pretending to be a psychic. See also *The Mentalist* for a similar series.

James Roday and Dule Hill. *USA Network/Photofest © USA Network; photographer: Alan Zenuk*

## SHAWN SPENCER

*Parents:* Henry (a retired police officer with the Santa Barbara Police Department) and Madelyn Spencer (Cybill Shepherd), a psychologist; they are currently divorced. Henry enjoys fishing from his boat, *Kanaka*, and was later hired by the police department to monitor Shawn's actions as its "psychic" consultant.

*Yearly Christmas Tradition:* Each year, Shawn and Henry exchange gifts but do not open them; each has to guess what the other has given him first.

*Place of Birth:* San Diego, California, in 1977.

*Girlfriend:* Juliet O'Hara (see below).

*Prior Girlfriend:* Abigail Lytar (Rachel Leigh Cook), who Shawn calls "Abbs." When an opportunity arises for Abigail to teach children in Uganda in a project called "One Kid, One World," she leaves Shawn to become a part of establishing it.

*Background:* Flashbacks of a young Shawn show him being taught by his father how to use his senses to their best advantage. Shawn developed a keen sense of observation but mentions he wanted to become a fireman, not a police officer like his father. Shawn attended high school but after graduation had no set goal and took and quit 57 jobs; these include driving an Oscar Meyer Weinermobile; steward on Emerald Cruise Lines; counselor at Camp

Durango; the deejay "Cold Cuts" at the Curbs, a nightclub; and an Arby's employee. He also mentions working as a lobbyist for M&M's "to bring back the little brown ones." As a child, Shawn attended Camp Tikihama and was the batboy for the Seabirds, a local minor league baseball team (as an adult, he becomes a member of the Santa Barbara Police Department's softball team, seen as "SBPD"; he wears jersey 44). He mentions creating "The Toaster Alarm" as a child, but it didn't work ("It woke you up by hitting you in the face with a waffle"), and as an adult he tried to sell an idea called "The Bed Comb" (a machine that combs your hair while you sleep).

*Pet Cat as a Child:* Sherman Meow.

*Character:* Shawn is fascinated by crime scenes and studies these by reading the newspaper (specifically, the *Sun)* and watching TV coverage on Channels 5 and 8. When he realizes that he has found something that was overlooked, he calls the Santa Barbara Police Department with a tip, as nothing escapes his razor-sharp mind. Although he does not possess any actual clairvoyant abilities, Shawn convinces the police he is a psychic, and, impressed by his "abilities," Karen Vick, the interim (and later) police chief, hires him as a psychic consultant to help them solve difficult cases. Immediately, he approaches his best friend, Gus (see below), to join him as his partner in a psychic private detective agency (a dream they have had since they were eight years old). Shawn is quite manipulative and an expert liar and thinks outside the box. He has an eye for detail and a photographic memory and can take a hunch and follow it through to solving a case. In order to keep up his appearance, Shawn has to play the part and often has "visions" of what has happened and/or what will happen. He can read people and tell them what they want to hear. He is so adept at lying that he can pass any lie detector test (as his father taught him "to believe the lie"); he introduces himself to people as "Shawn Spencer, Psychic Detective." When Shawn spots evidence, it is highlighted in colors for the viewing audience.

*Business:* Psych. Private Psychic Detective, an agency that will also allow him to service private clients. By dialogue, fees range from $1,500 to $3,000 per case; in others, Gus asks for a $2,000 retainer. Shawn mentions that when he was 15, he took a practice police academy test and scored a perfect 100.

*Affiliation:* Member of the Monarch Lodge, a secret society similar to the Masonic Lodge.

*Education:* Leland Bosseigh High School (Class of 1995).

*Medical Issue:* Shawn claims to have attention deficit disorder.

*Fault:* Talking too much (also his weapon, as his endless ramblings can exonerate him from perilous situations by stalling for time). Shawn appears to lack fear (just the opposite for Gus), as he will rush into dangerous situations without a plan or even thinking first.

*Aliases:* During cases, Shawn often gives himself (and Gus) an alias; Shawn's include T-Bone Turner, Die Harder, Scotch MacIntosh, and Dr. Howser.

*Phone Number:* 555-0135.

*TV Appearance:* Played Chad on the Spanish telenovela *Explocion Gigantesca de Romana*.

*Favorite Fruit:* Pineapple.

*Favorite Soda:* Sprite.

*Favorite Candy:* Clark Bar, Skittles, and saltwater taffy (which he makes himself).

*Favorite Frozen Treat:* Popsicles.

*Favorite Sports:* Football (a fan of the local Thunderbirds; he also mentions the San Diego Chargers) and baseball (of the local Seabirds team).

*Favorite TV Series:* *Grey's Anatomy*, *True Blood*, *Leverage*, *Step by Step*, and the mythical reality show *American Duos*.

*Favorite Cereal:* Kellogg's Fruit Loops (first seen as the mythical Fruit Puffs).

*Favorite Gift for His Father:* Snow globes (in real life, Corbin Bernsen has one of the world's largest collection of snow globes).

*Favorite Houseplant:* Jim (ficus).

*Favorite Food Truck Eatery:* Macho Taco.

*Video Game Play:* Nintendo.

*Book:* With Gus, Shawn wrote *Psych's Guide: Crime Fighting for the Totally Unqualified*.

*Fear:* The supernatural (especially spirits of the deceased). While not fearful, he is quite uncomfortable around funerals (a situation that developed in his childhood when he had to put his pet hamster and lizard to rest; as he says, "They're depressing, and there is organ music").

*Quirk:* Shawn often relates his observations of crimes based on obscure facts from movies (mostly those of the 1980s) and 1980s TV series.

*IQ:* 187.

*Hero:* Sylvester Stallone (when his father asks); "My father" when other people ask.

*Obsession:* His hair, which has to always appear perfect (he carries a travel size packet of Johnson & Johnson No More Tears baby shampoo with him in his wallet).

*Dream:* To have his own hair analyst and stylist.

*Flashbacks:* Young Shawn (Liam James, Skyler Gisondo, Josh Hayden, and Kyle Tejpar).

## BURTON "GUS" GUSTER II

*Relationship:* Friends with Shawn since they were three years old (another episode says since they were five); now business partner in Shawn's fake psychic business.

*Parents:* Bill (Ernie Hudson) and Winnie Guster (Phylicia Rashad); they married after Gus was born (whom they consider "our perfect little miracle").

*Older Sister:* Joy Guster (Faune Chambers Watkins); he also has an unnamed brother living in Connecticut. Gus is very protective of Joy (a lawyer) and becomes upset if she dates any of his friends (he was at first unaware that Shawn and Joy had a tryst 10 years earlier when he was away at college). Joy also doubts that Shawn has psychic abilities.

*Ex-Wife:* Mira Gaffney (Kerry Washington). She and Gus met during college spring break in Mexico, got drunk, and married. Gus realized it was a mistake and, even though he considers her "the one woman I can't resist," broke off the relationship, and both agreed to have the marriage annulled.

*Girlfriend:* Rachael (Parminder Nagra).

*Occupation:* Sales representative for Central Coast Pharmaceuticals (in one episode, the Alfaxan line [anesthesia for small animals] is mentioned as his responsibility).

*Salary:* $48,000 a year.

*Education:* Leland Bosseigh High School (Class of 1995); Pomona University.

*Talent:* Tap dancing (took lessons as a child). He is also an expert safecracker and reads *Safecracker's Monthly* magazine (also referred to as *Modern Safecracker* by Shawn) online and has an enhanced sense of smell (he calls himself "Super Smeller"). He also has the ability to verbally imitate the sounds of the gunfire from an AK-47.

*Fears:* Blood, heights, airplanes, tight spaces, jumpsuits, toupees, and corpses.

*False Diagnosis:* Gus is first fearful of riding on a boat due to his suffering from seasickness; he is later seen traveling on a boat with no problem. He can also be seen as fearing bombs (running away from them in one episode, then diffusing one in another).

*Address:* A house on Demarious Avenue.

*Character:* Gus was a gifted child and babied by his parents. He hoped to attend the Meitner School for Gifted Students, but it was too far from his home (his parents were also concerned that separating Gus from Shawn would be traumatic for him; it is later said that Gus's parents disliked Shawn because he was a bad influence on their son). In high school, Gus was voted "King of Howdy Day" (for his friendly greetings), "Most Likely to Succeed," and "Most Well-Liked." It is also mentioned that in sixth grade, Gus took one semester of prelaw. Gus and Shawn also had their own business ("Pet Baptisms" and a lawn-mowing operation). At one point after high school, Gus and Shawn did go their separate ways when Gus attended Pomona University. He is also a conversationalist and a lover of sea life (especially sea lions); he holds a lifetime pass to the sea aquarium. He attended Camp Tikihama with Shawn as a child, was called "Big Head Burton" in grammar school, and is named after his Uncle Burton (John Amos). He hides spare money in his socks and cries when he sees adults cry.

*Medical Issues:* Asthma and lactose intolerance.

*Breakfast Cereal:* Post Cocoa Pebbles.

*Favorite Beverage:* Seen drinking Minute Maid Orange Juice.

*Aliases:* Shawn has given Gus a number of aliases while on a case; these include Jazz Hands, Longbranch Pennywhistle, Chesterfield McMillan, Scorch Macintosh, Lavender Goums, Dr. McTock, Gus "Silly Pants" Jackson, Magic Head, and Control-Alternate-Delete.

*Suppressed Desire:* To shoot Shawn for all the stress he causes him (like getting him kicked out of PetSmart and the Salvation Army [although Shawn calls this "an honorable discharge"]).

*Favorite TV Series: Leverage, Airwolf,* and *America's Next Top Model*; he also makes references to "Sookie" (a character from *True Blood*).

*Favorite Pudding:* Tapioca with a sprinkling of cinnamon.

*Favorite Sport:* Football, especially the Los Angeles team, the Thunderbirds.

*Favorite Food Truck Eatery:* Macho Taco.

*Pets as a Child:* Mr. Bee (cat); Miss Mugglesworth (Cockatoo).

*College Band:* Blackapella (with three friends).

*Favorite Singers:* Gladys Knight and the Pips (he mentions meeting "one of the Pips").

*Catchphrase:* "You must be out of your damned mind" (which he says when Shawn suggests a plan of action during a case).

*Blue Car License Plate:* Seen as 4TR I019, 50LPT 46, and 5PC I371. Gus also owned a gold 1972 Mercury Cougar.

*Most Disliked Story: The Tell-Tale Heart* by Edgar Allan Poe ("It gives me the creeps").

*Internet Dating Site:* Gus is a member of SoulMateConnection.com.

*Expertise:* Spelling bees (he entered the American Spelling Bee in 1989 but lost; it has since become his obsession to know everything possible about spelling bee history); knows all the country's area codes and periodicals and is an expert on comic books (his favorite is *The Green Spirit*) and dinosaurs.

*Belief:* Ghosts are real.

*Hobby:* Coin collecting ("I have a collection with over 85 buffalo head nickels").

*Company Computer Password:* Chocolate Thunder.

*Flashbacks:* Young Gus (Carlos McCullers II, Isaiah Brown, and Julien Hill).

## JULIET LYNN O'HARA

*Parents:* Frank O'Hara (William Shatner), a con artist, and Maryann O'Hara (Susan Hogan).

*Place of Birth:* Miami, Florida, in 1981. She mentions being a Libra.

*Brother:* Ewan O'Hara (John Cena).

*Heritage:* Scottish.

*Childhood:* It is known through episodes that Maryann raised Juliet and Ewan after Frank deserted the family. Juliet felt that her father was never a part of her life, but he actually was, as he would attend important events, such as graduations, but not reveal himself to her. At an unspecified time, Maryann remarried a man named Lloyd (who became Juliet's stepfather). Juliet, however, contradicts her childhood by later saying that she and Ewan were raised by their parents, who were married for 30 years.

*Education:* University of Miami.

*Occupation:* Officer, then detective, with the Santa Barbara Police Department. As the series concludes, Juliet accepts a position as head detective with the San Francisco Police Department. Shawn Spencer (see above) relocates his psychic business to join her. It is later mentioned that before she became a police officer, Juliet worked for the mayor of Santa Barbara.

*Inspiration:* Juliet mentions that Ewan instilled in her the desire to become a police officer when he joined the military.

*Address:* 101 Shadow Lane (appears to be an apartment complex).

*Computer Screen Saver Image:* Shabby, the Sea Lion.

*Nickname:* Called "Jules" by Shawn and mostly "O'Hara" by her partner, Lassiter (see below).

*Character:* Pretty, sensible, not one for rushing into a situation, and often reluctant to deviate from the rules of the system. When she is outside of her comfort zone (warm states), she complains about being cold or chilly "because I grew up in a subtropical climate." Juliet likes to be liked; "I hate to think people hate me. I even get Christmas cards from people I arrest."

*Detective Test Score:* 98.4.

*Car Code:* "Car 7-0" (she rides with Lassiter).

*Favorite TV Series: The Mentalist* (the CBS series that uses a format similar to *Psych*).

*Expertise:* Baseball history and facts.

*Camp:* Juliet attended Cheerleader Camp for two weeks. ("I got kicked out. I don't like to talk about it.") With the skills she learned, she performed in a stage show called *Everybody Hip Hops*; it closed after two performances.

*Replacement:* After relocating to San Francisco, Juliet is replaced by Betsy Brannigan to work alongside Lassiter. Betsy (Mira Sorvino) is much like Shawn in her observational and deductive abilities and able to solve cases with the same skill as Shawn. In the pilot episode, Detective Lucinda Barry (Anna Dudek) is seen as Lassiter's partner; Juliet appears from the second episode on.

*Flashbacks:* Young Juliet (Bailey Herbert).

## CARLTON JEBEDIAH LASSITER

*Place of Birth:* Miami in 1968.

*Mother:* Mona Lassiter; his father is not named. At one point, Mona revealed that she was a lesbian and is in a relationship with a woman named Althea (who is said to be Carlton's stepmother).

*Sister:* Lauren "Lulu" Lassiter (April Bowlby), a graduate student (appears to be a film student, as she is seen making a documentary on the police department).

*Ex-Wife:* Victoria Parker (Justine Bateman).

*Current Wife:* Merlowe Lassiter (Kristy Swanson). They married in 2012, and as the series ends, they become the parents of a daughter they name Lilly Nora.

*Occupation:* Head detective, then police chief, with the Santa Barbara Police Department; he also served time as a patrol car officer when he was demoted at one point.

*Partner:* Juliet O'Hara (see above).

*Address:* Condo 536 at 1101 McBride Street, San Francisco, California 93101 (he sleeps with a gun in his hand). For added protection, he has hidden eight guns in his house.

*Education:* University of Miami (degree in criminology).

*Detective Test Score:* 97.3.

*Belief:* Shawn is a fake but can't prove he does not have psychic abilities. He dislikes Shawn for stealing his glory by solving the cases he feels he should be solving. Lassiter also cringes when Shawn accompanies him on a case because he likes old-fashioned police work, while Shawn uses unconventional methods and complicates situations with his nauseating sense of humor.

*Nicknames:* Called "Lassie" and "Detective Dipstick" by Shawn. His mother called him "Booker"; in grammar school, he had the nickname "Binky."

*Character:* Lassiter has a no-nonsense approach to crime solving and is hard on all his detectives, including himself. He has what he calls a "Crap List" on his desk that has the names of people he does not like (including Shawn) and "a little black book" containing the names of criminals he has arrested. Lassiter is continually upset by Shawn's actions, and tap dancing seems to put him at ease.

*Dislike:* Squirrels.

*Allergy:* Anything that contains mint but enjoys all varieties of cheese.

*Cell Phone Ringtone:* The theme to the TV series *Cops*.

*Sport:* Mentions fishing.

*Expertise:* Weapons (even land mines). He is a member at the Red Chief Firing Range, where he won first place at the Lucinda Barry Memorial Tournament ("Event Two, All Targets Thrown, Yellow Class").

*Coffee Mug Slogan:* "Shoot First, Drink Coffee Later" (he takes three creams and four sugars in his coffee).

*Car Code:* "Car 7-0."

*Car:* Department-issued Ford Fusion.

*License Plate:* 2 DDT 465, then 2SB 1653.

*Blood Type:* O-negative.

## FINAL EPISODE

Juliet and Karen have transferred to San Francisco, where Karen has become the police chief and Juliet continues as a detective. Realizing that he needs Juliet in his life, Shawn gives up his business and joins her in San Francisco. Gus, missing Shawn, joins him with the hope of helping the police department via Shawn's abilities. Karen tells them this cannot be "because we already have a psychic; he's alphabetizing the pantry as we speak" (referring to Adrian Monk from the series *Monk*). As Shawn proposes to Juliet outside the police station and is about to place his grandmother's wedding ring on her finger, a thief runs by, steals the ring, and escapes in a waiting car. Shawn and Gus take to Gus's car and begin a pursuit, indicating that the life they led in Santa Barbara may well be duplicated in San Francisco. Jane Lynch appears as Karen's sister, Barbara Dunlap, a Coast Guard commander.

*Series Note:* It can be seen that Shawn uses Apple-related products (seen with a silver computer), while Gus uses Microsoft-related products (has a black computer). In first-season episodes, it is seen that before brand-name computers were used, Shawn and Gus used a silver computer with the name "Alien Ware" printed on it. Virtually every episode features a fist bump between Shawn and Gus, and a running gag in most episodes is a visual of a pineapple. When pretzels are in a scene, Snyder's of Hanover bags are visible. The program uses real names of people, TV shows, and movies, and product placement (showing real products) is clearly visible.

# *Reba*
(WB/CW, 2001–2007)

*Cast:* Reba McEntire (Reba Hart), Christopher Rich (Brock Hart), Melissa Peterman (Barbra Jean Booker), JoAnna Garcia (Cheyenne Montgomery), Steve Howey (Van Montgomery), Scarlett Pomers (Kyra Hart), Mitch Holleman (Jake Hart).

*Basis:* Reba Hart, a divorced mother of three children (Cheyenne, Kyra, and Jake), struggles to overcome all the instances that constantly try her patience. How? As Reba says as the final words in the last episode, "We got though it all because we're survivors," which refers to the show's theme song, "I'm a Survivor."

## REBA NELL HART
*Place of Birth:* McAlester, Oklahoma, on March 28 ("The year is not important," as Reba says).
*Maiden Name:* Reba McKinney.
*Ex-Husband:* Brock Hart (see below). They were married from 1981 to 2001.
*Children:* Cheyenne, Kyra, and Jake Hart (see below).
*Education:* University of Oklahoma (acquired a degree in education).
*Dream:* To become a professional country-and-western singer.
*Background:* After graduating from college in 1976, Reba traveled to Texas to begin her teaching career. She also followed her dream and began moonlighting as a singer at a local bar (where she met Brock Hart, a dental student working as a bartender; they dated, married, and five years later, after Brock begins his dental practice, start a family). When the series opens, Reba is divorced, the children live with her, and Brock is now married to his dental assistant, Barbra Jean Booker (see below), the woman he had an affair with while still married to Reba.

*Address:* 4280 Oak Street in Houston, Texas.

*Income:* Reba first appears to be living off the child support and alimony provided by Brock. She is next seen as a substitute teacher at Westchester High School, then as Brock's dental office receptionist (suite 312); as receptionist for Dr. Eugene Fisher (Dan Castellaneta), the dentist across the hall from Brock (suite 314); and, finally, as a real estate agent for her own company, Cameron Realty (with Van Montgomery as her partner).

*Quirk:* Often talks to herself (due to the fact that she has a lot to say but no one will listen to her). It also bothers Reba that no one ever puts milk on the shopping list.

*Relationship with Barbra Jean:* A bit hostile for stealing her husband (but Barbra Jean believes they can put that behind them, as she is struggling to become Reba's friend).

*Catchphrase:* "Crap" (which she often says when something doesn't go her way).

*Computer Screen Name:* Red Rose.

*Car:* Said to be a gold Volvo station wagon.

*Allergy:* Lemonade (as Reba says).

*Beauty Pageant:* Won the Parker Elementary School Pageant of Grandmas.

*Laundry Bleach:* Clorox.

*Coffee Brand:* Chock Full o' Nuts.

*Medical Issue:* High blood pressure.

*Volunteer Work:* St. Raphael's Mission.

## BROCK HART

*Mother:* Elizabeth "Liz" Hart (Jenny O'Hara).

*Wife:* Barbra Jean Hart (maiden name Booker).

*Ex-Wife:* Reba Hart.

*Children:* Cheyenne, Kyra, and Jake (with Reba); Henry (with Barbra Jean).

*Occupation:* Dentist; in 2004, he retires to become a golf pro (with the Hooter's Tour; he is proud of the fact that he won the Presto Dry Cleaning Invitational).

*Address:* 4282 Oak Street (next door to Reba).

*Age:* In 2003, Brock is revealed to be 43 years old and three years older than Reba (making Reba's previously unmentioned birth year 1961).

*Favorite Sport:* Golf (he uses "naked lady golf tees").

*Fear:* Barbra Jean's father, called "Big Daddy," and her brother, Buzzard, who simply do not like him.

*In College:* Smoked marijuana.

*Transportation:* A Harley-Davidson motorcycle he calls "Crotch Pig."

*Trait:* According to Reba, "stupid, cheap, and greedy."

*Computer Screen Name:* Golden God.

**BARBRA JEAN HART**

*Parents:* Big Daddy (Dion Anderson) and Big Mamma Booker.

*Place of Birth:* Fisheye Bottom (a small town near Lubbock, Texas; it is noted for having the biggest slaughterhouse in the county).

*Sisters:* Katie Ann (Rachel York), Lori Ann (Park Overall), and Luanne (Rini Bel).

*Brother:* Bryan, called "Buzzard" (Bryan Callen).

*Husband:* Brock Hart.

*Son with Brock:* Henry Jesus Hart (Alexander and Jackson McClellan, then Jon Paul DeFabry).

*Education:* Lubbock High School (on the volleyball team; played the tambourine in the school's orchestra); her college is not mentioned.

*Occupation:* Brock's dental assistant. She retired (to spend more time with Henry) when Reba replaced her. She was also a TV weather girl (Cable Channel 34) who went by the name "Stormy Clearweather." She later became the channel's hard-news street reporter, Babs Jansen (she billed her segment as "Babs Jansen, Street Walker"). When Barbra Jean was in her teens, her mother bought her a pair of jeans that Barbra made more fashionable by attaching "shiny metal studs." During the "Storm of '82," Barbra was caught in the rain and struck by lightning in her left butt cheek. Now, anytime it is going to rain, her butt cheek (which she calls her "buttrometer") tingles (hence her qualifications to become a weather girl). At one point, Barbra Jean coached a women's prison football team (where "Little Arson Annie" was her star quarterback).

*Breast Nicknames:* Barbra Jean calls them "The Fellas"; Brock calls them "Puppies."

*Beauty Pageants:* Miss Value Mart, Miss Knox County, and Miss Tasty Freeze (in all of which she came in last), then a wet T-shirt contest (that she lost because she didn't know it was for gay men).

*Moneymaking Venture:* Joined with Reba to sell designer patchwork shirts designed by Reba.

*Quirk:* For unexplained reasons, Barbra Jean spoke nothing but Klingon (from *Star Trek*) for a week.

*Pet Dog:* Brock (named after her husband).

*Character:* Nosey, annoying, and a bit naive, and, according to Reba, "Barbra Jean laughs like a horse and doesn't have the sense God gave to paste." Barbra Jean is a full-figured woman and claims that in the second grade she experienced a sudden growth spurt and was called "Blondzilla" by her classmates. She is very religious and oversees her church's Bowling for Jesus Fund and shops at the Joy for Jesus Gift Shop. She takes art classes, reads to the blind on Tuesday evenings, and volunteers at the Church Service Camp (teaching blind high school children to cook).

*Character Change:* Final-season episodes show a much slimmer Barbra Jean (due to Melissa Peterman's dieting and weight loss).

*Computer Screen Saver:* A picture of Reba.

*Secret:* In her youth, Barbra Jean was a smoker (two packs a day).

*Nickname:* Called "B. J." by Brock.

*Pet Cat:* Clap Clap Kitty Cat.

*Famous For:* Her tuna casserole ("three kinds of tuna and two kinds of potato chips").

*Collection:* Beanie Babies (she has 450 of them and celebrates each new arrival with a cake and ice cream party).

*Quirk:* She has 14 plush animals that have to be arranged in a specific order with the exception of Binky and Lulu "because they have a history" (unexplained).

*Most Proud Of:* Her ability to stuff seven eggs in her mouth.

*Favorite Singer:* Sting.

*Dislikes:* TV game show host Bob Barker (who said "I wasn't perky enough to become a contestant on *The Price Is Right*" [which Barker hosted at the time]).

## CHEYENNE MONTGOMERY

*Parents:* Reba and Brock Hart.

*Husband:* Van Montgomery (see below).

*Daughter:* Elizabeth Montgomery (Alena and Gabrielle LeBerger, then Lila Braff), whom she had at 17 years of age (as a senior in high school).

*Education:* Westchester High School; Houston University; an unnamed dental school (attended when she chose to follow in her father's footsteps and become a dental hygienist; she scored a "B plus" on her entrance test).

*Background:* Cheyenne, cocaptain of the Wildcats football cheerleading team (the Peppettes), and fellow student Van Montgomery, a member of the football team, had an affair when Cheyenne was 17. Cheyenne became pregnant and had to drop out of school (she went into labor at her high school graduation and was voted "Prom Queen"). Van, disowned by his wealthy parents for what happened, moved in with Cheyenne (at Reba's home). They lived in Cheyenne's bedroom (until they purchase their own home in final-season episodes) and raised their daughter Elizabeth.

*Childhood:* Cheyenne took ballet lessons, karate, and piano lessons but gave up on them ("I'm flaky and don't stick with things"). At summer camp, Cheyenne took a self-defense course and was called "Most Lethal and Most Peppy."

*Favorite Store:* Donna's Outlet.

*Wardrobe:* Cheyenne dresses according to her mood (you don't want to get her angry "because the clothes are not sexy").

*Secret:* Revealed in the final season that Cheyenne has a drinking problem.

*Favorite Beauty Parlor:* Salon Verona.

*TV Appearance:* Appeared on the cable program *The Huddle* (airs on Channel 200) with Van in a segment profiling the wives of football players.

## VAN MONTGOMERY

*Parents:* Dan (Mark Tymchyshyn) and Sue Montgomery (Robin Riker); Sue called Van "Vonny."

*Wife:* Cheyenne Hart.

*Daughter:* Elizabeth Montgomery.

*Education:* Westchester High School (wore jersey 24 as a football team member); Houston University (on a football scholarship).

*Occupation:* Van worked as the groundskeeper at college while also playing on the football team. He quit school to become an aspiring linebacker with the Houston Thunderbirds, an Arena Football League (AFL) team (wore jersey 88). He also worked as the "Sauce and Cheese Captain" at Fat Tony's Pizza Parlor. Van's football career ends when he injures his tailbone (called a "broken butt" by Cheyenne and Reba), and an X-ray reveals he has spinal stenosis (a narrowing of the spine). He receives a $100,000 settlement from the AFL and joins with Reba in her business, Cameron Realty (which she operates from her garage); when Reba fires him, Van joins the Steve Norris Realty Company.

*Shoe Size:* 12.

*Favorite TV Show: 24* (he appears to admire Jack Bauer, the lead character).

*Car:* A red Ford Mustang he calls "Rhonda" (with the license plate K5L DNS).

*Nickname for Reba:* "Mrs. H."

*Favorite Dinner:* New York steak and apple pie.

*Favorite Superhero:* Underdog (from the 1960s cartoon series of the same title).

*Favorite Toothpaste:* Aquafresh.

*Fear:* Spiders (claims to have seen "a huge man-eating spider") and small dogs (due, he says, to his watching the movie *Cujo* on a nine-inch TV screen).

*Allergy:* Cats.

*Dream:* To be like the adventurous Jack Bauer (on the TV series *24*); if his life were to be made into a motion picture, he would like Denzel Washington to play him.

*Favorite Card Game:* Poker (his online screen name is Screen Name).

## KYRA AND JAKE HART

Kyra, Reba's middle child, is a very pretty but sassy 12-year-old (when the series begins). Her middle name is Eleanor, and she is a straight "A" student at Oak Elementary School (she later attends Westchester High School). She reads *Teen* magazine, is an expert chess player, and earns money by babysitting. She is an honor roll student and plays first clarinet (then tuba) in a school band. She is very independent and often defies Reba's authority (as a child, Reba says that Kyra would respond to answering questions regarding her actions "by holding her breath and pulling her dress up over her head"). Kyra mentions pot roast and macaroni and cheese as being her favorite meals. Pinwheel cookies are her favorite snack (although she can be seen eating candy bars). As the series ends, Kyra, as academically smart as she is, chose not to attend college to focus on a music career (singer and musician; she was also in a metal pop-rock band called Demi-Teen). Kyra can also be seen as the only child to have inherited Reba's red hair (Cheyenne has blonde hair; Jake has brown). Reba was also in labor with her for 56 hours.

Jacob Mitchell, called Jake, attends Parker Elementary School. He has a pet turtle named Speedy and attends jazz and tap classes. He is seven years old when the series begins and is a Cub Scout. He claims he can't eat fast food because it upsets his stomach, but likes chunky peanut butter and banana sandwiches (although at one time he swallowed $1.20 because Reba told him it was his lunch money). He is a member of the local children's soccer team (wears jersey 2, later jersey 22) and a member of the Hustlers basketball team at the recreation center.

# *Scrubs*
## (NBC, 2001–2008; ABC, 2009–2010)

*Cast:* Zach Braff (J. D. Dorian), John C. McGinley (Perry Cox), Sarah Chalke (Elliot Reid), Donald Faison (Christopher Turk), Judy Reyes (Carla Espinosa), Neil Flynn (Janitor), Ken Jenkins (Bob Kelso), Christa Miller (Jordan Sullivan).

*Basis:* The antics of doctors at Sacred Heart Hospital, where patients are treated in ways that can be accomplished only on television.

### DR. JOHN MICHAEL "J. D." DORIAN

*Parents:* Sam (John Ritter) and Barbara Dorian (Margaret Easley). They divorced when J. D. was seven years old; they were expecting a girl, and for the first three years of his life, J. D. was called "Joanna." Since the divorce, Barbara has been married (and divorced six times); Sam, a traveling office supply salesman, passed away while J. D. was a resident at Sacred Heart Hospital. Barbara's maiden name was Hobbs.

*Brother:* Dan Dorian (Tom Cavanagh), a real estate agent.

*Occupation:* Doctor of internal medicine (at Sacred Heart Hospital; later becoming New Sacred Heart Hospital); residency director (at St. Vincent's Hospital). At Sacred Heart, J. D. served as the co–chief resident with his future wife, Elliot Reid (see below). He was also a staff internist at Sacred Heart.

*Prior Romantic Interest:* Kim Briggs (Elizabeth Banks), with whom he had a son named Sam.

*Education:* William and Mary College in Virginia. In his unnamed high school, J. D. was the mascot for the girls' volleyball team.

*Likes:* Unicorns and pirates.

*Dislikes:* Beer (although he is seen drinking it), sharks, clowns, water parks, change (especially pennies), and robots.

The cast of *Scrubs. Touchstone TV/NBC/Photofest © Touchstone TV/NBC; photographer: Chris Haston*

*Social Security Number:* 987-65-4320.

*Transportation:* A Volvo, a scooter he called "Sasha," and a Toyota Prius (that he calls "Malik").

*Fear:* Afraid of commitment.

*Favorite TV Series: Sanford and Son, Candid Camera, Lost, Grey's Anatomy,* and *The Transformers.*

*Quirk:* Can't eat and watch TV at the same time; has constant daydreams (allows the viewer to see what he thinks through J. D.'s narration).

*Good-Luck Charm:* The top hat from the game "Monopoly."

*Hobby:* Collecting scarves.

*Nicknames:* Throughout the series, Dr. Cox had numerous female and dog names for him; these include the female names Shirley, Maria, Gloria, Judy, Marjorie, Sally, Clarabelle, Belinda, Reba, Gidget, and Sabrina; for dogs, he was called Lassie, Hooch, Toto, Scooby-Doo, Fido, Rin-Tin-Tin, and Astro.

*Address:* An unnamed apartment building with the street number 12629 (which he shares with Turk and Carla before they move out).

*Flashbacks:* Young J. D. (Cody Estes, then Zach Mills).

## DR. ELLIOT REID

*Parents:* Lily (Markie Post) and Simon Reid (Lane Davies). Simon is the chief of medicine at St. Augustine's Hospital in Connecticut.

*Place of Birth:* Greenwich, Connecticut.

*Husband:* J. D. (see above).

*Background:* Although Elliot was raised in an atmosphere of wealth (her family owned an orchard), her parents literally neglected her, and she was raised by their housekeeper (Consuelo). Elliot's mother was quite abusive to her, and her father, who was hoping for a boy, gave her a male name. He also refused to accept anything less than Elliot's becoming a doctor (as he and her brothers are all doctors). She played the tuba in high school and even attempted to commit suicide (by drowning herself in a lake; she was rescued by the school's rowing team). She attended Brown University (was a member of the Omega Beta Gamma sorority) and suffers a number of psychological issues, as her mother considered her the black sheep of the family and constantly told her that nobody would ever love her. Her mother also discouraged her from wanting to become a prima ballerina.

*Siblings:* Elliot has four brothers, but only two are named: Bradley and Barry (the latter is gay).

*Occupation:* Doctor of internal medicine; she later establishes a private practice. She began as an intern and then became a resident (including chief resident) and a senior attending physician; she did an internship at the North County University Medical Center.

*Political Affiliation:* Republican.

*Favorite Candy:* Anything with chocolate.

*Favorite Video Game:* "Pac-Man."

*Favorite Animals:* Horses (especially ponies) and rabbits.

*Favorite Soda Flavor:* Orange.

*Favorite Drink:* Red wine.

*Physical Issues:* Her eyebrows, which she feels are not right for her face; her feet, which she considers "large man feet"; and hands, which are always at temperatures below normal.

*Dislikes:* Cats (she claims they attack her, but she is seen with them), skimpy lingerie (like thongs), foul language, and explicit sexual terms or names.

*Fears:* Camping (mentally affected when she saw the movie *The Blair Witch Project*) and gorgeous redheaded women (makes her very angry when she sees one).

*Nicknames:* "Blondie," "Blonde Doctor," "Marshmallow," and "Barbie."

*Quirks:* Sneezes with her eyes open; during her pregnancy, she ate cereal with ketchup instead of milk; becomes unusually strong when she gets mad.

*Second Languages:* French and German.

*Food Preference:* Vegetarian (although some episodes show her eating meat).
*Elliot's Derriere:* Often made fun off, although Turk claims that "she has a nice ass for a white chick."
*Favorite Music Group:* U2.
*Catchphrase:* "Frick" (which she says with other words when she gets upset).
*Flashbacks:* Young Elliot (Alexandra Lee).

## DR. CHRISTOPHER DUNCAN TURK

*Mother:* Margaret Turk (Hattie Winston), a Jehovah's Witness. It is revealed that Christopher is one-eighth Japanese.
*Brother:* Kevin Turk (D. L. Hughley).
*Occupation:* Chief of surgery at Sacred Heart Hospital; professor at Winston University. He is commonly called "Turk."
*Wife:* Carla Espinosa (see below).
*Medical Issue:* Type 2 diabetes.
*Favorite TV Shows: The Jeffersons, The Transformers,* and *Sanford and Son.* As a child, he watched *The Smurfs, The Brady Bunch,* and *Webster.*
*Favorite Foods:* Pizza, cheese, sausages, and steak and ribs.
*Favorite Singers:* Marvin Gaye and Neil Diamond.
*Favorite Sport:* Basketball.
*Favorite TV Personality:* Tyra Banks.
*Favorite Holiday:* Christmas.
*Favorite Snacks:* Donuts.
*Fetish:* Women's feet.
*Favorite Made-Up Word:* "Brinner" (combining "breakfast" with "dinner" as a time to eat).
*Dislikes:* People singling him out because he is African American, hugging in public, his middle name (named "Duncan" by his father because he liked Dunkin' Donuts), being thought of as a sexist, and buying clothes that appeal to him but are called "girly clothes" by others.
*Nicknames:* Called "Chocolate Bear" (by J. D.), "Gandhi" (by Dr. Cox, because he is bald), and "Turk Turkelton" (by Dr. Kelso, because he believes it is Turk's real name).
*Phone Number:* 916-CALL TUR.
*Alter Ego:* Cal Turk, a white insurance salesman.
*Allergy:* Shellfish.
*Address (with Carla):* 56 Walnut Drive.
*Flashbacks:* Young Turk (T. J. Hall, then David S. Robinson).

## DR. PERCIVAL ULYSSES "PERRY" COX

Perry, born in 1959, is a doctor of internal medicine at Sacred Heart Hospital (where he was also an attending physician and the chief of medicine). He was then a professor at Winston University (where he believes his students will graduate to become murderers and assassins). He is divorced from Jordan Sullivan and is the father of Jack and Jennifer Dylan Cox. He is rather sarcastic and mentored J. D. (and, although he belittles him, he believes he will make a great doctor).

Perry was born in Pittsburgh and has a younger sister named Paige, who is now a born-again Christian. They were raised by alcoholic parents. He enjoys a scotch on the rocks and despises the nicknames his staff call him (from "Big Cheese" to "Dr. Professor Cox"). *Days of Our Lives* is his favorite TV show, Lindsay Lohan is his favorite actress, and the Pittsburgh Steelers and the Detroit Lions are his favorite sports teams. His hate list is rather large; he mentions TV awards shows, low-carb diets, and then President George H. W. Bush's children, high-definition TV (prefers his old analog TV set), and Republicans—in short, "everything that exists—past, present, and future."

Perry was voted "Best Physician" by a medical journal and attended Yale University and Johns Hopkins University. He is an atheist and mentions that his father showed affection to him by throwing a beer bottle and purposely missing his head. He has restrictions on which staff members can enter his office and despises actor Hugh Jackman. He takes his coffee with sugar and no cream, and his trademark (copied from the film *The Sting* with Robert Redford) is rubbing his nose and then crossing his arms.

Perry and ex-wife Jordan Sullivan are the parents of Jack and Jennifer Dylan Cox. Although divorced, they still live together as a family. She was a board member of Sacred Heart Hospital until she resigned to raise her children. She is sarcastic, mean, and rude (claiming she inherited it from her parents; in reality, her parents were just the opposite). Jordan likes vodka with soda crackers, being challenged, sparkling water with a lemon wedge, and fighting for the sake of it. She dislikes the pain of pregnancy, people who believe she is older than she looks, people taking advantage of her, and other people's children. She has a brother, Ben Sullivan (Brendan Fraser), and two sisters, Paige (Cheryl Hines) and Danni (Tara Reid).

## JANITOR

Janitor, as he is known, was born in 1964 and is the rather inefficient head of janitorial services at Sacred Heart Hospital. He was married to Ladinia "Lady" Williams (Kit Pongetti), a woman who had a fear of the unknown, lusted for Dr. Elliot Reid, and enjoyed playing pranks on J. D. In the season 8 finale, Janitor's name is revealed to be Glen Matthews (at which time he drops his mop and leaves the hospital; what happened after that is not known).

Information regarding a factual account of Janitor is unavailable, as he continually tells stories about his past, and what is actually true is unknown (from saying he believed his mother was his sister and his father was his brother [he called them "Sister-Mom" and "Brother-Dad"] to having a deaf sister and a brother who worked as a stripper). He was so proficient at lying that no one disbelieved him. Janitor mentions liking taxidermy (he has a license, but it was revoked for killing all the squirrels in the vicinity of the hospital; he had a collection he called his "Squirrel Army" but later traded them in for a stuffed dog named Steven), sharks, mops, floors (he tends to treat them like his children), and manipulating people.

On the other hand, Janitor dislikes Moon Pies (aka Scooter Pies) snack cakes, working (most of all), whales, not having an office, being thought of as stupid because he is only a janitor, and actress Audrey Hepburn. Janitor apparently tried his luck at acting but appeared in only one film (*The Fugitive* in 1993) as "Transit Cop" (under the screen name Neil Flynn, which is presumably a stage name that he used). Because of his height, he is called by such nicknames as "Lurch" (from *The Addams Family*), "Jolly Green," and "Stretch." Janitor also appears to be a fan of the TV series *The Addams Family* because he changed his hospital file address to 0001 Cemetery Drive (where Gomez and Morticia Addams lived). Janitor can speak Korean and American Sign Language and has several alter egos: Klaus (German), Nigel (British), and Roscoe (fake brother). His favorite reading matter appears to be the magazine *The Janitorial*, and because of his love of mops, he has a mop tattoo. He also has inconsistent religions—from Islam to Norse—and mentions that he has difficulty distinguishing colors.
*Flashbacks:* Young Janitor (Brandon Waters).

## CARLA ESPINOSA
Carla, the wife of Christopher Turk (see above) and the mother of two daughters (Isabelle, born in 2006, and the other unnamed, born in 2009), was born in Chicago in 1971. She worked as the head nurse at Sacred Heart Hospital before settling down to become a full-time mother. Carla continues to use her maiden name to preserve her cultural Dominican heritage (she was born in the United States but her mother in the Dominican Republic). She has a younger brother (Marco) and two sisters, Maria and Gabriella.

Carla likes to express her opinions and be heard but hates it when she is wrong about something. She enjoys pizza rolls and video games, and while working as a nurse, she found great pleasure in pointing out other people's faults and giving them advice. She dislikes people mistaking her heritage (believed to be Puerto Rican or Mexican), people pointing out her faults, and her fingers (which she calls "sausage fingers"). Carla has a pierced navel, is left-handed, and wears a size 36C bra (because of the cup size, J. D. uses them like water balloon launchers). Carla, a Democrat, used hypnotism to cure her smoking habit and has had numerous nicknames, none of which actually stuck; these include "Scary Nurse-Wife" (by Janitor), "Pickle" (by J. D.), and "Ex-Nurse Turkelton" (by Kelso, who believes Christopher's last name is Turkelton). Carla has a middle name that is never revealed, but Christopher believes it is Juanita.

## ROBERT "BOB" KELSO

Bob was born in Altoona, Pennsylvania, in 1942 (another episode claims 1947) and was the chief of medicine at Sacred Heart Hospital (he was previously a minor league shortstop, apparently wanting a career in baseball). He served as a medic during the Vietnam War and is a stickler for maintaining the hospital's budget but often oblivious to staff and patient problems. After his wife Enid's passing, he began teaching at Winston University. He is also the father of two children with Enid (Harrison [gay] and Thong Tri Kelso, the result of an affair with a Vietnamese woman).

Although Bob was married to Enid (who was ill and wheelchair bound), he had numerous affairs (mostly with prostitutes) and mistresses. He has a dog (Baxter) and a car he calls "Bessie." He is especially fond of Korean call girls (also mentioned as "Southeast Asian prostitutes"), eating peanut butter from the jar, playing video games (like "Pac-Man"), bobblehead dolls, and muffins.

On the other hand, he dislikes having to part with money, most of his staff (and patients), bicycles, and having sex with Enid. And, like Carla, he has numerous nicknames; these include "Mr. Doody-Head" (by Elliot) and "Beelzebob," "Bob-O," "Bobarino," and "Bob-a-Tron" (by Dr. Cox). Bob attended Stanford University (Class of 1968), called Enid (married for 44 years) "Bunny," and hung out at Coffee Bucks (where he enjoyed muffins).

*Series Note: Scrubs* aired on NBC (2001–2008) and then ABC (2009). ABC revised the series as *Scrubs: Med School*, which ran for three months in 2010. Lucy Bennett (Kerry Bishe), Denise Mahoney (Eliza Coupe), Drew Suffin (Michael Mosely), and Cole Aaronson (Dave Franco) were added as interns at Sacred Heart Hospital.

# *Sheena*
## (Syndicated, 2000–2002)

*Cast:* Gena Lee Nolin (Sheena); Margo Moorer (Kali); John Allen Nelson (Matt Cutter); Vickie Phillips, then Denise Loden (the Darak'na).

*Basis:* A young white girl, raised in Africa and known as Sheena, protects her adopted homeland from evil.

## SHEENA

*Real Name:* Cheryl Hamilton.

*Parents:* Amanda Hamilton (Carol Grow); unnamed father (Robb Chamberlain).

*Background:* Cheryl, the daughter of archaeologists, was five years old when her parents moved to Africa. At an unspecified time thereafter, Amanda and her husband were exploring a cave when a rock slide crushed the cave and they were killed. Cheryl, waiting outside the cave, becomes unsure of what to do and begins wandering in the jungle. She is found by Kali, the medicine woman of the Kia tribe, who raises her as her own (after investigating and discovering that Cheryl's parents are dead). Kali names her "Shi-na," but Cheryl prefers "Sheena." Sheena, 25 years old when the series begins, had been raised to respect humans and animals but to be fearful of humans who come to Africa with evil on their mind.

*Home:* A cave in the La Mista, a dangerous area in the Maltoka region of the jungle.

*Ability:* Morph (change into animals). Kali's people possessed the power to change into animals many decades ago. When civilization came to Africa, the Kai tribe (with the exception of Kali) chose to become animals. Kali passed on the knowledge of morphing to Sheena. To become an animal, Sheena must feel the spirit of the animal inside her (what she calls the "Manta"). Once she has chosen the animal she wishes to become, she looks into its eyes, and the transformation begins.

*The Animal:* Sheena retains her human memories as well as the instincts of the animal she possesses. Sheena, however, is not protected. She is prone to two dangers: retaining part of the animal if she remains in that form for too long and injury if she is hurt in her animal form (she will retain that injury when she returns to human form). She can track animals and humans by their scents and will kill a human only if one threatens to kill her.

*Inability:* Sheena cannot talk to animals, but she can communicate with them—except rogues (because there is no focus).

*Education:* Taught to fight by Kali; learned the ways of life through reading.

*The Legend:* La Mista is also home to a horrifying and legendary creature called the "Darak'na" (the "Shadow" in English). It is said that "whenever evildoers come to Africa, the Darak'na will strike." The Darak'na is actually Sheena, who uses a power that Kali gave her to battle evil when evil fights unfairly.

*The Darak'na:* It is a vicious catlike creature with razor-sharp claws that, as the creature, Sheena will kill. To become the creature, Sheena first covers herself in mud and then concentrates, and the creature emerges. Sheena retains her human thought processes but loses her bralike top, exposing her mud-covered breasts (although it appears that the stunt actress is actually topless, the mud prevents anything from being seen; it is not explained how Sheena regains her top when she becomes her normal self).

*Assistant:* Matt Cutter, the only other person who is aware of Sheena's secrets. Matt owns Cutter Enterprises (later called Cutter Unlimited) and offers safaris to search for the Darak'na (he is actually conning people, he knows that Sheena is the Darak'na and that it will not appear unless evil is present; people say, "Matt Cutter would sell his liver if he could profit off of it"). Matt, a graduate of Florida State University, previously worked for the CIA as the agency's best sniper (his code name was Jericho; he was also an instructor at the Farm, the CIA training camp). One morning, after killing an innocent man by mistake, he quit the agency and retreated to Africa. Sheena and Matt became friends after Matt, trying to escape from diamond smugglers, fell into a pond of quicksand and was rescued by Sheena. Sheena thinks she is pretty and attractive and has a crush on Matt, but feels Matt does not see her in the same light as he always calls her "Good Buddy" ("I wonder if he knows I'm a girl," Sheena says to herself, "or just a good buddy?").

*Flashbacks:* Cheryl, age five (Brittney Robertson).

## PRIOR VERSION

In 1955–1956, Irish McCalla played the title role in *Sheena, Queen of the Jungle*. Here, Sheena, the only survivor of a small-plane crash in the African jungle, was found and raised by a noble tribe as Sheena, a protector of animals who is feared as a white jungle goddess. She is assisted by her chimpanzee, Chim, and Bob Rayburn (Christian Drake), a white trader in Kenya.

# *Still Standing*
## (CBS, 2002–2006)

*Cast:* Mark Addy (Bill Miller), Jami Gertz (Judy Miller), Renee Olstead (Lauren Miller), Taylor Ball (Brian Miller), Soleil Border (Tina Miller), Jennifer Irwin (Linda Michaels).

*Basis:* Events in the lives of a middle-class family living in Chicago: parents Bill and Judy and their children, Lauren, Brian, and Tina.

## WILLIAM "BILL" MILLER

*Parents:* Al (Paul Sorvino) and Louise Miller (Sally Struthers); Al is a retired steel worker.

*Place of Birth:* Chicago.

*Education:* Thomas Jefferson High School (Class of 1981). He was all-city linebacker on the football team and the school's hot dog–eating champion (ate 32 in one sitting).

*Occupation:* Bathroom fixture salesman at Berenson's Department Store at the Oak Street Mall.

*Address:* 209 Evergreen Place.

*Favorite Beer:* Miller High Life.

*Favorite Eatery:* The Churchill Room (a restaurant that features voluptuous waitresses).

*Favorite Activity:* Avoiding work (e.g., it was easier to cut down the tree in their backyard than it was to rake up leaves).

*Disciplining the Children:* Pretends to be the "Big Angry Guy."

*Nickname as a Child:* Called "Silly Billy" by his mother.

*Natural Ability:* Lying (because he does it all the time).

## JUDITH "JUDY" MILLER

*Parents:* Helen (Swoosie Kurtz) and Gene Michaels (Steve Gilborn).

*Place of Birth:* Illinois.

*Education:* The Pixey Preschool, Hamilton Grammar School, and Jefferson High School (Class of 1981). It was here that Judy and Bill first met. She was an activist and stood up for what she believed was right.

*Occupation:* Prior to marriage, Judy worked as a dental office receptionist; after returning to work, she became a dental assistant. She also tried to make extra money by selling hand-painted outdoor chairs at flea markets.

*Childhood Affiliation:* A Blue Bell Girl Scout.

*Disciplining the Children:* Becomes "tight-lipped, scary-voice Mom." She feels she is the better parent ("Bill isn't a bad parent; he's just a stupid man doing the best he can").

*Trait:* Sings all the time (although she can't carry a tune), overcooks meals (especially chicken), constantly talks (especially when Bill is trying to watch TV), and constantly puts words in Bill's mouth.

*Favorite Movie: Terms of Endearment.*

*Favorite Beauty Parlor:* Hair by Gary.

*Appliance Shopping:* Judy wears a sexy, cleavage-revealing halter top to get discounts from male salesmen.

## LAUREN MILLER

*Place of Birth:* Illinois on June 3, 1989 (she is 13 years old when the series begins).

*Education:* The Radford Academy Grammar School, then Jefferson High School (where she was a member of the school choir until she learned it was for losers). School does not really excite Lauren, and she finds that doing her household chores makes her look forward to school.

*Favorite Breakfast Cereal:* Post Alpha-Bits.

*Musical Ability:* Attempting to play the cornet.

*Favorite Pillow:* "Dawson" (which she named after her favorite TV show, *Dawson's Creek*).

*First Job:* Babysitter (she also created but couldn't sell "Goose Clothes"—outerwear for plastic lawn geese). She also likes it when her grandfather visits "because I can really use the money."

*Favorite Activity:* Shopping for clothes with her mother (because Judy knows how to manipulate people to get what she wants).

*Fashion Choice:* Not into the latest styles and enjoys wearing what she likes.

*Nickname:* Called "Pumpkin" by Bill.

*Trait:* Has a tendency to break rules (at home and school). She does not apply herself to her schoolwork and is thus an average student. She does not hold a high opinion of herself (she does not believe she is as pretty as others see her), and she appears to hate everything about herself (even though Bill and Judy often spoil her).

*Favorite Music:* Hip-hop.


## BRIAN MILLER

*Place of Birth:* Illinois in 1987 (he is 14 years old when the series begins).

*Education:* The Radford Academy Grammar School, then Thomas Jefferson High School. He is a member of the debate team and the engineering, chess, and math clubs. He was also a member of the football team (the Cougars), first as a player and then a cheerleader, the mascot, and, finally, the team statistician. He later attends the University of Chicago.

*First Job:* Salesman in a bookstore.

*Character:* Excessively neat and quite intelligent.

*Nickname:* Called "Bry Bry" by his mother.

*Fear:* Clowns.

*Homemade Robot:* Mr. Nuts and Bolts.

*Trait:* Is he gay? Although he is smart, he is not very popular at school and is considered a geek (even his parents consider him lame). But certain situations make him appear gay. He reads *Vogue* magazine (hoping to see models in see-through clothes), twirls a baton (as a cheerleader; his reason: to interact with girls), and was asked out on a "boy gay date" by the football team's top player.


## TINA MILLER

Tina is the youngest child of Bill and Judy. She attends the Radford Academy Grammar School (in second grade) and is rather sassy and manipulative for one so young (learned by observing her mother). Bill and Judy believe Tina is just an ordinary six-year-old and unaware that she is just pretending to be normal. Judy has named one cup in the house "The Sickly Cup," which Tina uses when she has a cold.

## LINDA MICHAELS

Linda is Judy's younger sister, a legal secretary. She is as beautiful and sexy as Judy but does not feel she is attractive to men (she suffers from low self-esteem and high self-pity). She visits often, but she and Bill simply do not get along and constantly insult each other. She is later seen marrying a musician named Perry. It also stresses Linda out that when her mother comes to visit her, she would rather sleep on the sofa at Judy's house than in the spare bedroom at Linda's home.

# 30 Rock
## (NBC, 2006–2013)

*Principal Cast:* Tina Fey (Liz Lemon), Alec Baldwin (Jack Donaghy), Tracy Morgan (Tracy Jordan), Jane Krakowski (Jenna Maroney).

*Basis:* A behind-the-scenes look at what happens before a television series airs (here, the mythical NBC series *The Girly Show*, which is produced in Manhattan at 30 Rockefeller Plaza, a building referred to as "30 Rock").

### ELIZABETH "LIZ" LEMON

*Parents:* Dick and Margaret Lemon (Anita Gillette).

*Place of Birth:* White Haven, Pennsylvania.

*Brother:* Mitch Lemon (Eric Ruffin).

*Occupation:* Head writer of the TV series *The Girly Show with Tracy Jordan*; also host of the relationship talk show *Deal Breakers*. Liz also did a TV commercial for a sex hotline called "1-900-OK FACE."

*Famous For:* Wearing her *Star Wars* Princess Leia costume.

*Address:* 160 Riverdale Drive (from her building awning) in Manhattan (Apartment 3B).

*Husband:* Jack Donaghy, divorced; Criss Chros (James Marsden).

*Children:* Janet and Terry-Lemon Chros (adopted).

*Education:* Northwestern University (where she met Jenna Maroney and together they created a comedy skit called *The Girly Show*). In high school (unnamed), Liz appeared nerdy but was actually the school bully.

*The Girly Show:* Liz and Jenna performed their skits for Second City audiences in Chicago before moving to New York City, where they sold their idea to NBC (Liz became the head writer; Jenna the principal star). Jack Donaghy (see below) felt the idea did not appeal to a male audience, hired an off-the-wall comedian (Tracy Jordan), and retitled it *The Girly Show with Tracy*

Tracy Morgan, Tina Fey, Jack McBrayer, Alec Baldwin, and Jane Krakowski.
*NBC/Photofest © NBC*

*Jordan* (seen as *THS with Tracy Jordan*). Liz bills *The Girly Show* as a late-night "live show of comedy and music"; she also says the show's audience is composed of "men between 9 and 13 and the morbidly obese."

*Favorite Movies:* The *Star Wars* trilogy (although she considers *Star Wars Episode II: Attack of the Clones* to be the worst of the films).

*Favorite Magazine: Playgirl.* She also subscribes to the *New Yorker* (through her iPad).

*Medical Issue:* Sleepwalks, sleep eats, and sleep smokes.

*Middle Name:* Miervaldi (it is of Latvian origin).

*Immortalized:* In a black-and-white portrait painted by Leonard Nimoy (as Jack says, "You can almost see her breasts").

*Award:* The W.I.M. (Women in Media) honor.

*Talent:* Transitioning her pajamas into day wear.

*Flashbacks:* Young Liz (Marcella Roy, Michal Aztonov, and Amy Poehler); Liz in her twenties (Tina Fey).

## JACK FRANCIS "JACK" DONAGHY

*Mother:* Colleen Donaghy (Elaine Stritch). Due to Colleen's affairs, Milton Greene (Alan Alda) is revealed to be his biological father, while Jimmy Donaghy (Brian Murray) was presumed to be his father.

*Ex-Wives:* Bianca Donaghy (Isabella Rossellini), Avery Jessup (Elizabeth Banks), and Liz Lemon (see above).

*Daughter:* Elizabeth "Liddy" Donaghy (by Avery).

*Half Brothers:* Eddie Donaghy (Nathan Lane) and Patrick Donaghy (Boris Mc-Giver).

*Half Sisters:* Patricia Donaghy (Siobhan Fallon) and Katherine Donaghy (Molly Shannon).

*Education:* Jack claims he won the Avery Blaine Handsomest Scholarship to Princeton University but attended Harvard Business School instead.

*Occupation:* NBC vice president of East Coast television (Programming Division); CEO of Kabletown (a channel for women); executive at General Electric (GE), where he created the Trifection oven (uses three kinds of heat to cook foods). Jack later creates his own job title: "vice president of East Coast television and microwave oven programming." He is also the owner of Donaghy Estates, a Long Island winery that he purchased but produces rather off-tasting wine. Prior to acquiring a job with GE, he worked as an intern for Senator Ted Kennedy.

*Allergy:* Peanuts.

*Political Affiliation:* Republican.

*Character:* Appears to be a slick confidence man but is totally scrupulous. His first order of business is to run his division as best he can, even if it means demeaning people (especially Liz).

*Religion:* Irish Catholic (he has named his fists "St. Michael" and "St. Patrick").

*Hobby:* Collecting cookie jars (at cookie jar conventions, he displays them under the name "Victor Nightingale").

*Cooking Specialty:* Chili.

*Honor:* The centerfold for *Fortune* magazine (three years in a row).

*GE Environmental Spokesman:* "Greenzo" (David Schwimmer); hired by Jack to promote his company products.

*Public Service Announcement:* Jack appeared as the spokesman for GE in "product integration" (placing GE products into NBC series as a means of product placement).

*Favorite TV Show: The Simpsons.*

*Favorite Newspaper: New York Post.*

*Flashbacks:* Young Jack (Benjamin Cook).


## TRACY JORDAN

*Wife:* Angie Jordan (Sherri Shepherd, then Sharon Wilkins).

*Children:* Tracy Jr., Virginia, and George Foreman Jordan.

*Occupation:* Actor and comedian (star of the NBC series *THS with Tracy Jordan*).

*Character:* Self-centered, dim-witted, and known to exhibit strange behavior at times. He can be seen wearing a necklace with the letters "T" and "J" attached.

*Medical Issue:* Mental health issues brought on by the publicity he receives (his disillusioned psychiatrist, Dr. Leo Spaceman [Chris Parnell], uses experimental treatments to, it is hoped, cure Tracy).

*Address:* 42-22 22nd Street in Manhattan.

*Background:* Born to a prostitute named "Liquorish" (she became pregnant by one of her johns and after a failed attempt to have the baby aborted gave birth to it at Yankee Stadium in the Bronx). Liquorish raised Tracy alone until he began working as a stand-up comedian. As a child, he performed on the mythical Nickelodeon series *Ray Ray's Mystery Garage* and was discovered performing his comedy act at the Apollo Theater in Manhattan in 1984.

*Belief:* He is a descendant of Thomas Jefferson and his slave, Sally Hemings (Tracy attempted but failed to produce a film called *Jefferson*, wherein he plays the roles of Thomas Jefferson, Sally Hemings, and King George III).

*Movies:* Starred in *Aunt Phatso, Fat Bitch, Sherlock Homie, Who Dat Ninja, Black Cop/White Cop*, and *President Homeboy* (America's first black president).

*Favorite Singer:* Pat Benatar.

*Novelty Song:* Wrote "Werewolf Bar Mitzvah" (for Geffen Records).

*Ebony Magazine Column:* "Musings."

*Favorite TV Show: Family Guy.*

*Fear:* The Black Crusaders (a supposed group of avengers who are after Tracy for his stereotyped portrayal of African Americans in his films).

*Hobby:* Playing video games (especially "Halo 3").
*Flashbacks:* Young Tracy (Eric Ruffin, then Elijah Cook).

**JENNA MARONEY**
*Place of Birth:* Santa Barbara, California, in 1969.
*Parents:* Verna (Jan Hooks) and Werner Maroney (worked as a fast-food burger server but left Verna for a surfer named Roberta).
*Husband:* Paul L'Astname.
*Children:* Jessica, Judy, and Jerome.
*Education:* Northwestern University (studied voice; met future friend Liz Lemon).
*Occupation:* Actress and singer.
*TV Series: The Girly Show* (created by her and Liz; later changed to *TGS with Tracy Jordan*).
*TV Appearances: Gossip Girl, Law and Order: SVU, America's Kids Got Singing* (where she performed her first live song), *The Mickey Mouse Club* (the 1977 revival), *Arli$$*, and a pilot film called *Good Looking.*
*Theater Shows: The Jenna Chronicles: A One-Woman Show, Con Air: The Musical,* and *Mystic Pizza: The Musical.*
*Feature Films: The Rural Juror, Sing Them Blues, White Girl* (not released), *Emmanuelle Goes to Dinosaurland* (update of a series of 1970s sexy *Emmanuelle* films), and *Take My Hand.*
*Exercise Video: Jenna Gets Hard.*
*Music Videos: It's Your Birthee Slut, Muffin Top, Rural Juror,* and *I Caught Crabs in Paradise.*
*TV Commercials:* Shop-Rite Supermarkets, the Wool Council, and Enorme, "the fragrance for plus-sized women" (seen in an exaggerated weight costume).
*Clinical Test Subject:* Jenna volunteered to be the subject for a military antisleeping pill.
*Awards:* Cable Ace Award (for her guest role on *Arli$$*); Funniest Woman in New York (by *Time Out* magazine); Best Actress (for *Mystic Pizza: The Musical* by the New York Critics Association).
*Flashbacks:* Young Jenna (Athena Eleanor Ripken).

# *Tru Calling*
(Fox, 2003–2005)

*Principal Cast:* Eliza Dushku (Tru Davies), Zach Galifianakis (Davis), Jason Priestley (Jack Harper).

*Basis:* A young woman (Tru Davies) with the ability to travel back in time for 24 hours uses her abilities to help people who will become victims of crime.

## TRU DAVIES

*Parents:* Richard (Cotter Smith) and Elise Davies (Sherry Thorson, then Jena Halley).

*Place of Birth:* Manhattan in 1981.

*Siblings:* Meredith (Jessica Collins) and Harrison Davies (Shawn Reaves).

*Education:* Grover Cleveland High School (Class of 1999); New York University (star of the track team; graduated with a medical degree); intern at a local, unnamed hospital.

*Measurements:* 34-24-34; she stands 5 feet, 5 inches tall.

*Home Address:* 1723 Oakland Street, Apartment 3.

*Cell Phone Number:* 555-0119.

*Car License Plate:* RTM 356.

*Favorite Eatery:* The Standard Diner.

*Occupation:* Medical examiner with the New York City Morgue (located at 330 West 7th Street in Manhattan). Her job requires her to work at nights in the crypt (where bodies are stored) and to assist on autopsies.

*Gift:* Tru believes that her ability to relive the past 24 hours is not a blessing: "A calling gives you something you're destined to do; that gives your life meaning. What I do is more like a curse."

*The Change:* In 1991, when Tru was 10 years old, an intruder broke into her home. Elise, alone with Tru at the time, felt something was going to happen and hid Tru in her bedroom closet. Although Tru could not see what was happening, she heard the intruder shoot her mother. The killer was never found, and the incident has haunted Tru ever since (unknown to Tru, her father hired a hit man to kill Elise so that he could marry another woman). At the funeral, Tru believed she heard her mother's voice say, "I'm okay." At that moment, Tru wished she could go back in time and change that fatal day, but nothing happened. It is assumed that Tru, Meredith, and Harrison were raised by relatives. Tru's wish becomes a reality in 2003 when, on her first night in the crypt, she hears a female voice call her name. She traces the voice to a recent victim who says, "Help me." Instantly, Tru is transported back in time 24 hours to relive the events of the day to alter the destinies of those who die too soon.

*Revelation:* Tru calls these experiences "rewinding" or "the day has rewound." She suspected (but didn't know at first) that her mother possessed the same ability; her mother, however, couldn't save herself, and Tru believes it is a condition that is handed down to certain members of the Davies family (but why her, as her sister and brother do not have the ability?). Tru has no idea why she was chosen or how it is possible to relive a day (her memories of what happened on the day she is reliving are the key to her saving lives).

*Catchphrase:* "I have 24 hours to relive the past to change the future."

*Supervisor:* Davis (no other name given) is Tru's superior at the city morgue. He knew that Tru's mother had special abilities when she warned him about an impending car crash but didn't listen to her. She saved his life by flattening his car tires. Davis is a fan of games (especially "Dungeons and Dragons") and offers Tru the guidance she needs to help a person when she is called to go back in time.

*Flashbacks:* Tru as a young girl (Victoria Tennant); Meredith at age 15 (Tori Anderson).

## JACK HARPER

Jack works at the city morgue with Tru and has a mysterious link with the dead, as he himself was once dead. Jack was an emergency medical technician who felt that after five years on the job he needed a change of life. He worked at Sinclair Hospital, the Lexington Medical Center, Pearson Health Services, and St. Vale's Children's Hospital prior to his job at the morgue. During an emergency call to help a child who had become the victim of a shooting, Jack was shot, and his heart stopped beating for three minutes and 28 seconds before he was brought back from the dead (for an unknown purpose at first). It is revealed in the 2004 season finale that Jack is also capable of reliving days—but to see that people who die are not saved by Tru. He claims that if someone was meant to die, it should happen; if Tru saves that person's life, it creates a dangerous rift in time, and he needs to prevent that from happening. Situations also change for Tru when she learns from Jack that if she saves someone who was meant to die, someone else will have to die to take his or her place. Jack lives at 109-567 Charleston Road (address on his ID card), 555-0183 is his phone number, and jharper@exgent.web is his e-mail address.

# *True Blood*
## (HBO, 2008–2014)

*Principal Cast:* Anna Paquin (Sookie Stackhouse), Stephen Moyer (Bill Compton), Alexander Skarsgard (Eric Northman), Ryan Kwanten (Jason Stackhouse), Deborah Ann Woll (Jessica Hamby), Sam Trammell (Sam Merlotte), Tina Wesley (Tara Thornton), Nelsan Ellis (Lafayette Reynolds).

*Basis:* A young woman's (Sookie's) involvement with a supernatural world that exists in her hometown of Bon Temps, Louisiana. Vampires are the most prominent, and it was through the Japanese creation of "Tru Blood" (a synthetic blood that "tastes metallic and vile") that allowed vampires to feed without killing humans and become a part of society.

## SOOKIE STACKHOUSE

*Parents:* Michelle (Jenni Blong) and Corbett Stackhouse (Jeffrey Nicholas Brown).

*Brother:* Jason Stackhouse (see below).

*Nickname:* "Sook."

*Place of Birth:* Bon Temps, Louisiana, on May 24, 1983.

*Species:* Halfling (part human and part Fae [also known as a fairy]).

*Religion:* Christian.

*Occupation:* Waitress at Merlotte's Bar and Grill.

*Medical Issue:* Carrier of hepatitis C.

*Background:* Sookie and Jason are descended from Niall Brigant (Rutger Hauer), the ancient king of an original tribe of Fae. Niall is estimated to have been born in the 3000s B.C., making him more than 5,000 years old for the series.

*Sookie:* As Sookie grew, she began to develop the powers of a Fae, the first being her ability as a telepath. Concerned over her unusual ability to tune into other people's thoughts, her parents had her examined by a doctor who misdiagnosed her as having attention deficit disorder based on his observations of Sookie's being perceptive and observant. Michelle knew this was not the case and refused to allow Sookie to take medication. Ten years later, Sookie's life again changed when her parents were killed by a vampire named Macklyn Warlow (Robert Kazinsky)—but their deaths were not attributed to a vampire (Michelle and Corbett were found in their car, which, it was assumed, crashed into a swamp during a flash flood; the bite marks on their bodies were attributed to alligators). Sookie and Jason were sent to live with their paternal grandmother, Adele Stackhouse, where Sookie suffered another trauma: she was sexually abused by her great uncle, Bartlett (who was banished from their lives when Sookie told her grandmother); it was revealed that Bartlett had done the same thing to Adele's daughter, Linda. Sookie's upbringing continued to worsen as her ability made it difficult for her to concentrate on her schoolwork and teachers assumed she was a slow learner. Her only friend at this time was Tara Thornton, a girl considered an outcast because she was being raised alone by an alcoholic mother. Until she was able to control her telepathic abilities through concentration, Sookie never dated or had a boyfriend, as she could "hear" their thoughts, which were anything but pure.

*Powers:* Because Sookie is a hybrid, she has not acquired the abilities of pure-bred Fae. Her telepathic abilities allow her to "hear and see" the thoughts (and even pick up on the memories) of humans. She cannot "read" the minds of vampires, as they are dead and have no brain waves. Sookie can also touch a person to force memories to be revealed and also delve deeper into a person's thoughts. She next acquires photokinetic abilities that are emitted through her hands (in a glowing blue and white light) and allows her to cross into alternate dimensions or defend herself (as a single ball of energy). Faes attain their beauty based on the dimension in which they are living, and Sookie has attained the physical attributes of the world in which she now lives.

*Side Effect:* Sookie, like all Faes, emits an aroma that is especially appealing to vampires, but her blood, which has no distinct type, is not as appealing to vampires as that of a full Fae. Sookie is well versed in the martial arts, but because she is a half-breed, she endures the same aging process as normal humans. She feels that her life is in constant danger because "I'm basically vampire crack" and has suddenly become bisexual, lusting after women as well as men.

*Flashbacks:* Young Sookie (Zenali Turner, Lilac Emery-Haynes, and Lily Bigham).

## WILLIAM "BILL" COMPTON

*Place of Birth:* Bon Temps, Louisiana, on April 9, 1835.

*Parents:* William Thomas Compton and Margaret Lattermilk.

*Wife:* Caroline Shelby (Gabrielle N. Brown; flashbacks); they married in 1855.

*Children:* Sarah (Deborah Puette; flashbacks) and Thomas Compton.

*Alias:* "Vampire Bill."

*Civil War Service:* First lieutenant in the 28th Louisiana Infantry (1862–1865).

*The Turning:* Bill, discharged from the army in 1865, began a journey home. En route, he became lost (thinking he knew a shortcut) and found refuge at the home of Lorena Krasiki (Martina Klaveno), an evil but seductive vampire who posed as a widow to draw humans to her. When Bill refused her advances, she turned him, leaving him unable to return to his family.

*New Life:* Bill, with Lorena by his side, journeyed to San Francisco, where they lived off the blood of prostitutes, mostly those associated with the Comstock Brothel (owned by Pamela de Beaufort). Fearing exposure, they moved to Chicago, where they posed as French tourists and again fed on humans. They next moved to Los Angeles, where Bill, fed up with his and Lorena's vagabond lifestyle, pleaded with her to let him out of her grip. She refused until Bill threatened to kill himself and Lorena freed him.

*The Meeting:* Sookie first meets Bill when he enters Merlotte's Bar, and they are instantly drawn to each other. Only Sookie realizes he is a vampire but cannot read his thoughts.

*Character:* Sookie's main love interest. Although Bill can become violent, he suppresses that trait and appears as kind, polite, and well mannered. He has the unique ability to mimic, which he uses to his advantage. He is also capable of sustaining sunlight for short periods of time, has exaggerated fangs, can control people with his mind and levitate, and has blood that is intoxicating to other vampires.

*Bill's Fate:* As the series ends, he succumbs to the disease hepatitis D (a strain of the disease that is relatively harmless to humans).

## ERIC NORTHMAN

*Place of Birth:* Sweden in A.D. 900 (he is close to 1,100 years old when the series begins, but he appears as a 30-year-old-man).

*Parents:* Astrid and Ulfrik (a Viking king).

*Childhood:* Enjoyed spending days by the ocean with no interest in marriage, as being single appealed to him.

*The Change:* One night in A.D. 919, a pack of werewolves attacked Eric's home, killing his mother and sister and mortally wounding his father. Eric, away at the time, returned to discover what happened from his dying father and made a vow to find those responsible and destroy them. Eleven years later, while serving as a Viking in Scandinavia, Eric was wounded and lay dying when a mysterious figure (Godric [Allan Hyde], a 1,000-year-old vampire) appeared to him and, having witnessed Eric's strength in battle, offered him a new chance at "life" by turning him into a vampire. Eric accepted.

*New Life:* It is many centuries later when Eric and Godric are again seen (London in 1665). Eric's father's killers have still eluded him, but an outbreak of the plague brings Eric in contact with Nora Gainesborough (Lucy Griffiths), who has become infected with the plague while helping others and now lies dying. Hoping to save Nora, Eric brings her to Godric, who turns her into a vampire (Eric becomes her "brother"). Eric eventually makes his way to Louisiana, where he becomes the owner of Fangtasia, a vampire bar in Shreveport (it was originally a video rental store that Eric transformed).

*Character:* A vampire drawn to Sookie (and vice versa). He is calculating and not one to kill humans without a reason. He is unlike other vampires in that he is loyal and shows affection (especially to Sookie and his vampire sister, Nora). He is capable of controlling his emotions but can become violent when angered.

*Ability:* To move at an accelerated speed that makes him appear as a blur. He can heal rapidly after any nonfatal injury. With the exception of hepatitis D, Eric is immune to all diseases. He can see in darkness, has heightened senses, and has the gift of flight. His cell phone ringtone is the 1921 song "Ain't We Got Fun."

## JASON STACKHOUSE

Jason, Sookie's older brother (age 35), is a deputy sheriff for the Bon Temps Police Station (also said to be the Renard Parish Sheriff's Department) in Louisiana. He worked previously as a road crew supervisor and in high school was a quarterback on the football team. He is married to Brigette (Ashley Hinshaw), a microbiologist, and is the father of three unnamed daughters (although before his marriage he was known as the town's notorious woman-izer). Jason is quite impulsive and is seen displaying bigotry toward vampires (he was once a member of the Fellowship of the Sun [also called Soldiers of the Sun], an antivampire church). Jason is a full human and, although descended from Niall Brigant, has not inherited Fae abilities like his sister (although he contends that his heritage did endow him with good looks and natural seduc-tiveness). In his time with the antivampire church (which is also called a para-military group), Jason acquired sharpshooting expertise as well as proficiency in hand-to-hand combat.
*Flashbacks:* Young Jason (Labon Heston).

## JESSICA HAMBY

Jessica, the daughter of Jordan (Ben Lemon) and Annabeth Hamby (Cheryl White), was 17 years old when she was turned into a vampire. She has a younger sister named Eden and works as a waitress alongside Sookie at Merlotte's Bar and Grill. She lives in Shreveport, Louisiana, and was raised in a very strict Christian family. Over time, Jessica developed a rebellious attitude toward her father for all the restrictions he put on her life. One night, in defiance of her father, Jessica secretly attended a classmate's party with friends and was turned into a vampire. She was now capable of exploring different feelings and the world around her but deeply regretted killing humans for their blood to survive. She acquired the powers of all vampires (like speed, enhanced senses, immortality, and strength) but was also cursed with an aversion to sunlight, silver, and a stake to the heart (any of which could end her immortality). She also established a video blog at Babyvamp-jessica.com.

## SAM MERLOTTE

Sam is the mayor of Bon Temps, Louisiana, and previously owned Merlotte's Bar and Grill (the bar is taken over by Arlene Fowler Bellefleur [Carrie Preston], a medium who renames it Bellefleur's Bar and Grill [there is also a werewolf bar in town called Lou Pine's]). He is married to Nicole Merlotte and the father of Victoria and Tommy Merlotte. Sam, who appears to be about 35 years of age, was born to a shape-shifter (Melinda) when she was 16 years old. Her human boyfriend, Joe (Lee Mickens), was incarcerated for a crime, and Melinda (T. J. Smith Cameron), unable to care for Sam, gave him up for adoption. He was taken in by Sue Anne (Judy Prescott) and Mitch Merlotte and grew up in a loving household. His life seemed normal until he reached puberty and discovered, at the light of a full moon, that he is a shape-shifter (on his first change, he involuntarily shape-shifted into an exact image of the family dog in front of his parents). The following day, after returning home from school, Sam discovered that his adopted family, fearing for their lives, had abandoned him. Sam, now a teenager, quit school and began to drift and learned to control his ability to change. At an unspecified time later, Sam broke into a home where he found a considerable amount of cash, stole it, and used it to establish his bar and grill. Sam can become any animal he wants (as long as there is such an animal on which he can concentrate), and it appears that he prefers shifting into a border collie. Sam is also comfortable living amongst vampires, as he supports the Vampire Rights Amendment.

*Flashbacks:* Young Sam (Martin Spanjers).

## TARA MAE THORNTON

Tara was born in Bon Temps in 1982 and is a close friend to Sookie. She is the daughter of Joe and Lettie Mae Daniels (Adina Porter) and is the cousin of Lafayette Reynolds (see below). She was turned into a vampire at the age of 27 (in 2009) by Pamela de Beaufort (Kristin Bauer van Straten), her maker (Tara is her student and learns through Pamela how to live and survive as a vampire). Tara currently works at the vampire bar Fangtasia as a bartender (she worked previously at Merlotte's Bar). Because of her abusive upbringing (from her alcoholic mother), she is cynical and confrontational and speaks her mind, often isolating herself from those around her. As the series progressed, Tara made amends with her mother, but in a battle with a vampire seeking her mother's blood, Tara was overpowered and killed (as Pamela mentions that she could feel Tara's passing). Tara, like Pamela, belongs to the Godric vampire bloodline (it can also be seen that both women are bisexual, having sex with both men and women as well as with each other).

*Flashbacks:* Young Tara (Layla Crawford, Dara Iruka, and Avion Baker).

## LAFAYETTE REYNOLDS

Lafayette, the head chef at Merlotte's Bar (then Bellefleur's Bar), was born in Bon Temps, Louisiana. He is the son of Ruby Jean Reynolds (father not named), a cousin of Tara Mae Thornton (see above), and the nephew of Lettie Mae Daniels. He is a medium and able to contact the spirits of the dead. He is also gay and, because of his sexuality, was kicked out of his home by his mother when he revealed it to her. While he does earn an honest living as a cook, he supplements his income in various illegal activities (particularly drugs) to make ends meet. Lafayette believes that he inherited his abilities from his great grandmother (a practitioner of magic) and can communicate with the spirit of his late lover, Jesus Velasquez (a demon who perished in the process of transferring his powers into Lafayette's body).

# 24

## (Fox, 2001–2010)

*Principal Cast:* Kiefer Sutherland (Jack Bauer), Elisha Cuthbert (Kimberly Bauer), Dennis Haysbert (David Palmer), Carlos Bernard (Tony Almeida).
*Basis:* Real-time depiction of the assignments of CIA agent Jack Bauer.

### JACK BAUER
*Place of Birth:* Santa Monica, California, on February 18, 1966.
*Father:* Philip Bauer (head of the company BXJ Technologies); his mother (not named) is deceased.
*Late Wife:* Teri Bauer.
*Daughter:* Kimberly "Kim" Bauer.
*Brother:* Graeme Bauer.
*Education:* University of California, Los Angeles (acquired a bachelor of arts degree in English literature); University of California, Berkeley (master of

Kiefer Sutherland as Jack Bauer. *Fox/Photofest © Fox*

science degree in law and criminology). In high school (unnamed), Jack rode motorcycles and enjoyed surfing.

*Position:* Head of the U.S. president's Counter Terrorism Unit (CTU). He was previously a special agent in charge of the Los Angeles Domestic Unit, then director of field operations for the unit.

*Military Service:* The Combat Alliance Group and the Delta Force Counter Terrorist Unit. He completed the Special Forces Operations training course and graduated from the John F. Kennedy School of Special Warfare. He served as an instructor for the Special Forces Robin Stage Exercises and Q-Course Phase III Training Programs. Jack was a member of the Delta Force (acquired the rank of captain), then a member of the Green Berets.

*Los Angeles Police Department Service:* Enrolled first in its SWAT (Special Weapons and Tactics) school after graduating from Berkeley, then in a Special Forces Operations training course.

*Character:* Experience has taught Jack to be careful, as the slightest mistake could have serious repercussions. He handles each assignment with kid gloves and executes each carefully planned maneuver with precise accuracy.

*Languages:* English, German, and Russian (he can also speak, but not as fluently, Spanish, Arabic, and Serbian).

*Badge Number:* 9431006.

*Employee Number:* 68025638X.

*Cars:* A GMC Yukon, a Ford Expedition (owned by the CTU), a Toyota, and a Chevrolet (all issued to coordinate with the sponsor of the show).

## KIMBERLY "KIM" BAUER

*Parents:* Jack and Teri Bauer.

*Place of Birth:* Santa Monica, California (most likely in mid-1985).

*Husband:* Stephen Wesley.

*Daughter:* Teri Wesley.

*Address:* 12 Blue Tree Drive in Hancock Park, California. She previously lived in Santa Monica, then Woodland Hills, California.

*Occupation:* Agent with the Domestic Unit of the Los Angeles Counter Terrorism Unit.

*Position:* Level 1 analyst.

*Education:* Santa Monica High School (dropped out but later acquired her GED); Santa Monica College (acquired an associate of arts degree in computer programming).

*Favorite Music Performers:* Linkin Park, 2Pac, Coldplay, and Green Day.

*Member:* Teen Green (a teenage environmental group).

*Target:* During a rally with Teen Green, Kim was targeted by a terrorist and infected with cat's claw virus, which manifested itself in a dangerous fever (cured when Jack acquired a vial of the antidote and injected it into her).

*E-Mail Password:* Life Sucks.

## DAVID PALMER

*Position:* The mythical first African American president of the United States and personally in command of the CTU.

*Marital Status:* Divorced.

*Children:* Nicole and Keith.

*Prior:* David was a senator from Maryland and a member of the Senate Commerce Subcommittee, the Senate Appropriations Committee, the House Ways and Means Committee, and the House of National Security Subcommittee.

*Education:* Maryland School of Law (acquired his law degree); Georgetown University (economics degree). Another episode claims he attended the University of California, Berkeley.

*Awards:* In college (Berkeley), he played basketball and was named College Player of the Year by *Sporting News*; he won the Wooden Award as Player of the Year and was named Defensive Player of the Year by the Big East Conference. He was also an NCAA All-American in men's basketball.

*Character:* A powerful force for justice. He doesn't rule with an iron fist and expects only the best from the agents he commands as head of the CTU.

## ANTHONY "TONY" ALMEIDA

*Place of Birth:* Chicago, Illinois.

*Position:* Agent with the Los Angeles CTU; he was formally with the CIA.

*Wife:* Michelle Dessler (Reiko Aylesworth), an employee of the CTU (under her maiden name).

*Expertise:* Hand-to-hand combat (he is also a certified instructor).

*Education:* Stanford University (master's degree in computer science); San Diego State University (bachelor's degree in engineering).

*Military Service:* First lieutenant with the Marines (where he gained experience at the Marine Scout Sniper School); Surveillance and Target Acquisition Platoon School.

*First Assignment:* Teamed with Jack Bauer in 2000 in Operation Proteus. He was next the special agent in charge of the Los Angeles Domestic Unit (where he also served as the systems validation analyst).

*Character:* A bit impulsive, and while he follows orders, he sometimes finds that his gut instinct is more reliable than what he has been told to do.

*Address:* 21048 Kipling Place, Los Angeles.
*Favorite Baseball Team:* Chicago Cubs.
*Allergy:* Penicillin.

## OTHER CHARACTERS

Chloe O'Brian (Mary Lynn Rajskub) is a senior intelligence analyst with the Los Angeles CTU as well as the internet protocol manager; she was later transferred to the unit's New York Office. She possesses a bachelor of science degree from the University of California and is an expert in operational security, computer vulnerability, and intrusion detection. She drives a blue Toyota Prius, her badge number is 99A-12, and her e-mail address is co-brian@CTUGOV.net. She also served with the Washington Bureau of the CTU as a field operations analyst and cyber-terrorist expert. Her first husband, Miles, is deceased; she then married (then divorced and remarried) Morris O'Brian; they are the parents of Prescott O'Brian.

Teri Bauer (Leslie Hope) was Jack's wife until she was killed by an enemy agent named Nina Myers. She has a sister named Carol and is the mother of Kimberly with Jack. She was an artist and designer and was the creative director of Click California Design, graphic artist for Los Angeles Design, graphic artist for Chiat-Day Advertising, curator of the Museum of Contemporary Art, consultant to the director of the Los Angeles County Museum, advertising art director for Greenpeace, colorist for Dark Horse Comics, conservator for the Isabella Gardner Museum, restorative assistant for the Uffizi Galleria (where she lived in Florence, Italy), and co-owner (with her friend Kitty) of the firm Graphic Eye. She attended the Rhode Island School of Design (has a bachelor of arts in painting) and the University of California, Berkeley.

# *Two and a Half Men*
## (CBS, 2003–2015)

*Cast:* Charlie Sheen (Charlie Harper), Jon Cryer (Alan Harper), Ashton Kutcher (Walden Schmidt), Angus T. Jones (Jake Harper), Holland Taylor (Evelyn Harper), Conchata Ferrell (Berta), Melanie Lynskey (Rose), Marin Hinkle (Judith Harper), April Bowlby (Kandi).
*Basis:* The events that enliven the life of Charlie Harper, a womanizer who earns a living as a jingles writer.

## CHARLES "CHARLIE" FRANCIS HARPER
*Place of Birth:* California in 1967.
*Parents:* Evelyn (see below) and Frank Harper. Frank died of food poisoning, which led to Evelyn marrying three additional men: Harry Gorsky (left

Evelyn for a younger woman), Don Thomas (a bisexual Texan who left the family for a gay life; he called Charlie and Alan "Buckaroos"), and Luther King (an obese man whom Evelyn eventually divorced).

*Brother:* Alan Harper (see below).

*Wives:* Betsy (divorced) and Rose.

*Daughter:* Jenny (resulted from an affair Charlie had in the early 1990s; he distanced himself from Jenny and her mother's lives but did send money to help support them).

*Occupation:* Jingles writer (for TV commercials); writer of children's songs.

*Nickname:* "Charlie Waffles" (the name under which he performs as a children's singer).

*CD Producer:* Fluffy Bunny Records (produces "Charlie Waffles" albums).

*Character:* A womanizer. Although Charlie is seen with numerous women, he is actually faithful to each of them (except Rose) as long as the relationship lasts. His judgment regarding whom he dates is often impaired by his love of alcohol, and although he has only one daughter, Berta, his maid, is surprised that with all his affairs there aren't other children. Charlie is very charming and persuasive but also manipulative when it comes to seducing women.

*Home:* A Malibu beach house. Charlie and Lisa, the girl he was dating at the time, were in love. They purchased the beach house together and hired a maid (Berta). Constant fighting led to their breakup; Charlie got the house and Berta.

*Stalker:* Rose. After a one-night stand with Rose, his neighbor, Charlie discovers that she has become obsessed with him (so much so that she uses a mannequin she names "Manfred Quinn" as her pretend husband). In a strange twist of fate, Charlie develops romantic feelings toward Rose and dates her, and they marry. While in Paris on their honeymoon, Rose catches Charlie in bed with another woman, a mime, and a goat. As Rose storms out of the room, Charlie follows her (as does the goat) to a train station. Bitter at Charlie for cheating on her, Rose attempts to push Charlie onto the tracks, but instead the goat is shoved and killed by an oncoming train. In a continually strange story, Rose takes Charlie captive; somehow gets him back to California, where she buys a house; and locks Charlie in the basement. Meanwhile, it is told by everyone that the ashes of the goat that was killed and cremated are those of Charlie, who slipped on a train platform and was killed by a train. It was at this time that the beach house was put up for sale and purchased by Walden Schmidt (see below). In season 12, after having spent four years in Rose's basement prison, Charlie manages to escape and is now seeking revenge. While it appeared that Charlie would achieve his goal, the series ends when a helicopter, carrying a baby grand piano, loses its cargo and the piano falls on Charlie, actually killing him this time.

*First Job:* Composing the jingle for an unnamed toothpaste brand (which was followed by a national commercial for Pepsi-Cola).

*Education:* Revealed only that Charlie attended Juilliard (but was expelled for an unknown reason).

*Medical Issue:* While it is not stated outright, Charlie appeared to have one sexually transmitted disease (this is mentioned during Charlie's [actually the goat's] funeral when several of his past girlfriends mentioned that he gave them an STD).

*Flashbacks:* Young Charlie (Dylan Minnette).

### ALAN JEROME HARPER

*Place of Birth:* California in 1968.

*Parents:* Same as Charlie (see above).

*Relationship:* Charlie's younger brother.

*Ex-Wives:* Judith Harper-Melnick (see below) and Kandi, one of Charlie's ex-girlfriends, who is beautiful but extremely dense (Kandi's mother claims that Kandi inherited her stupidity "from her moron father"). When they married, they bought a condo with money they won in Las Vegas on their honeymoon; Alan lost that in the divorce settlement.

*Son:* Jake Harper (see below).

*Occupation:* Chiropractor.

*Home:* Shares Charlie's Malibu beach house.

*Character:* Simply put, Alan is miserable. He is surrounded by failure and rejection (believes nobody likes him) and, if not for Charlie taking him and Jake in after his divorce from Judith, would be living in poverty (as his alimony payments to Judith are $3,875.32 a month; he also lost virtually everything he owned in the divorce settlement). He is a neurotic, penny-pinching moocher. If there is a way for him not to pay for something, he will find a way to do it. He has an extended vocabulary (speaks elegantly) and has a flamboyant fashion style. He is sometimes mistaken for being gay for how he acts in certain situations.

*Favorite TV Show:* Glee.

*Favorite Entertainment:* Broadway theater plays that are on tour in California.

*Turn On:* Women who are angry (or even a little overweight).

*Medical Issue:* Lactose intolerant.

*Car:* A Volvo station wagon.

*Office:* Located in the San Fernando Valley.

*Award:* Won the San Fernando Valley Chiropractic Award.

*Resentment:* Alan is literally jealous of Charlie for how women and money come easily to him (Alan has worked hard his entire life and has nothing to show for it).

*Liquor:* Alan opposed Charlie's drinking of hard liquor and will drink only beer (but as the series progressed and Alan became more neurotic, he tended to follow in Charlie's footsteps).

*Girlfriends:* Although Alan claims nobody likes him, he did have girlfriends after his divorce but allows them take full advantage of him ("a doormat," as he describes himself with women).

## JACOB "JAKE" DAVID HARPER

*Date of Birth:* March 14, 1993. He is the "Half-Man" of the title with Charlie and Alan being "The Men."

*Parents:* Alan and Judith Harper (each of whom accidentally dropped Jake when he was an infant).

*Character:* He is rather lazy, loves to eat, is not a good student at school (excels in poor grades), and appears to have no general smarts. He has trouble understanding certain words, lacks self-confidence, and is always unaware of the fact that he is being made fun of.

*Musical Ability:* Plays the guitar.

*Favorite Snack:* Popcorn.

*Change:* While schools are not mentioned for Jake, he does join the army (season 10 in 2012) and is stationed on a base in Japan (where he becomes the company cook). It is also revealed that Jake smoked marijuana.

## WALDEN THOMAS SCHMIDT

*Position:* Replaced Charlie Harper (seasons 9 to 12) when Charlie Sheen left the series.

*Mother:* Robin Schmidt (Mimi Rogers); his father is not named.

*Ex-Wife:* Bridget Schmidt (Judy Greer).

*Occupation:* Entrepreneur (owner of Walden Loves Bridget Enterprises, which he named after his ex-wife and owns with her and her mother).

*Background:* Walden was raised by his mother, a scientist, after his father, a magician, deserted the family. For the first four years of his life, Walden had an "older brother" named Magilla (named after the TV series *Magilla Gorilla*), who was actually a gorilla used by Robin in an experiment to see if gorillas could learn as fast as humans. Walden flunked the eighth grade but was permitted to attend high school (where he met his future wife, Bridget). Somehow, he managed to attend MIT and designed a website that Microsoft purchased, making him a billionaire.

*Character:* Emotionally immature, not very imposing (more childlike in appearance), and often depressed (most likely due to his divorce from Bridget).

*The Meeting:* After Bridget divorced Walden and threw him out of their house, he devised an "ingenious" plan to win Bridget back by pretending to commit suicide by jumping into the ocean (hoping Bridget will take him back). When he realized it would not work (the water was too cold), he found his way to a house (belonging to Charlie) and rang the doorbell (wanting to use the phone). It is at this time that he meets Alan (who is still living there with Jake after Charlie's passing) and buys the beach house when he learns that it is up for sale (Alan cannot pay the property taxes and three mortgages on the house; Alan also convinces Walden to let him and Jake live there for free).

## BERTA

Berta is Charlie's, then Walden's, housekeeper. She can be seen as rude, crude, sarcastic, and simply disrespectful. She is treated with respect (out of fear) by Charlie, Alan, and Walden. Berta has a sister, Daisy (Camryn Manheim), but they are always at odds. She has been married and divorced twice and has three daughters (who she says "are sleazy and easy"); Megan Fox played her daughter Prudence. Berta's past includes her serving time in prison (why perhaps she is so mean) and working as the prison barber. Through dialogue, it is learned that Berta smoked pot and takes valium with her coffee to control her violent temper. Berta was a groupie (with the Grateful Dead), and it is suggested that she had a lesbian affair during that time. Berta's nickname for Alan is "Zippy." Her catchphrase is "I ain't cleaning that up."

## EVELYN NORA HARPER

Evelyn is Charlie's and Alan's mother (and Jake's grandmother). Although she is 58 years old when first introduced, vanity gets the best of her, and she changes her birth year as she ages. She is not only superficial but also an unfit mother (the family often refer to her as "The Devil"; Charlie calls her "The Unholy Mother of Us"). Charlie has made "666" (the Devil's number) her number on his cell phone. It can be seen that she is more interested in affairs than she is in raising her children. Evelyn could also be seen as being a witch (not the ugly type but the powerful type) when one of Charlie's girlfriends, a Devil worshipper, appeared frightened when she met Evelyn. Evelyn sells real estate, is wealthy, and lives in Beverly Hills.

## JUDITH HARPER-MELNICK

Judith, Alan's first wife not only is self-absorbed but also lacks a sense of humor and is vindictive and coldhearted. Judith was the first woman with whom Alan had sex (which apparently did not please Judith, as she mentions that the only time she was ever sexually happy was when she became pregnant with Jake). Judith enjoyed spending Alan's money, living in luxury, and, at first unknown to Alan, hooking up with numerous men. After divorcing Alan, she has since remarried (Dr. Herb Melnick, played by Ryan Stiles, Jake's pediatrician). She has a child with Herb whom she names Millie (when Jake and Berta meet Millie, each claims that she looks nothing like Judith or Herb, implying that Alan could be the biological father [as Judith left Herb, came back to Alan, and then returned to Herb]).

# Veronica Mars

(UPN/CW, 2004–2007)

*Principal Cast:* Kristen Bell (Veronica Mars), Enrico Colantoni (Keith Mars), Jason Dohring (Logan Echolls), Percy Daggs III (Wallace Fennell), Francis Capra (Eli "Weevil" Navarro), Ryan Hansen (Dick Casablancas).

*Basis:* The events that befall a high school student (Veronica Mars) as she turns detective to help her father (Keith Mars) solve crimes.

## VERONICA MARS

*Parents:* Keith (a private detective) and Lee Ann Mars (Corinne Bohrer), an alcoholic; they are now separated.

*Place of Birth:* Neptune (located in Balboa County), California, in August 1987. Veronica claims that "Neptune is a town without a middle class. There are two types of people in Neptune—millionaires and people who work for millionaires. I fall into the second group."

*Address:* Apartment 101 of the Sunset Cliffs Apartments.

*Education:* Neptune High School (junior when the series begins); Hearst College (sociology and criminal courses). After one year, she transferred to Stanford University (where she acquired a bachelor of fine arts degree in psychology). She then enrolled in Columbia Law School, where, on graduation, she was offered a job by Truman-Mann & Associates, a law firm in Manhattan.

*Job:* Secretary to her father, the owner of Mars Investigations (she tails philanderers and cheating spouses and investigates false insurance industry claims).

*Agency Phone Number:* 555-0137.

*Character:* Not a fan of high school ("My grades are okay") and attends only because she has to (she joined the pep squad for the physical education credits). Two years earlier, Veronica was a victim of date rape and became very vengeful; if you cross her, she will find a way to get even ("I believe in the

Kristen Bell as Veronica Mars. *UPN/Photofest © UPN*

old school—an eye for an eye"). She is a computer whiz and enjoys working as a photographer for the school newspaper, the *Navigator*. ("Every girl's gotta have a hobby. Photography is mine.") While very pretty, she never lets that get in the way of who she really is—a gutsy girl who will not take nonsense from anyone. She lies, steals evidence, and cheats to accomplish a goal. Veronica seems to attract trouble, and she will help someone for reasons that are sometimes known only to her. Veronica claims that the most disturbing part of her job is uncovering information that could prove harmful to her client. "Should I tell them, or is it better if they do not know?"

*Childhood:* The Balboa County Courthouse was like a second home to Veronica (as she would often do her homework in an empty interrogation room). Her father was a deputy (later the sheriff), and Veronica and her mother would visit him at lunchtime.

*Skills:* Can pick locks with a hairpin and goes undercover when she has to "as a dumb blonde or a brunette." When she can't pick a lock, she goes old school, using bolt cutters.

*Teenage Trauma:* Veronica crashed her friend Shelly Pomeroy's party and was given a drugged drink. She was raped but has no memory of the party and recalls only that "I woke up in my bra and panties." She is now very careful with whom she associates and where she goes.

*Private Eye Test Score:* 95 percent.

*Frequently Used Word:* "Frack."

*Pet Dog:* Buddy.

*Car License Plate:* 6B1 A504.

*Favorite Movie: South Park: Bigger, Longer & Uncut.*

*Favorite Website:* www.preyingeye.com (for research).

*Favorite Dessert:* Ice cream and waffles.

*Favorite Food:* Italian.

*Baking:* When Veronica makes a cake, "They tend to lean a little to the left."

*Measurements:* 34-24-34. She stands 5 feet, 1 inch tall and has blonde hair and blue eyes.

*Nicknames:* "V" and "Ronnie."

*Best Friend:* Lilly Kane (Amanda Seyfried). She and Veronica were members of the prestigious "09er" clique at Neptune High School. Lilly's murder (her body found near her family's swimming pool) devastated Veronica, and it became her goal to uncover the killer (also the subject of the first season).

*Books Seen in Veronica's Office: Collier's Encyclopedia* and *The Encyclopedia of Photography.*

*Computer:* An Apple PowerBook, then a MacBook Pro.

*Flashbacks:* Young Veronica (Carsyn Spencer).

## KEITH MARS

*Occupation:* Deputy sheriff, then sheriff, of Balboa County; private investigator. When Veronica was nine years old, Keith became sheriff. It is said that Keith previously worked as a deputy in Fresno, California, when he was 22 years old.

*Place of Birth:* Omaha, Nebraska (where, as a teenager, he drove a 1978 GTO). He was also a member of a local rock band.

*Address:* Same as Veronica.

*Favorite Food:* Italian.

*Favorite Music:* Jazz.

*Favorite Singers:* Aretha Franklin, Louis Armstrong, and Miles Davis.

*Favorite Recording Group:* The Beatles.

*Favorite Movies: The Big Chill, Rear Window, Blazing Saddles,* and *Slap Shot* (he also mentions enjoying film noir).

*Favorite Actor:* Humphrey Bogart.

*Favorite Sport:* Baseball.

*Published Book: Big Murder, Small Town.*

*Favorite TV Networks:* PBS (for the show *Austin City Limits*) and the Food Network.

*Private Investigator Test Score:* 97 percent.

*Skills:* Surveillance, tracking, an expert shot.

# *What I Like about You*
(WB, 2002–2006)

*Principal Cast:* Jennie Garth (Valerie Tyler), Amanda Bynes (Holly Tyler), Leslie Grossman (Lauren).

*Basis:* The relationship between two sisters (Valerie and Holly) as they share each other's dreams, ambitions, and sorrows.

## VALERIE TYLER

*Place of Birth:* Manhattan on April 21, 1974.

*Address:* An apartment (34C) on Bleecker Street; she later lives in a loft (3D) on Spring Street in Manhattan.

*Occupation:* Account executive (later managing director) of the Harper and Diggs public relations firm. She previously worked as the assistant manager of the Hobby Hutch. She later forms her own public relations firm, Valco; the series concludes with her as the co-owner (with Lauren) of a cupcake shop called Sugar Babies Bakery.

*Education:* Stuyvesant High School (where she was a cheerleader and called "Pickles" ["Because I like pickles"]); Columbia University (majoring in business).

*Favorite Actress:* Meryl Streep.

*Favorite Singer:* Michael Bolton.

*Favorite Board Game:* "Scrabble."

*Favorite Childhood Teddy Bear:* "Biddy Bear" (when she outgrew it, she gave it to Holly, who renamed it "Lorenzo").

*Favorite Donut:* Chocolate with chocolate sprinkles.

*Favorite Eatery:* The Liberty Diner (owned by Jeff [Simon Rex] and Valerie's boyfriend during first-season episodes).

*Measurements:* 34-26-35. She stands 5 feet, 5 inches tall and has green eyes and blonde hair.

*Nickname for Her Breasts:* "The Girls."

*Collects:* Plush animals.

*X-Rated Movie:* In college, Valerie played a bartender in a low-budget student film that was shelved when the director ran out of money. Years later, he reworked the film by adding sex scenes, and Valerie became known as "The Butt Tender."

*Quirks:* Carries a toothbrush and toothpaste with her at all times ("So I can brush after every meal"), eats a Mounds candy bar when something bothers her, and alphabetizes her soup cans.

*Quality:* Bright, beautiful, and fun loving. She cares for other people and will do what she can to help someone in an uncomfortable situation. She prides herself on being fashion conscious and as perfect as she can be—"That's who I am, and that's what I do."

*Husband:* Vic Maladao (Dan Cortese), a New York City firefighter. Val and Vic had a date and got drunk, and Valerie woke up married.

## HOLLY TYLER

*Place of Birth:* Manhattan on April 3, 1986.

*Address:* Holly originally lived at her childhood home (at 128 Amsterdam Avenue) with her father (her mother is deceased). When her father, a salesman, receives a transfer to Japan, he sends Holly, now 16, to live with her older sister, Valerie.

*Education:* Stuyvesant High School (she dreams of attending Columbia University but rejected the idea because she felt she would be living in Valerie's shadow). After graduating from high school, she spent the summer of 2004 on a scholastic internship in Paris; she enrolled at New York University in the fall of that year (but later dropped out when she couldn't handle the workload).

*Hangout:* The Liberty Diner.

*Character:* Holly is bright, independent, trouble prone, inquisitive, and very nosey. She likes to do things her way and frowns when a situation doesn't always turn out as she expected. She claims to be "a loose cannon"—"I do whatever comes to my mind."

*Measurements:* 34-26-37. She stands 5 feet, 5 inches tall and has green eyes and brown hair.

*Cooking Specialty:* Omelets.

*Favorite Hot Dog Topping:* Ketchup.

*Favorite Breakfast Cereal:* Various Post brand products: Fruity Pebbles, Honey Bunches of Oats, and Blueberry Morning.

*Occupation:* Busgirl at an unnamed restaurant (responsible for "bread, water, and clearing tables"); Valerie's assistant (then mailroom girl) at Harper and

Diggs; assistant salesgirl at a duplicating company called Copy That; junior manager at Marquee Records (she hopes to become a rock musician manager and promoter).

*Allowance:* $60 a week from her father; Valerie takes out $20 and adds $30 of her own for Holly's college fund.

## LAUREN

*Date of Birth:* October 25, 1971.

*Occupation:* Lauren (no last name given) works with Valerie at Harper and Diggs. Lauren was first portrayed as a backstabber and would stop at nothing to get what she wants. She and Valerie eventually became friends and started their own public relations firm called Valco. When this fails, Valerie and Lauren open a cupcake store called Sugar Babies Bakery.

*Character:* Lauren knows she is beautiful and alluring. She uses her sex appeal, especially her breasts, to get whatever she wants from men (even women); she says, however, "I didn't always look like this. In high school I was considered big boned and undatable." She is impulsive, doesn't think before she acts, and claims to be a people person (but is pushy). She also claims to be an overachiever, but when Valerie asks her to do something, she says, "No way." She appears to always give meaningless advice and is shocked when someone accepts it.

*Dream:* Marry a rich man (Lauren worships money, "and I would roll around in it if I had any").

*Background:* Lauren has a criminal record for robbery. She was overweight in grammar school and had her nose fixed when she was 16 years old (she felt it didn't fit her face).

*Bra Size:* 36C (as mentioned by Lauren). She stands 5 feet, 5 inches tall and has hazel eyes and blonde hair.

*Breast Nickname:* "The Maids of Honor" (later, "The Girls," duplicating what Valerie calls her breasts).

*Dating:* Lauren says, "I am not just a hot piece of meat, I have a lot to offer." She hates sports, and if she dates a man who likes sports, she says, "I'll change him." If she is with a man she doesn't like, she gets out of the date with her remark, "I'm a lesbian."

*Address:* An apartment (42) in Greenwich Village.

*Addiction:* Sweets ("Sugar is my pimp").

*Favorite Snack:* Peanut butter brownies.

# Index

Hale, Michael, 9
Hall, Michael C., 77
Halley, Jenna, 204
Hannigan, Alyson, 122
Hardin, Melora, 150
Harris, Neil Patrick, 122
Hatcher, Teri, 7
Hayden, Josh, 175
Hayes, Isaac, 107
Haysbert, Dennis, 211
Headly, Glenne, 155
Heaton, Patricia, 141
Hedaya, Dan, 149
Helberg, Simon, 18
Helgenberger, Marg, 60
Helin, Megan, 50
Henggeler, Courtney, 18
Hennessy, Jill, 58
Herbert, Mailey, 178
Herrmann, Edward, 95
Heston, Labon, 209
Hewitt, Jennifer Love, 93
Hill, Dulé, 172
Hill, Julien, 177
Hines, Cheryl, 191
Hinshaw, Ashley, 209
Hirsch, Judd, 157
Hofmann, Isabella, 55
Hogan, Susan, 177
Holbrook, Hal, 115
Holleman, Mitch, 181
Hooks, Jan, 203
Hope, Leslie, 214
Hornsby, Russell, 107
Howard, Ken, 58
Howard, Ron, 9
Howard, Traylor, 149
Howell, C. Thomas, 52
Howey, Steve, 181
Hoyos, Terri, 51, 171
Huckabee, Maxwell, 80
Hudson, Ernie, 176
Huertas, Jon, 44
Huett, Zane, 73
Huffman, Felicity, 72

Hyde, Allan, 208
Hyland, Sarah, 142

Irving, Amy, 8
Irwin, Jennifer, 195

Jackson, Jeannie, 132
Jackson, Kate, 54
James, Liam, 175
James, Tyler Patrick, 93
Janes, Dominic, 80
Jenkins, Ken, 187
Jerald, Penny Johnson, 45
Johnson, Ashley, 83
Johnson, Eric, 52
Jones, Angus T., 214
Jones, Jill Marie, 103
Jones, Mary-Charles, 112
Jordan, Montana, 30

Kaczmarek, Jane, 131
Kain, Khalil, 106
Kaling, Mindy, 161
Kamel, Stanley, 150
Kasch, Cody, 77
Katic, Stana, 41
Kazinsky, Robert, 206
Keibler, Stacy, 123
Kemper, Ellie, 161
Kennedy, Jamie, 93
King, Erik, 77
King, Hunter, 81
King, Joey, 93
King, Tim, 134
Kinsey, Angela, 161
Kinsman, Brent, 73
Kinsman, Shane, 73
Klaeno, Martina, 207
Knowles, Shanica, 112
Krakowski, Jane, 199
Krasinski, John, 161
Krumholtz, David, 157
Kruntchew, Luke Andrew, 77
Kuroda, Emily, 102
Kurtz, Swoosie, 196

# About the Author

**Vincent Terrace**, a television historian for BPOLIN Productions, LLC, has written more than 40 books on television and radio history, including *Television Introductions: Narrated TV Program Openings since 1949* (Scarecrow Press, 2013) and the following books in this trivia series: *Television Series of the 1950s, Television Series of the 1960s, Television Series of the 1970s, Television Series of the 1980s,* and *Television Series of the 1990s* (all published by Rowman & Littlefield). He is also the author of the only set of Internet TV series books that is available: *Internet Horror, Science Fiction and Fantasy Television Series; Internet Drama and Mystery Television Series; Internet Lesbian and Gay Television Series; Internet Comedy Television Series;* and *Internet Children's Television Series.*